THE

S·A·B·E·W

STYLEBOOK

Also by Chris Roush

"A Century of Progress: Celebrating Progress Energy's History of Service"

"A Good Night's Sleep: The Pacific Coast Feather Story"

"Inside Home Depot: How One Company Revolutionized an Industry"

"Profits and Losses: Business Journalism and Its Role in Society"

"Show Me the Money: Writing Business and Economics Stories for Mass Communication"

THE S·A·B·E·W STYLEBOOK

2,000 Business and Financial Terms Defined and Rated

Chris Roush
and Bill Cloud

Marion Street Press
Portland, Oregon

To Susan Johnston, the greatest woman I have never met.—Chris Roush

Published by Marion Street Press
4207 S.E. Woodstock Blvd. # 168
Portland, Ore. 97206-6267
USA
http://www.marionstreetpress.com/

Subscribe to the book online at http://www.fiwords.com/

Orders and desk copies: 800-888-4741

Printed in the United States of America

ISBN 978-1-933338-38-5

Cover Art Direction by Nicky Ip

Library of Congress Cataloging-in-Publication Data Pending

Contents

S·A·B·E·W

The Society of American Business Editors and Writers Inc., formed in 1964, is committed to sharing and promoting best practices in covering financial news, and in maintaining the highest ethical standards. Recognizing that economic freedom is inextricably linked to political freedom and that an informed citizenry is critical to sustaining these freedoms, the not-for-profit organization seeks to encourage comprehensive reporting of business and economic events without fear or favoritism and to upgrade skills and knowledge through continuous educational efforts.

SABEW offers a growing spectrum of member services, including:

Awards and Competitions

- The Best in Business Contest, which highlights overall excellence in newspaper business sections and pages, weekly business journals and wire services. The news contest rewards superior coverage of breaking news and enterprise stories.
- The Distinguished Achievement Award, presented annually to outstanding business journalists.

Education and Training

- An annual national conference that includes specialized workshops, field trips and panel discussions geared to expose SABEW members to new ideas in business and economic journalism. The annual event features speeches by important figures in the news and a provocative ethics discussion.
- Specialized onsite and online programming, call-ins and webinars.
- Boot camps for special groups.
- SABEW Endowed Chair in Business and Financial Journalism at the University of Missouri in Columbia. Martha "Marty" Steffens occupies the chair. The SABEW chair develops business journalist curricula for undergraduate, graduate and mid-career professionals.

Networking Opportunities

- Active social networking sites (Facebook, Linked In, Twitter) with all the latest news and SABEW information.

Publications

- A new vibrant website. Redesigned with additional features, our web site (www.sabew.org) offers an up-to-date look at business journalism. The site also contains contest and registration materials for training.
- Occasional newsletters. The Business Journalist features articles designed to improve the quality of business and economics reporting and to inform members about industry trends.
- An online, searchable membership directory.
- Coming soon: a freelancer listserv for editors who need new talent. See also http://sabew.org/resources/freelancers/

How to Join

See page 237 for a complete list of membership opportunities.

Acknowledgments

As with any book, credit must be given to those behind the scenes.

This stylebook is the product of a number of people besides the authors. Allan Sloan, the current Fortune magazine senior editor at large and perhaps the best business journalist out there today, gave invaluable guidance early on and then read the entire manuscript — twice — to give feedback.

Herb Greenberg, a former business columnist for Marketwatch.com, TheStreet.com, The San Francisco Chronicle and others who is now with CNBC, also provided feedback, as did Adam Levy, a former business journalist, former Loeb Award winner, former Wall Street analyst and friend.

The legal section at the end of the book could not have been compiled without the help of Michael Hoefges, an attorney who teaches mass communication law at the University of North Carolina at Chapel Hill, and two Dow Jones & Co. attorneys — Mark Jackson and Jason Conti. The accounting and financial definitions were reviewed by Ed Maydew, the David E. Hoffman Distinguished Professor of Accounting at the University of North Carolina at Chapel Hill.

I also gave versions of the stylebook to several business journalists — and some college students who want to be business journalists — and asked for their opinions. Those who gave me feedback were Bloomberg reporters Amy Thomson and Sapna Maheshwari, and former students Sarah Frier and Andrew Dunn.

I look at this stylebook as a work in progress. While it's something that I wish I had while working as a business reporter, it will get even better in the future. Don't hesitate to let us know how we can add to or fine-tune the entries. Readers who want to make a stylebook entry suggestion can e-mail Chris Roush at croush@email.unc.edu. Please put 'SABEW Stylebook suggestion' as the header.

Also, this stylebook is available online at www.fiwords.com and might be more useful to business journalists who prefer reference material online. If you have bought a copy of the book, you can email customer.service@marionstreet-press.com for access to the site.

— Chris Roush, University of North Carolina at Chapel Hill

Foreword

Business has its own language. Unfortunately, it's not English. It's what I call bizspeak, a pseudo-language full of terms and shorthand and buzzwords that none but the initiated understand. And even many of the initiated can't explain to the uninitiated what these terms mean.

This stylebook helps you translate bizspeak into English, both for yourself and for your audience. Think of it as a foreign language guide, and also as a reminder that even though you may now understand the term after reading about it, much of your audience probably doesn't.

So make sure to use as much English and as little bizspeak as you can. That way, you're serving the initiated and uninitiated alike.

Many of the words that we business journalists use and understand — or think we understand — are, in fact, euphemisms that we'd do well to avoid. My favorite: "correction," used to describe a big decline in prices of stocks or houses or some other asset. If the new, lower prices are in fact correct, which is what "correction" implies, did we call the price rise preceding the decline a "mistake"? Obviously not. Use words that convey substance, not spin.

This book also gives you an objective reason to avoid using the absurd exclamation marks that the likes of Yahoo and Yum Brands insist are part of their names. So if Yahoo folk want to know why you didn't call them Yahoo! folk, invoke the stylebook.

Unlike other stylebooks I've seen during my 40 years in business journalism, this one isn't written for a particular organization. It's written for all of us. A feature I especially like is that the book recognizes that business audiences, general audiences and trade audiences are different from each other, and makes allowances for those differences.

This book isn't perfect — what is? But even if, like me, you don't agree with all the definitions and second-use suggestions here, that's small beer. The book is an invaluable guide to helping you get business right, understand it and explain it. Which is, of course, what we all should be trying to do.

— Allan Sloan, senior editor at large, Fortune magazine
2001 SABEW Distinguished Achievement Award winner

Introduction

I once got into a debate with a reporter who had written that natural gas was selling at $2.50 (as I recall) per million cubic feet. I didn't know much about commodity pricing, but a million cubic feet of anything, I argued, would cost more than that. The figure's right, the reporter replied, because the figure was listed as "mcf" and his source told him what it meant. Thankfully, a reporter experienced in the market settled the argument: The "m" represented 1,000, as in a Roman numeral. The gas was priced per 1,000 cubic feet.

What I needed then, and what both editors and writers need now, was access to this manual. It's a quick way to decode a business term and get guidance on how to use the term in a story. I could have shown the entry to the reporter, and both of us could have quickly gotten back to work. (The manual also would have saved me embarrassment on the many times I've raised similar questions and turned out to be wrong.)

Sadly, as media organizations downsize, there are fewer experienced business writers and even fewer specialized business copy editors. But at least with this manual, there is more help for those still on, or new to, the job.

What you'll find in these pages are explanations for more than 1,100 terms that might pop up in corporate documents, regulatory filings and government reports, as well as phrases that come out of the mouths of corporate CEOs and press representatives. We'll tell you what the terms mean, when they should or shouldn't be used and defined for readers (check our rating system) and how to use them. Some will be fun to know even if they should never appear in print.

It gives guidance on what all those abbreviations (APR, CUSIP, LLC, TARP) mean and when they are acceptable. There's a section devoted to the rapidly growing and changing list of technology terms. And it provides an up-to-date roll call of tricky company names and trademarks as well and guidance on their punctuation and capitalization.

Keep this book handy. You'll find it will improve your reporting, speed up your editing and let you avoid overly long discussions on what mcf means.

— Bill Cloud, University of North Carolina at Chapel Hill

Listings Key

Here is a typical entry for this stylebook:

> **buyback** (n.), **buy back** (v.) The repurchasing of shares by a company to decrease its number of shares outstanding. A company *will buy back* those shares. Just because a company announces a buyback plan doesn't mean that the shares will actually be repurchased. Some companies will announce a buyback plan to support its stock price, but not actually repurchase the shares. Also, a company may buy back its stock to inflate its **earnings per share** number. Earnings per share is net income available for common stock divided by total number of shares outstanding. With fewer shares outstanding, the EPS number may rise. The term *share repurchase* is also acceptable. **($$)**

The **bold word** or **words** at the beginning of an entry illustrate the accepted usage. An acceptable abbreviation of the word or phrase might be included at the end of an entry. Unacceptable abbreviations are also mentioned when necessary.

If the part of speech is necessary to distinguish usage, it will be indicated in parentheses after the word.

The dollar signs in parentheses after the entry are used to provide a guideline on when the word or term should be defined in business journalism. See p. xiii for the stylebook's rating system.

Italicized words in an entry show how the term can be used in writing or show similar acceptable terms.

The words that follow an entry in ***indented bold italics*** indicate where you can find similar terms in the Browse by Industry section of fiwords.com.

Bold words in an entry can refer to another entry in the stylebook or to a related term.

Every attempt will be made to define the entry and provide an explanation of what it means in the business world.

In some cases, an entry might provide tips on how to use it in reporting or writing. For example:

earnings story guidelines: Nearly every business journalist at some time will write a story about a public company's earnings. Some will even write a story about a private company's results. The following guidelines are important to consider in such stories:

- When calculating the earnings growth or decline, focus on the net income or net loss, not the earnings per share. Companies can manipulate their earnings per share growth by decreasing the number of shares outstanding through share repurchase programs.

- Leads need to emphasize why a company's earnings rose or fell during the quarter. Don't just tell the reader that the earnings rose or fell by a certain percentage. They'll want to know the reason.

- Context, context, context. If a company's earnings have fallen after quarters of increases, then you'll need to tell the reader the last quarter in which earnings fell. Was there a loss in the quarter? Then tell the reader when the last quarterly loss occurred. Net income rose 49 percent? When was the last quarter that profits rose faster?

- Listen to the conference call. Sometimes, the story is not the press release with the numbers, but what the executives say to the analysts and investors later in the day. One telltale sign is to watch how the stock price reacts while you're listening to the call. If the price begins to move up or down dramatically, then something newsworthy was said.

- Compare a company's quarterly earnings with the same quarter from the previous year, not the previous quarter. Many businesses are cyclical, making the better comparison the same time a year ago. You can't compare, for example, Coke's second-quarter earnings with the first quarter because it's hotter in the second quarter and more people are thirsty.

- When writing about earnings, focus on the most-recent earnings first before mentioning the same quarter a year earlier. For example, write *Earnings rose 25 percent to $4.5 billion from $3.6 billion in the same time period a year ago,* not *Earnings rose 25 percent from $3.6 billion in the time period a year ago to $4.5 billion.*

- Whom are you going to quote? Increasingly, investors in the stock are being quoted in stories about the earnings, not buy-side analysts. While both have a bias, the investors have less of a conflict of interest.

This style guide is not intended to be the business reporter's sole reference when it comes to style. It should be used in conjunction with another stylebook, such as the latest edition of the Associated Press Stylebook and Libel Manual. This stylebook, however, is intended to fill in the many gaps for business journalists when it comes to other reference materials, which historically have downplayed or ignored the special needs required to report and write business news.

If you cannot find an entry in this stylebook, please refer to the AP stylebook or the Webster's New World Dictionary of the American Language. If you are still not satisfied, or don't have an answer to your style question, please drop us a line and we will consider adding an entry in a following edition.

Rating System

Many words and phrases in this style guide have dollar signs listed after them.

The dollar signs, based on a five-level scale, make it easy for a business journalist to decide whether the term or phrase needs defining for his of her audience.

A term or phrase with no dollar sign next to it means that it does not need to be defined in any media form. A term or phrase with a **$$$$$** next to it means that it should be defined in all media.

Here is how we've delineated the different levels of this five-point scale:

$ Daily newspaper business page or section.

$$ Weekly business newspapers, such as those operated by Crain Communications and American City Business Journals, as well as trade publications, such as Nation's Restaurant News or Beverage Digest.

$$$ Television networks or shows devoted to business news, such as "Nightly Business Report" on PBS or CNBC and Fox Business Network, as well as websites and blogs that focus on business and financial news, such as TheStreet.com, Marketwatch.com, Moneywatch.com and SeekingAlpha.com.

$$$$ Personal finance publications such as Money, SmartMoney and Kiplinger's Personal Finance, and weekly and semi-weekly business magazines such as Bloomberg Businessweek, Forbes and Fortune.

$$$$$ Daily business newspapers such as The Wall Street Journal, Investor's Business Daily and The Financial Times, as well as publications designed for the hard-core investor, such as Institutional Investor and Bond Buyer.

In other words, if a term or phrase is rated a **$$$$**, and The Wall Street Journal is a **$$$$$**, then every media outlet that falls into a category rated at or below **$$$$** should define the term or phrase, but The Journal need not.

When ranking words and phrases, we've taken into consideration how these are currently being used in business publications, as well as where we think improvements could be made for the benefit of the readers.

Bibliography

Any business journalist who cares about his or her craft needs to have some, if not all, of the following books. These offer further explanation of topics in this stylebook.

"Bottom Line Writing: Reporting the Sense of Dollars." By Conrad Fink. Ames, Iowa: Iowa State University Press: 2000.

"Covering Business: A Guide to Aggressively Reporting on Commerce and Developing a Powerful Business Beat." By Robert Reed and Glenn Lewin. Oak Park, Ill.: Marion Street Press: 2005.

"Profits and Losses: Business Journalism and its Role in Society." By Chris Roush. Oak Park, Ill.: Marion Street Press: 2006.

"Show Me the Money: Writing Business and Economics Stories for Mass Communication." By Chris Roush. Mahwah, N.J.: Lawrence Erlbaum & Associates: 2004.

"The Bloomberg Way: A Guide for Reporters & Editors." By Matthew Winkler. New York: Bloomberg News: 2009. 11th edition.

"The Economist Style Guide." London: Profile Books: 2005.

"The Wall Street Journal Guide to Business Style and Usage." By Paul R. Martin. New York: Simon & Schuster: 2002.

"The Wall Street Journal Guide to Understanding Money & Investing." By Kenneth M. Morris and Virginia B. Morris. New York: Lightbulb Press: 2004. Third edition.

"Writing About Business: The New Columbia Knight-Bagehot Guide to Economics and Business Journalism." Edited by Terri Thompson. New York: Columbia University Press: 2000.

"Understanding Financial Statements: A Journalist's Guide." By Jay Taparia. Oak Park, Ill.: Marion Street Press: 2003.

I. Stylebook

A&W Restaurants Inc.

Use the ampersand and the capital W in all references. The restaurants exclusively sell draft A&W Root Beer, though that brand is owned by Dr Pepper Snapple Group. A&W was a subsidiary of Yum Brands Inc. but is now owned by A Great American Brand LLC, a partnership set up by A&W franchisees.

Company Name, Restaurant

A.C. Moore Arts & Crafts Inc.

The Berlin, N.J.-based craft store chain uses the ampersand in all references.

Company Name, Retail

Abbott Laboratories

The Abbott Park, Ill.-based company uses no Inc., Co. or Corp. after its name. Abbott Labs is acceptable on second reference.

Health care

abbreviations

Many companies, such as **GE**, **GM** and **IBM**, are more commonly known by an abbreviation. Some companies, such as **FedEx** and **Alcoa**, are now referred to by a shortened version of their names. Do not abbreviate a company name on first reference unless it is commonly known by its abbreviation. The Associated Press Stylebook says to use IBM on first reference, but GE and GM on second reference only. We agree.

AbitibiBowater Inc.

The paper and pulp company is based in Montreal. Its name is always one word. The company uses all lowercase letters in its logo, but capitalize the A and the B in its name.

Company Name

above water

Refers to the value of an asset and implies that the value is above its cost. Although being above water is a good thing, avoid this term in writing except in direct quotes because many consumers are unfamiliar with it.

acceleration clause

A situation in real estate where the lender can require payment of all money owed because of a breach of contract, such as a delinquent payment. (**$**)

Real estate

accounts payable

Amounts owed to suppliers that must be paid off within a short time period. They are included on a company's balance sheet as a liability. (**$$**)

accounts receivable

Reflects the amount of goods or services that a company has sold but has yet to receive payment for. These are listed as an asset on a company's balance sheet. **($$)**

accreditation
A process by which a health care organization such as a preferred provider is evaluated to determine whether it meets the qualifications of an accrediting body. An accreditation is held to ensure that a level of quality of health care is met.
Health care, Insurance

accretive
An adjective used to describe when a merger, acquisition or stock buyback will add to a company's profits. Specify the amount and the time period in a merger or acquisition story. **($$)**

accrual accounting
The standard accounting method for most companies. It differs from the **cash basis accounting** method by recognizing revenues when earned rather than when received and expenses when incurred rather than when paid. Publicly traded firms are required to use the accrual method per **generally accepted accounting principles**. **($$$)**

Ace Hardware Corp.
Capitalize only the A in the first name of the Oak Brook, Ill.-based hardware store chain.
Company Name, Retail

Ace Ltd.
Lowercase the Swiss-based insurance company's name after the A even though it uses all capital letters.
Company Name, Insurance

acid-test ratio
The ratio of current assets minus inventories compared to current liabilities. Companies with a ratio of less than 1 should be viewed with caution because they don't have enough to pay their liabilities. **($$)**

ACNielsen Corp.
The New York-based information services company does not use periods in its name, and spells ACNielsen as one word. It's best known for its Nielsen television viewer ratings.
Company Name

acquisition
When one company purchases a stake in another company. It can be either a majority or a minority position, although many acquisitions are for 100 percent of the company being sold. When an acquisition is announced, it often has not closed yet, so avoid writing that Company A has acquired a stake in Company B. The story should be written as Company A has agreed to acquire a stake in Company B.

When writing about acquisitions, make sure that the following facts are included in the story:

1. The total price, including debt that the buyer will have the responsibility to pay, which should be in the lead;

2. If stock is part of the purchase, the terms, such as how many shares of stock in company A will

be given to shareholders of company B;

3. The reason for the deal;
4. Whether the deal is **accretive** or **dilutive**;
5. The stock price reaction;
6. A price comparison to other deals in the same industry;
7. Whether there were unusual trading levels in either company before the deal was announced;
8. The investment banks that advised each company. (**$$**)

acquisition indigestion

A slang term in which the two companies involved in an acquisition have had trouble integrating their operations. It can also be used to describe a company that has made multiple acquisitions and is now having trouble integrating those businesses. (**$$**)

across-the-board

A term often used to describe the stock market when virtually every sector is seeing increases in stock prices.

Wall Street

activity

A term often attached to a noun, such as manufacturing, market or trading that is redundant.

actuary

An employee of an insurance company who analyzes the insured to determine what premiums will be charged. In effect, an actuary is an oddsmaker. (**$$**)

Health care, Insurance

Adidas AG

Capitalize the first letter of the Herzogenaurach, Germany-based sporting goods company even though it lowercases its name.

Company Name, Retail

adjustable-rate mortgage

A mortgage where the interest rate paid by the consumer fluctuates. It's also known as a floating-rate mortgage or a variable-rate mortgage. ARM is acceptable on second reference. The Federal Reserve Board has a section on its site about these mortgages. (**$**)

Real estate

adjusted gross income

A measure of taxable income for tax purposes. It is your total income minus items such as deductions related to business activities, moving expenses, alimony paid and deductible student loan interest. It should not be confused with **taxable income, disposable income** or **discretionary income**. (**$$**)

administrative supervision

A situation in which a state insurance department takes over control of an insurance company.

Health care, Insurance

Advance Auto Parts Inc.

The auto parts retailer is based in Roanoke, Va. Avoid the AAP abbreviation in all references. Advance is acceptable on second reference.

Company Name, Retail

Advanced Micro Devices Inc.

The chip manufacturer is based in Sunnyvale, Calif. AMD is acceptable on second reference.

Company Name, Manufacturing, Technology

adverse opinion

A statement by the auditor about a company's financial statements that the statements do not fairly represent the company's operations. Adverse opinions signal a disagreement between the auditor and the company, and they are typically viewed as a negative for the company. An adverse opinion found in a company's **Securities and Exchange Commission** filings is considered a news story. **($$$)**

Aecom Technology Corp.

The engineering and architecture company is based in Los Angeles. Its name is an acronym for architecture, engineering, consulting, operations and management. Do not use all capital letters for AECOM.

Company Name

Aegon NV

Capitalize only the first letter in the first name of the life insurance company based in The Hague, Netherlands.

Company Name, Insurance

AES Corp.

The energy company is based in Arlington, Va. Use AES on second reference.

Company Name, Energy

Aetna Inc.

The health insurance company is based in Hartford, Conn.

Health care, Insurance

AFL-CIO

The American Federation of Labor and Congress of Industrial Organizations. It is the largest union organization in the United States. AFL-CIO is acceptable on first reference.

Aflac Inc.

Capitalize only the first letter in the first name of the Columbus, Ga.-based insurance company.

Company Name, Insurance

after the bell

A term commonly used to describe an event after the market closes. When a company makes an announcement after 4 p.m., it is considered after the bell. Hyphenate before a noun: an after-the-bell announcement.

Wall Street

after-hours trading

Trading that occurs after the major U.S. markets close at 4 p.m. EST by electronic communication networks, or ECNs. Trading after hours is voluntary, so there may not be a market for all public stocks. **Dow Jones Newswires** uses the term after-hours session to refer to such trading. **($)**

Wall Street

after-tax income

The amount of money left over after an individual or a company has paid federal, state and local taxes. For a consumer, this is also called **disposable income**. (**$**)

AG
See **PLC** entry.

Agco Corp.
Do not capitalize all of the letters in the name of the Duluth, Ga.-based manufacturer of agriculture equipment.
Company Name, Manufacturing

Agilent Technologies Inc.
The electronics company is based in Santa Clara, Calif.
Company Name

Air Products and Chemicals Inc.
The Allentown, Pa.-based company sells industrial chemicals and gases. Air Products is acceptable on second reference.
Company Name

Airgas Inc.
The distributor of industrial and medical gases, as well as welding equipment, is based in Radnor Township, Pa.
Company Name, Manufacturing

Alamo Rent A Car
The St. Louis-based company does not hyphenate its name.
Company Name

Alcoa Inc.
Alcoa is acceptable on all references to the company formerly named Aluminum Co. of America.
Company Name, Manufacturing

Aldi Inc.
The Essen, Germany-based grocery store chain, which has locations in the United States, should be spelled with lowercase letters after the A, in contrast to the company's all-cap spelling.
Company Name, Retail

Allergan Inc.
The pharmaceutical company is based in Irvine, Calif.
Company Name, Health care

Alliant Techsystems Inc.
The aerospace and defense contractor is based in Arlington, Va. ATK is acceptable on second reference.
Company Name

allotment
A term used to describe the number of shares given to each underwriter of a public offering, either initial or secondary, to sell to its customers. (**$$**)
Wall Street

Allstate Corp.
Do not use the "the" before Allstate on any reference to the Northbrook, Ill.-based insurance company.
Company Name, Insurance

Ally Financial Inc.
The Detroit-based bank holding company was formerly known as GMAC Inc. GMAC stood for General

Motors Acceptance Corp. Ally Bank is a subsidiary.

Company Name, Finance

alpha

A technical ratio that measures performance on a risk-adjusted basis. An alpha compares the performance of a mutual fund with a benchmark index. A mutual fund with a positive alpha of 1 has outperformed the benchmark by 1 percent. A negative alpha of 1 would mean the mutual fund has underperformed the benchmark by 1 percent. **($$$$)**

Wall Street

alternative investment

An investment other than stocks, bonds and cash. It can be used to describe investments such as commodities, real estate, private equity, **venture capital** and **hedge funds. ($$$)**

Wall Street

alternative minimum tax

A tax imposed on individuals, corporations and estates by the federal government. The rate is 26 percent or 28 percent for individuals and 20 percent for corporations. Taxpayers must pay the greater of the alternative minimum tax of a regular tax. AMT is acceptable on second reference. Be careful not to use the word "tax" after AMT, however. The Internal Revenue Service site contains information about calculating the AMT. **($)**

Economy

Altria Group Inc.

The name of the tobacco company formerly known as Philip Morris Cos. It is based in Henrico County, Va., just west of Richmond. There is a **Philip Morris International Inc.** that is a separate company that was spun off from Altria in 2008.

Company Name

Amazon

When referring to the online retail company, write Amazon.com Inc. on first reference and Amazon on subsequent references. When referring to its website, write Amazon.com on all references.

Company Name, Retail

AMC Entertainment Holdings Inc.

Capitalize the letters AMC in the name of the Kansas City, Mo.-based movie theater chain.

Company Name

Ameren Corp.

The utility company is based in St. Louis. Its name comes from the words American and Energy.

Company Name, Energy

American City Business Journals Inc.

The parent company of 40 weekly newspapers across the country. Its headquarters is in Charlotte, N.C. Although commonly used, avoid the abbreviation ACBJ on second reference. American City is preferred. The company's site lists its newspapers and publications.

Company Name

American Depositary Receipt

A certificate issued by a bank that represents shares of a foreign company traded on a U.S. stock exchange. All three words are capitalized. ADR is acceptable on second reference, but this term should be defined somewhere in the story. Note that the second word is depositary, not depository. **($$$$)**

Wall Street

American Electric Power Co.

An electric utility company based in Columbus, Ohio. Avoid the AEP abbreviation in all cases.

Company Name, Energy

American Express Co.

The New York-based financial services company can be referred to as *AmEx* on second reference.

Company Name, Finance

American Family Insurance Group

The insurance company is based in Madison, Wis. Avoid the AmFam abbreviation.

Company Name, Insurance

American Financial Group Inc.

The insurance and financial services company is based in Cincinnati. Its major insurance division is Great American Insurance Co. Use American Financial on second reference, not AFG.

Company Name, Finance, Insurance

American International Group Inc.

The name of the New York-based insurance company can be abbreviated to *AIG* on second reference.

Company Name, Insurance

American Stock Exchange

Now formally known as *NYSE Amex Equities* because the American Stock Exchange was acquired by NYSE Euronext, the parent of the **New York Stock Exchange**, in October 2008. The American Stock Exchange was once a major competitor to the NYSE. Use NYSE Amex Equities on first reference, and either the *Amex* or the exchange on second reference.

Wall Street

Amerigroup Corp.

Capitalize only the first letter in the first name of the Virginia Beach, Va.-based health insurer. The company uses all capital letters for Amerigroup.

Company Name, Health care, Insurance

Ameriprise Financial Inc.

The financial services company is based in Minneapolis.

Company Name, Finance

AmerisourceBergen Corp.

The drug wholesale company based in Chesterbrook, Penn., spells its name as one word. Capitalize the B in all references.

Health care

Amgen Inc.

A biotechnology company based in Thousand Oaks, Calif. Its current name came from shortening its original name, Applied Molecular Genetics. Use Amgen in all references.

Company Name

amortization

An accounting practice that over time deducts from profits the purchase price of an asset. When a company purchases a new computer mainframe for $30 million, it may amortize the value of that computer over three years. That means the value of that asset decreases by $10 million on its books each year for three years. A company may change its amortization schedule to a longer time period to slow the decline in value of its assets on its books and thus increase its reported profits. Strictly speaking, amortization goes with intangible assets while **depreciation** goes **with** tangible assets. **($$$$)**

ampersand

Use when part of a company's formal name. Otherwise, do not use in place of "and."

AMR Corp.

The Fort Worth, Texas-based parent company of American Airlines. Capitalize AMR in all references.
Company Name

Anadarko Petroleum Corp.

The oil and gas company is based in The Woodlands, Texas.
Company Name, Energy

analyst

A financial professional who gives opinions about whether investments should be bought or sold. There are two types of analysts. A **sell-side analyst** works for a brokerage and places recommendations such as "buy," "hold" or "sell" on an investment based on his or her research. A **buy-side analyst** works for a mutual fund company or money manager and researches investments for purchase by his or her firm. Both types of analysts typically focus their research on companies in a specific industry, such as banking or retail. Business journalists commonly quote both. With sell-side analysts, however, it has become increasingly common to disclose whether the analyst owns the stock personally and whether the analyst's firm has done any investment banking business with the company within the past two years. These disclosures are typically found at the end of a sell-side analyst's report. If a reporter doesn't have the report, ask the analyst at the end of the interview. Once a common source for business journalists, sell-side analysts are now less willing to talk on the record because of these disclosure rules. Many brokerage firms now require journalists to seek approval from their public relations staff before talking to an analyst. Note that there are also analysts who work for the rating agencies and evaluate the debt issued by a company. These analysts are considered to have fewer ethical conflicts. Many companies list the sell-side analysts that follow their stock on their website. A business reporter should ask analysts to put him or her on their distribution lists so that the reporter may receive their reports. Many analysts now distribute research via e-mail.
Wall Street

anesthesiologist

A medical doctor who delivers anesthesia to a patient before surgery. (**$$$**)

Health care

angel investor

An individual who provides start-up money for a new company in exchange for an ownership position. Angel investors typically invest their own money rather than investing money for others. (**$$$**)

Finance, Wall Street

Anheuser-Busch InBev

The St. Louis-based brewery Anheuser-Busch is now part of this company after its 2008 takeover by InBev. The headquarters is in Belgium.

Company Name, Manufacturing

Anixter International Inc.

The distributor of wire and cable is based in Glenview, Ill.

Company Name

annual meeting

A meeting held by a company for its shareholders to vote on matters such as the election of directors, the approval of an **independent auditor**, and outside shareholder proposals. Although annual meetings are not open to the general public, many companies allow business reporters to attend and provide access to company executives either before or after the meeting. (See the annual meeting entry in the "business news legal issues" section of this site.) Annual meetings are also a good place for reporters to meet investors in the company. *Shareholders meeting* is also acceptable.

annual percentage rate

The annual interest rate that is charged for borrowing money. A credit card that charges a 1 percent monthly interest rate has a 12 percent annual percentage rate. APR is acceptable on second reference. (**$**)

Finance

annual report

A once-a-year publication required of public companies to provide financial and operating information to its shareholders. The report typically begins with a letter from the company's **chief executive officer** The document sometimes has news in it. The formal annual report is filed with the **Securities and Exchange Commission** and is the **Form 10-K**.

annual unit volume

Can mean either the number of items produced by a manufacturer or the dollar amount of sales a business unit produces. AUV is acceptable on second reference. In the fast-food world, AUV is an overall measure of brand health. A "million-dollar store," one with $1 million AUV, is considered successful. (**$$**)

Manufacturing, Restaurant, Retail

annuity

A financial product that typically has a variety of investments such as mutual funds for the purchaser to choose from. Ideally, these investments grow in value and provide a stream of income for the holder during retirement. Also, some annuities pay fixed returns for life of the annuitants. **($$)**
Finance

anti-takeover measure

A tactic by a company's **board of directors** to ward off unwanted acquisition overtures.

antitrust

No hyphen. Antitrust refers to government action to prevent a monopoly in an industry. Antitrust laws prohibit monopolistic control of an industry. The Federal Trade Commission has a guide to antitrust laws.

AOL Inc.

The formal name of the New York-based Internet company is no longer spelled out as American Online.
Company Name, Technology

Aon Corp.

The insurance and consulting company is based in Chicago.
Company Name, Insurance

Apache Corp.

An oil and gas company based in Houston.
Company Name, Energy

Apple Inc.

The Cupertino, Calif.-based consumer electronics company was formerly known as Apple Computer Inc., but the computer has been dropped from the name.
Company Name

application

A software program loaded into a smartphone such as a Droid, a social networking site such as Facebook or tablet such as an iPad. *App* or *apps* is acceptable on second reference. **($$$)**
Technology

Applied Materials Inc.

The Santa Clara, Calif.-based company makes equipment and software.
Company Name, Technology

appraisal

The valuation of a piece of property by an expert in that field. It can be real estate, an antique or an old car. Many appraisers have an official designation from a governing body. If you're writing about an appraisal, ask who did the appraisal and seek their qualifications. **($$)**
Real estate

Aqua-Lung

A trademarked brand name. Note the hyphen and the capitalization. The generic term is underwater breathing apparatus.
Trademark

Aramark Corp.

Lowercase the name of the Philadelphia-based food and facilities supplier and manager. The company capitalizes all of the letters.

Company Name

arbitrageur

An investor who attempts to profit from inefficiencies in the market by going long and short in assets that have similar characteristics but are trading at different prices. This is known as classic arbitrage. Another kind of arbitrageur, a risk arb, speculates on announced takeovers. An arbitrageur might buy shares of a company making an acquisition and short on the targeted company, hoping to profit both ways if the deal falls through. **($$$$)**

Wall Street

arbitration

A hearing regarding a dispute. Many investor disputes with brokerage houses are settled by arbitration. The decision is typically final.

Arby's Restaurant Group Inc.

Arby's features roast-beef sandwiches at its nearly 3,700 restaurants. It was acquired by Roark Capital Group in 2011.

Archer Daniels Midland Co.

The Decatur, Ill.-based company's primary businesses are providing ingredients for food and beverage and animal feed. The *ADM* abbreviation can be used on second reference.

Company Name

Arms Index

A measurement that gauges supply and demand for stocks in an index. It is measure by subtracting the number of declining stocks from advancing stocks and dividing that number by the number of stocks with declining volume by the number of stocks with increasing volume. The equation is written as (advancing issues - declining issues)/(advancing volume/declining volume). The name is capitalized because it was created by Richard W. Arms. Also called the *trading index*. **($$$)**

Wall Street

Arrow Electronics Inc.

The Melville, N.Y.-based company distributes electronics components and computer products.

Company Name

Arthur Andersen

A now-defunct accounting firm that was involved in the Enron scandal. Note the "en" at the end of Andersen.

Company Name

articles of incorporation

Documents filed with the government that detail the creation of a corporation. These documents, typically filed with a **Secretary of State's Office** in a state government, can include information about the corporation's location, owners and officers.

Ashland Inc.

The Covington, Ky.-based company's best-known product is Valvoline motor oil.

Company

ask (n., adj.)

The price that a stock seller is willing to accept for his or her shares. Also called the offering price, although this term should be avoided because it also refers to the price at which shares in an initial public offering are sold. Can be used as a noun as the ask or an adjective as the ask price. **($$$)**

Wall Street

aspirin

Although it's a generic term, Bayer still holds the trademark in about 80 countries, including Canada.

Health care, Trademark

assessed value

The value given to a piece of property such as real estate or a vehicle for assessing taxes.

Real estate

asset stripping

The process of buying a company and then selling some of its operations to make a profit. Asset stripping often occurs when a company is valued at less than the sum of its assets.

Company Name

asset-backed securities

Investments that derive their value from an asset, such as mortgages or credit card loans. Theoretically, such assets spread the risk of the investment because the securities are spread among borrowers and the securities are owned by many investors. Do not use ABS on any reference. **($$$$)**

asset-turnover ratio

The amount of sales generated by a company for every dollar in assets it owns during a certain time period, such as a quarter or a fiscal year. The ratio is calculated by dividing revenue by assets. The higher the number, the better. Companies with low profit margins, such as grocery stores, have high asset-turnover ratios. **($$$$)**

assets

Items that a company or individual owns that have value. Current assets include cash and short-term investments, such as stocks. Fixed assets include property, machinery and equipment.

assisted living facility

A medical facility where the residents receive health care and other services. Assisted living facilities do not provide as much care as a nursing home. Assisted living residence is also acceptable. Assisted living facilities are regulated by state governments.

Health care

Associated Press

Do not capitalize "the" when used before the name. The current business editor of the Associated Press is Hal Ritter.

Company Name

assumable mortgage

A loan that allows the buyer to take over the seller's mortgage when purchasing a home. (**$**)

Real estate

Assurant Inc.

The insurance company is based in New York.

Company Name, Insurance

AstroTurf

A trademarked name that is one word. Note the capital T. The generic term is artificial surface.

Trademark

at the money

When the **strike price** of an option is equal to the price of the underlying security. So, if Coca-Cola Co.'s stock price is at $60, then the Coca-Cola $60 option is at the money.

Wall Street

AT&T Corp.

Headquartered in Dallas. AT&T is acceptable on second reference. Do not spell out American Telephone & Telegraph in any reference. Its name is now AT&T.

Trademark

Atmos Energy Corp.

The Dallas-based company is the largest natural gas distributor in the United States.

Company Name, Energy

attribution

An important issue in any business news story, attribution needs to be specific in some cases to let the reader know where important facts and information came from. Use according to when referring to documents such as **Securities and Exchange Commission** filings, lawsuits, depositions, contracts, etc. Use said or another verb that describes how the person talked when attributing something to a person.

auction

A sale to the highest bidder.

audited financial statement

Describes a company's financial statements that have been prepared and certified by a **certified public accountant**. The statements must meet generally accepted accounting principles, or GAAP. (**$$**)

auditor

A person or firm qualified to examine and audit a company's financial statement.

auditor's report

A short statement by the auditing firm found in a company's SEC filings. It will explain the auditor's responsibilities, the scope of the audit, and the auditor's opinion about the financial statements.

authorization

A term used by health insurers to describe their approval of payment for services by a health care provider.

Health care

Auto-Owners Insurance Co.

the property and casualty insurance company is based in Lansing, Mich. The hyphen is used in all references.

Company Name, Insurance

Automatic Data Processing Inc.

The **outsourcing** company is based in Paterson, N.J. ADP is acceptable on second reference.

Company Name

AutoNation Inc.

Maintain the capital N in the name of the Fort Lauderdale, Fla.-based auto dealership chain.

Company Name

AutoZone Inc.

The automotive parts retailer is based in Memphis, Tenn. Its name is one word, with a capital Z, in all references.

Company Name, Retail

Avery Dennison Corp.

The maker of office supplies is based in Pasadena, Calif.

Company Name

Avis Budget Group Inc.

The Parsippany, N.J.-based company does not hyphenate the name of subsidiary Avis Rent a Car System LLC.

Company Name

Avnet Inc.

The Phoenix-based company is a distributor of electronics components.

Company Name

avoid

A rating given to a stock by a sell-side analyst. It is equivalent to a **"sell"** rating. **($$$)**

Wall Street

Avon Products Inc.

The cosmetics and perfume company is based in New York.

Company Name

B

Babies R Us

A division of Toys R Us. Do not use the single quotation marks around the R.

Company Name, Retail

baby boomer

A person born in the post-World War II growth period of 1946 to 1964. This demographic controls more than 80 percent of all personal finance assets and more than half of **consumer spending**.

Economy

back of house

Part of the restaurant that customers rarely enter, including the kitchen and storage areas.

Restaurant

back office

The administrative and support personnel of a financial services company. These are the employees who are involved in trade-clearing, regulatory compliance and accounting, for example. **($$)**

back up (v.)

To copy files or directories onto a separate storage device to protect it from being lost in case of a computer drive failure.

Technology

back-end

A database that is accessed by a user through an external application. For example, a lot of the data stored on Facebook using specific software by accessed through the Facebook application. **($$$$)**

Technology

back-of-the-napkin business model

A term used to describe a rough outline of a company's business model. Also common is back-of-the-envelope business model. **($$)**

backdating

The practice of placing an earlier date on a document than when the agreement was executed. In recent years, companies have been charged with backdating **stock** options given to executives so that the options are dated when the company's shares were at a lower price than when the options were granted. **($$$$)**

backlog

The total value of orders waiting to be filled, typically for a manufacturing company. An increase in the backlog could indicate a company is having trouble keeping up with its orders or that orders are increasing, or it could signal that the **economy** is improving. **($)**

Manufacturing

bad-debt reserve

An accounting entry that a company, especially a financial institution, sets up to reflect loans that it has made that might go bad. Also called **loss** reserve. **($$$)**

bailout

A term used to describe when a business, individual or the government provides funding to a company that might fail without the investment. In most cases, the government bails out a company to protect the economy. It's one word, with no hyphen. **($$)**

Bake-off

A trademarked event. Note the hyphen and the lower case o. The generic term is baking contest.

Trademark

Baker Hughes Inc.

The oilfield services company is based in Houston. Baker Hughes was formed in 1987 with the merger of Baker International and Hughes Tool Co. — both founded more than 100 years ago when R.C. Baker and Howard Hughes Sr. conceived groundbreaking inventions that revolutionized the fledgling petroleum era.

Company Name, Energy

balance sheet

A financial statement compiled by a company that shows its assets, its liabilities and its shareholder equity. Assets should always equal liabilities plus shareholder equity. On a balance sheet, look to see whether a company's **accounts receivable** or **accounts payable** have increased dramatically since the previous balance sheet. That could be a sign that the company is having trouble paying its bills or is having trouble collecting payments.

balanced fund

A mutual fund that invests in both stocks and bonds.

Ball Corp.

The packaging company is based in Bloomfield, Colo. It no longer makes Ball canning jars and lids. Those products are now produced under license by Jarden Home Brands (Hearthmark LLC).

Company Name

balloon payment

A loan that has a large amount of money due at the end of the loan. Balloon loans are attractive to short-term borrowers because they have a low interest rate. Some balloon loans allow the borrower to reset the interest rate at the end of the term to the current market rate. Do not use as a synonym for an interest-only loan. **($$$$)**

Bancorp

Do not use Bancorp as a standalone name. It's a common abbreviation of bank corporation used by banks throughout the country, the largest being U.S. Bancorp.

Finance

Band-Aid

A trademarked product. Note the hyphen and the capital A. The generic term is adhesive bandage.

Trademark

bank closure

When a bank is closed by federal or state regulators, the **Federal Deposit Insurance Corp.** sells the branches and the deposits to another bank in the market. No advance notice is given to the public when a financial institution is to be closed. Customers can continue to use their checks, debit cards and the ATMs of the closed bank. A bank closure typically happens on a Friday after the banks have closed for the day, and the banks re-open on Monday under the name of the new bank.

Finance

bank holding company

Any company that has control over a bank. It is required to register with the Federal Reserve System. Bank holding companies can issue stock with greater regulatory ease than other banks. The largest bank holding company in the country, as of Dec. 31, 2011, is JPMorgan Chase & Co. It had $2.26 trillion in assets on that date. Do not use BHC in any reference. A list of the 50 largest bank holding companies can be found on the National Information Center's website. (**$**)

Finance

Bank of America Corp.

The name of the bank company based in Charlotte, N.C. Its investment banking subsidiary is called Bank of America Merrill Lynch.

Company Name

Bank of New York Mellon Corp.

The New York-based financial services company can be referred to as BNY Mellon on second reference.

Company Name, Finance

bankruptcy

A legal proceeding that occurs when an individual or a business is unable to pay all its debts as they come due. The federal government runs the bankruptcy court system. The bankruptcy court system allows the person or company to reorganize its debt so that it can be paid off. With some bankruptcy filings, part of the debt can be eliminated.

When covering a bankruptcy court case, it's important to obtain the following documents:

- The initial filing, which will list the amount of the assets and the amount of the liabilities of the filer.

- The creditors' list, which will list every individual and business owed money. This list comes with addresses. Consider it a source list.

- The reorganization plan, which will detail how the debtor in a **Chapter 11** bankruptcy plans to pay off its debt and emerge from bankruptcy court protection.

- The judge's ruling approving the reorganization plan.

When writing about companies filing for bankruptcy, do not state that the business is closing its doors unless it has filed for **Chapter 7** bankruptcy. This is a liquidation. With a Chapter 11 bankruptcy, a company hopes to reorganize its debt and emerge from bankruptcy court as a continuing business. The U.S. court system has a guide and overview of the bankruptcy court process. A list of the 10 largest U.S. bankruptcy cases can be found on the CNNMoney.com site. **($$)**

Bankshares, Bancshares
Spell as one word if it is spelled that way in a company name.
Finance

barbell strategy
1. A bond investment strategy considered effective when interest rates are rising. Investors buy long-term bonds for good rates and short-term bonds so money will be available to buy other long-term bonds when their prices decline. 2. A pricing strategy used especially in fast food in which bargain items, such as a dollar menu, are offered along with higher-margin premium items, such as fancy coffee drinks. **($$$$)**
Finance, Restaurant, Retail, Wall Street

bargain hunting
Avoid this term. One investor's bargain may be expensive to another.

Barnes & Noble Inc.
The New York-based book retailer uses an ampersand in all references.
Company Name, Retail

barrels per day
The daily rate of production from an oil field or a country, or through a pipeline or refinery. A barrel contains 42 gallons of oil. The bpd abbreviation is acceptable after a number on second reference.
Energy

Barron's
A weekly business newspaper that is a subsidiary of **Dow Jones & Co.** Its first edition appeared in 1921, and it is named after former Dow Jones head Clarence Barron. The "Up and Down Wall Street" column is widely read. Note that the apostrophe is always used except when referring to its website, Barrons.com. The formal name, Barron's National Business and Financial Weekly, is not needed on any reference.

based
Use this term only when a business has branches or operations in more than one city: The Durham, N.C.-based company. Otherwise, say the Durham, N.C., company.
Company Name

BASF SE
Capitalize the name of the German-based company, the largest chemical producer in the world.
Company

basic earnings per share vs. diluted earnings per share

A publicly traded company will report both numbers. Basic earnings per share is net income divided by the total number of shares in the company outstanding. Diluted earnings per share includes the number of shares outstanding plus the shares that would be held by investors if all its **stock** options, warrants and convertible securities were exercised. For companies that have issued a lot of stock options to executives, the diluted earnings-per-share number is usually lower than the basic earnings per share number. Business news organizations differ on which number to use when writing earnings stories. Some use the basic earnings per share number, while others use the diluted earnings per share number. Check with your editor to determine which number to use. **($$$)**

basis point

One 100th of 1 percent. Written another way, 100 basis points equal 1 percentage point. Companies and analysts will talk about a change in ratios such as profit margins or net operating margin in terms of basis points. **($$$)**

basket of goods

A set of goods and services whose prices are compiled on a regular basis to track inflation. In the United States, a basket of goods tracks the consumer price index. **($$)**

Economy

Baxter International Inc.

A health care company based in Deerfield, Ill.

Company Name, Health care

BB&T Corp.

There are no spaces in the name of the Winston-Salem, N.C.-based bank holding company. The initials stand for Branch Banking & Trust, but BB&T is acceptable in all references.

bean counter

A slang term for a person in a company's finance or accounting department who tracks, or is concerned with, the company's spending. Use only in direct quotes and columns.

bear market

A period in which the broader stock markets fall. A bear market is considered by many to be at least a 20 percent decline in an index. Avoid using this term if the market has fallen by a smaller percentage. **($$)**

Wall Street

bear trap

When investors who are shorting an investment are forced to cover their position at a higher price because of a market rally.

Wall Street

beating the gun

A term that describes when an investor buys or sells a stock before the price has reacted to breaking news, such as a company issuing a warning that its earnings won't be as high as analyst expectations. **($$)**

Wall Street

Becton, Dickinson and Co.

The medical device manufacturer is based in Franklin Lakes, N.J. Note the comma between Becton and Dickinson. Avoid using the BD abbreviation.

Company Name, Health care

Bed Bath & Beyond Inc.

The home furnishings retailer is based in Union, N.J.

Beige Book

A report from the Federal Reserve that examines the economy around the country. It is released eight times a year — about two weeks before each **Federal Open Market Committee** meeting — and includes information gathered by each of the 12 Federal Reserve Banks about economic conditions in their regions. The release of the Beige Book, on the Fed's website, typically results in a story by major business wire services and other business media outlets. The markets typically focus on the summary. **($$)**

Economy

Belk Inc.

The Charlotte-based department store chain has stores called Belk and no longer uses Belk Hudson or Hudson Belk as store names.

Company Name, Retail

beneficial owner

The individual, or group of individuals, who owns a specific security. For example, shares of stock may be held by a 94-year-old woman from Thomasville, Ga., in a brokerage account. That woman is the beneficial owner even though the stock is under the brokerage account's name. **($$$)**

Wall Street

beneficiary

A person or group that receives benefits. The term can also refer to a person named in a will who receives a piece of property after the owner dies.

Health care

Berkshire Hathaway Inc.

The Omaha, Neb.-based company is best known for being run by Warren Buffett. It owns a number of other companies, including **Geico**.

Company Name, Finance

Bernanke, Ben

The chairman of the **Federal Reserve Board**. Acceptable to use Fed chair or Fed chairman on second reference. His biography can be found on the Federal Reserve's website.

Economy

Best Buy Co.

The Richfield, Minn.-based consumer electronics retailer's name is two words.

Retail

beta

A number that measures the volatility of a stock compared with the overall market, with a 1 rating being the average for the market. A beta above 1 means the stock is more volatile than the overall market. Utility stocks, for example, typically have betas below 1, but technology stocks typically have betas above 1. A company's stock with a beta of 1.5 can be described as a stock that is 50 percent more volatile than the overall market. (**$$$$**)
Wall Street

Better Business Bureau

A nonprofit organization that sets and upholds high standards for fair and honest business behavior. The Better Business Bureau has 124 local organizations across the United States and Canada that evaluate and monitor businesses and charities. The bureau is acceptable on second reference.

bid

The price at which an investor is willing to purchase a stock. A bid will also include the amount of shares the investor is willing to buy. (**$$**)
Wall Street

Big Blue

Acceptable after first reference for IBM.
Company Name

Big Board

A nickname for the **New York Stock Exchange**. Use only after referring to the exchange by its full name.
Wall Street

Big Lots Inc.

The discount retailer is based in Columbus, Ohio.
Company Name, Retail

Big Pharma

A term used to describe the large companies in the pharmaceutical industry. There are 33 companies in the industry with more than $3 billion in annual revenue and more than $500 million in annual **research and development** costs.
Health care

Big Three

The term can no longer be used to refer to **General Motors Co., Ford Motor Co.** and Chrysler Group LLC as they no longer are the three biggest auto makers.

big-box retailer

Another term for a retailer with large stores, typically more than 50,000 square feet in size. Examples include **Wal-Mart**, Target, **Home Depot** and Best Buy.
Retail

Biogen Idec Inc.

The biotechnology company is based in Weston, Mass. Its logo uses all lowercase letters, but the company does capitalize its name.
Company Name, Health care

Birds Eye Foods Inc.

No apostrophe in the name of the Rochester, N.Y.-based frozen food company.

Company Name

bitmap

A type of memory used to store digital images.

Technology

BJ's Wholesale Club Inc.

The warehouse club retailer is based in Natick, Mass. BJ's is acceptable on second reference.

Company Name, Retail

Black Friday

A phrase commonly used to refer to the Christmas shopping done on the Friday after Thanksgiving because it is the day that many retailers supposedly go "into the black," i.e., become profitable. It is not, however, the largest shopping day of the year in terms of the dollar value of products sold. That typically occurs on the Saturday before Christmas, according to the International Council of Shopping Centers. In eight of 10 years between 1996 and 2005, the Saturday before Christmas was the biggest shopping day in the United States. The council hasn't released data on the top shopping days since 2005. Also, Black Friday has a secondary meaning — the stock market crash in September 1869. **($$$$)**

Retail

Black Monday

A phrase commonly used to refer to the stock market drops that occurred in October 1929 and October 1987. The October 1929 drop led to the **Great Depression**, while the October 1987 drop was the largest one-day percentage decline in stock market history. **($)**

Wall Street

black swan

An event or occurrence that is not expected. The term was coined by finance professor Nassim Nicholas Taleb. For example, the failure of hedge fund Long Term Capital Management was considered a black swan event because none of the firm's computers were programmed to consider the default of Russia's debt, in which it was heavily invested. **($$$$)**

Economy, Finance, Wall Street

black-box accounting

A term used to describe financial statements that are so complex that they are difficult to understand. Avoid using unless you can explain the accounting method being used.

BlackBerry

A trademarked product from Research in Motion Ltd. Both B's are capitalized. The generic term is **smartphone**.

Technology, Trademark

blackout period

A time period in which a contract cannot be changed, such as a retirement plan or health benefits coverage. **($$$)**

BlackRock Inc.

The investment management company is based in New York. Its name is always one word with a capital R.

Company Name, Finance

blind pool

A limited partnership or stock offering with no stated goal for the funds received from the investors. Blind pools are considered risky investments and often result in hefty fees for their managers.

Wall Street

block trade

A trade of at least 10,000 shares of a stock or $200,000 worth of a bond. **($$)**

Wall Street

Blockbuster LLC

The video store chain is based in Dallas and is now a subsidiary of the **Dish Network Corp.**

Company Name, Retail

Bloomberg Businessweek

The business magazine is two words. The magazine was founded in 1929. After being owned by McGraw-Hill for 80 years, it was sold in 2009 to **Bloomberg L.P.**

Bloomberg L.P.

The New York-based parent company of Bloomberg News, a financial wire service that is delivered via its terminals and to media customers. When founded in 1990, the wire service was called Bloomberg Business News. It now also owns radio, television, magazine and book publishing operations. When writing about the wire service and the company together, or when mentioning its founder, Michael Bloomberg, make sure to distinguish which one is being referenced.

Blu-ray

A disc storage format for data and high-definition video. The trademark belongs to the Blu-ray Disc Association, of which Sony has a majority stake.

Technology, Trademark

blue chip

A term used to describe a large, financially secure company. Blue-chip stocks are considered to be high quality. **($$)**

Wall Street

Blue Cross and Blue Shield

Many different health insurers have the rights to use the name from the Blue Cross Blue Shield Association. Identify which one on first reference: Blue Cross and Blue Shield of Alabama.

blue sky laws

State laws designed to protect the public against securities fraud. The laws require that financial details be disclosed with a securities The name comes from a Supreme Court justice, Joseph McKenna, who once said that investment schemes had the equivalent value of a patch of blue sky. **($)**

Wall Street

BMW

The preferred usage for Bayerische Motoren Werke AG, the formal name of the German automobile manufacturer.

Manufacturing, Transportation

BNSF Railway Co.

The Fort Worth, Texas-based railway is now owned by Berkshire Hathaway Inc. Its initials stand for Burlington Northern Santa Fe, its name before it was acquired in 2010.

Company Name, Transportation

board of directors

A group of people who represent the interest of shareholders and make major policy decisions for a company. The **CEO** of a company reports to the board of directors, although this person may also be the chairman of the board. Board members are elected at a company's annual meeting. Always lowercase. There are inside directors and outside directors. Inside directors are employees of the company. Outside directors are not employed by the company, although they may be executives of other companies that do business with the company on whose board they sit.

boardroom

A room where the **board of directors** of a company usually meets. Business reporters sometimes state that a decision was made "in the boardroom" when it actually wasn't. Be cautious when using this phrase. It should

only be used to mean a decision by the board of directors.

Boeing Co.

The airplane manufacturer is now based in Chicago, not Seattle, where it still maintains a large plant.

Company Name, Manufacturing

boiler room

A term used to describe a brokerage that uses aggressive marketing tactics in an attempt to sell stocks or bonds. In some cases, the investments may be highly speculative or even fraudulent. (**$$$**)

Wall Street

boilerplate

Standardized language or common disclosures in a company's **Securities and Exchange Commission** documents, contracts or regulatory filings.

bond

An investment where a company or a government entity borrows money from investors for a certain amount of time. A bond offers a rate of return for the investor, and therefore is considered safer than stocks. Bonds are also called **fixed-income** securities or **debt**. When writing about bonds issued by companies, do not state that bondholders have an ownership stake similar to that of shareholders. Bonds do not convey ownership unless they are **convertible bonds**. (**$$**)

Wall Street

The Bond Buyer

A newspaper published five days a week founded in 1891 that covers the municipal bond industry.

bond fund

A mutual fund that invests primarily in corporate or government bonds. (**$$**)

Wall Street

bond indexing

Designing a portfolio of bond investments so that its performance will match that of a bond index.

bond rating

A grade given to a bond that indicates the financial security of the issuer. The highest rating is AAA. Anything below BBB, or Ba3 for Moody's, is considered a **junk bond**. Bonds rating D are in default for nonpayment.

Wall Street

bondholder

An investor who owns bonds. One word.

Wall Street

bonus

Additional compensation received by an employee of a company above his or her salary and other payments. A bonus is sometimes higher than the person's salary.

book building

Describes the process in which an underwriter determines the price of an initial public offering. When an underwriter takes orders from clients as to how many shares they want of the **IPO** and at what price, the underwriter is said to be building a book for the offer. Those orders help the underwriter set the overall price for the offering. (**$$$$**)

Wall Street

book runner

The managing underwriter who maintains the books of securities sold for a new issue. Also commonly called the **lead underwriter**. (**$$$$**)

Wall Street

book value

Another term for **shareholder's equity**. It equals the value of a company's assets minus liabilities. It is the dollar amount that investors in the company would receive if the company's assets were sold for their accounting value, which may not equal their fair market value, and its liabilities were paid off.

Books on Tape

A trademarked product. The T is capitalized. The generic term is audio books.

Trademark

Books-A-Million Inc.

Hyphenate the name of the Birmingham, Ala.-based book retailer.

Company Name, Retail

Boston Scientific Corp.

The medical device maker is actually based in Natick, Mass.

Company Name, Manufacturing

bottom fisher

An investor who likes to purchase stocks that have fallen dramatically in price. A bottom fisher believes the stock price will rebound. (**$$**)

Wall Street

bottom line

The line on a financial statement that shows how much money has been made or lost by a company or a specific project. **Net income** is the preferred term, though bottom line can be used in casual references.

Company Name

bourse

Another name for a stock market, especially in Europe. Avoid unless it's part of the organization's official name. Bourse can also be used, acceptably, for coin and stamp sales areas at collectors' shows and meetings. (**$**)

Finance, Wall Street

boutique

A small firm that specializes in offering services to a few clients. A boutique investment bank may cater to a specific industry.

boycott

In business, a term used to describe when consumers organize to stop using or purchasing a good or service because they disagree with a decision made by the manufacturer.

brand jacking

Occurs when a third party takes a company's name and slogan and uses it for its own purposes without the company's permission. (**$$$**)

brand names

Products or services that have distinguished themselves from competitors by quality, style, innovation or heavy advertising. Guard against using brand names to describe a product. For example, write photo copies rather than Xeroxes.

breakup fee

A settlement negotiated as part of a merger or acquisition that would be paid by the buyer or seller if that party terminates the deal. Breakup fees are often set at a high amount to discourage other bidders. There is no hyphen, per the AP stylebook. (**$$$**)

BRIC

An acronym that refers to Brazil, Russia, India and China. BRIC is acceptable on all references, but make sure that the countries are listed somewhere in the story. (**$$**)

Economy

bridge loan

A short-term loan that allows buyers to purchase a new home before closing on the sale of their existing home. After the closing of the existing home, the bridge loan is paid off using the proceeds.

Finance, Real estate

Bristol-Myers Squibb Co.

Note the hyphen in the name of the New York-based pharmaceutical company. Avoid the BMS abbreviation in all references.

broadband

An Internet connection that allows for faster interaction than dial-up access.

Technology

Broadcom Corp.

The integrated circuits manufacturer is based in Irvine, Calif.

Company Name, Manufacturing, Technology

broker

A person who charges a commission to execute a transaction. The term can also be used to describe a firm. See **dealer**.

brokerage

A company that employs stock brokers to execute trades for investors.

Wall Street

brokerage account

Similar to a bank account, a brokerage account is where an investor places money with a broker and that money is used to execute the investor's trades.

Wall Street

browser

A software program such as Internet Explorer or Mozilla Firefox that allows you to search the Internet for information.

Technology

BTU

Use the abbreviation for British thermal units, a measure for power, in all references.

Energy

bubble

A rapid and unrealistic rise in the price of an asset. When the bubble bursts, prices collapse.

Bubble Wrap

A trademarked product name. Note that it is two words. The general term is packaging bubbles.

Trademark

bucket shop

A brokerage firm that uses aggressive tactics to persuade investors to buy or sell stocks and bonds. The term is derogatory and should be used sparingly. Also known as a **boiler room** operation. **($$)**

Wall Street

build-out

An estimate of the amount of money and land needed for a development. **($$)**

Real estate

bulge bracket

A term used to describe the underwriting banks that sell the bulk of the stock in an initial public offering. These are the underwriters typically listed on the **tombstone** advertisement. **($$)**

Wall Street

bull market

A time when investments are rising. The terms bull market and bear market come from how the animals attack their prey. A bull thrusts its horns up, while a bear swipes its paws down. Bull market should be used sparingly and never for a one- or two-day increase. **($)**

Wall Street

bullet contract

A **guaranteed investment contract** purchased by paying just one premium. **($)**

Finance, Insurance

bullet strategy

An investment strategy in which all of the bonds in a portfolio mature near the same date. **($$$)**

Finance, Wall Street

Bureau of Economic Analysis

A division of the U.S. Commerce Department that tracks the country's **gross domestic product,** as well as the GDP for states and specific metropolitan areas. It also tracks foreign trade. Avoid BEA on all references.

Economy

Bureau of Labor Statistics

A division of the U.S. **Department of Labor** that tracks economic data such as unemployment, inflation, the producer price index and productivity. BLS is acceptable on second reference.

Economy

Burger King

The Miami-based hamburger chain operates more than 12,200 restaurants in all 50 states and in 76 countries and U.S. territories. About 90 percent of its operations are run by franchisors.

burn rate

A term used to describe how much money a company is consuming each month. Burn rate indicates how long it will be before the new business runs out of money. For example, a company with $15 million in funding with a burn rate of $1 million can only last for 15 months without finding additional funding or generating cash. **($$$$)**

bushel

A dry measure used in commodities trading, especially for grains, such as wheat.

Wall Street

business continuity

A plan for conducting the day-to-day business of a company. It includes instructions and procedures for how a company reacts to abnormal conditions, such as an earthquake, so that its operations continue.

Company Name

business editor

Capitalize when used as a formal title before a person's name.

business-to-business

Describes transactions where one business is selling to another, such as a manufacturer selling to a wholesaler. Avoid the B2B abbreviation.

buy (n. or v.)

A rating given to a company's stock by a sell-side analyst. Buy or strong buy are typically the highest ratings an analyst gives.

Wall Street

buy limit order

A conditional order that indicates that the **security** can only be purchased at the designated price or lower. (**$$**)
Wall Street

buy the dips

A phrase used to describe when investors purchase shares or bonds after a decline in their price. (**$$$**)
Wall Street

buy vs. bought

When writing about acquisitions, write "agreed to buy" when the deal is announced but has not yet closed. Do not use "bought" unless Company A has already acquired Company B.

buy-side analyst

An **analyst** who works for a money manager or investment firm whose research is used solely for in-house purposes. A buy-side analyst typically makes recommendations for stocks to buy and sell for the firm's internal funds it manages for investors. See **sell-side analyst**. (**$$**)
Wall Street

buyback (n.), buy back (v.)

The repurchasing of shares by a company to decrease its number of shares outstanding. A company will buy back those shares. A company's announcement of a buyback plan doesn't mean necessarily that the shares will actually be repurchased. Some companies will announce a buyback plan to support its stock price, but not actually repurchase the shares Also, some companies will buy back their stock to inflate their **earnings per share** numbers. The term share repurchase is also acceptable. (**$$**)

buyer's agent

A real estate agent who represents the buyer in a transaction.
Real estate

buyer's market

A situation in the real estate market where prices are depressed, allowing a buyer to pay less for a house than in normal circumstances.
Real estate

buyout

When a controlling interest of a company is acquired. Acquisition is also acceptable.
Company Name

buyout (adj., n.), buy out (v.)

Another term for an **acquisition**, or when a company buys out the contract of one of its executives so that he or she will leave. A buyout of a company occurs when one company buys a controlling interest of the stock in another company.

C corporation

A corporation that is taxed separately from its owners. Most major companies in the United States are C corporations. The Internal Revenue Service has information about C corporation taxes on its website.

Company Name

C-suite

A slang term referring to a company's top executives. Avoid using except when quoting someone.

C.H. Robinson Worldwide Inc.

A trucking logistics company based in Eden Prairie, Minn. C.H. Robinson is acceptable on second reference.

Company Name, Transportation

CA Technologies Inc.

The Islandia, N.Y., company formerly known as Computer Associates and CA Inc. should now be referred to as CA Technologies Inc. on first reference and CA Technologies on subsequent references. **($$)**

Company Name, Technology

Cablevision Systems Corp.

Cablevision is acceptable on second reference for the Bethpage, N.Y.-based cable television company.

Company Name

Caesars Entertainment Corp.

The Paradise, Nev.-based operator of casinos and hotels changed its name from Harrah's Entertainment in 2010. There is no apostrophe in Caesars.

Company Name

cafeteria plan

An employee benefit plan that allows workers to choose from a menu of options. The options will typically include items such as health insurance, disability insurance, life insurance, tax credits and retirement plans. **($$)**

Insurance

calendar year

From Jan. 1 to Dec. 31. While many companies report their financial performance based on the calendar year, others will report using the **fiscal year**. These terms are often interchangeable unless a company's fiscal year is not the same as the calendar year.

call options

An agreement that gives an investor the right but not the obligation to purchase a stock, bond or commodity at a specific price by a specific time. Owning a call option, however, does not mean that the investor actually owns the investment. See **put options**. **($$$$)**

Wall Street

Calpine Corp.
The energy company is based in Houston.

Cameron International Corp.
The Houston-based company makes equipment for oil wells and refineries.

Company Name, Energy

Campbell Soup Co.
The Camden, N.J.-based food company is known as Campbell's on second reference.

Company Name

capital
A vague term often used to describe the assets of a company. Capital can be cash, or a "capital asset" such as machinery, equipment or anything else of value.

capital controls
Government-imposed limits on how much money can enter or leave a country. Describe the actual limit. **($$)**

Economy

capital expenditure
The amount of money that a company spends each year to expand or maintain its operations. Many industries have large capital expenditure budgets each year, while others have small capital expenditure spending. Do not use the slang capex, often used by company **CFOs** and treasurers. **($$$)**

capital gain
An increase in the value of a business asset or investment from its purchase price. However, the gain is not realized until the asset is sold. The opposite is **capital loss**. **($$$$)**

Wall Street

capital gain distribution
A payment made by a mutual fund to investors based on the realized **capital gains** of its investment portfolio. **($$$$)**

Wall Street

capital loss
A loss when an investment decreases in value below its cost. The loss isn't actually recognized until the investment is sold. It's the opposite of **capital gain**.

Capital One Financial Corp.
The bank holding company is based in Richmond, Va. Avoid the COF abbreviation in all references.

capitation
A method of payment in health care. It is based on the number of patients covered for a specific health care service during a specific time period rather than the cost of the services actually provided. **($$$)**

Health care

captive insurance
A strategy in which a company insures itself against risk by setting up an in-house insurance operation instead of buying insurance from

another company. It might hire an outside insurer to manage the operation. The difference between captive insurance and a **self-insurance plan** is that with a captive, the company sets aside money for future losses. **($$)**

Company Name, Insurance

Cardinal Health Inc.

The health care services company is based in Dublin, Ohio.

cardiologist

A doctor who treats heart disorders. Cardiologists should be distinguished from cardiac, cardiothoracic and cardiovascular surgeons, who perform cardiac surgery, often via a sternotomy, an operation that cuts through the sternum or breastbone.

Health care

CarMax Inc.

The Richmond, Va.-based used-car retailer spells its name as one word with a capital M.

Company Name, Retail

carrying value

The value of an asset on a company's balance sheet. The carrying value of an asset is often lower than its actual value if it were sold. **($$)**

cartel

A group of producers of a service or a product that join together to control the supply in an effort to manipulate prices. **($$)**

Economy

carve out (n., v.)

A process where a health insurance company excludes one or more medical services from the benefits it provides. **($)**

Health care, Insurance

Casey's General Stores Inc.

The convenience store chain is based in Ankeny, Iowa. It has more than 1,540 stores, primarily in the Midwest.

Company Name, Retail

cash

The amount of money a company has on its books at the end of a reporting period. It is not to be confused with **cash flow**.

cash basis accounting

An accounting method that recognizes revenue or expenses at the time **cash** is paid out or received. It is simpler than the **accrual accounting** method. **($$$$)**

cash cow

A business line, product or asset that consistently produces money for its owners. This is a slang term. Use it sparingly, and carefully.

cash earnings

Also known as pro-forma earnings. Do not use this term because it excludes items such as charges. State what items aren't included.

cash flow

The amount of **cash** a company generates. It is calculated by adding noncash charges, such as depreciation, to the net income after taxes. Cash flow can be used as an indicator of a company's financial strength. A company can be described as having a positive cash flow or a negative cash flow. **($$)**

cash market

The market where you can actually purchase a commodity rather than a futures contract for that commodity. **($$)**

Wall Street

cash reserves

Cash deposits, short-term bank deposits, **money market** deposits and short-term securities, all of which can be converted quickly to cash. **($$)**

casual dining

When a restaurant offers table service and a casual atmosphere — usually at moderate prices.

Restaurant

casualty insurance

Insurance against loss of property, damage or other liabilities. A type of casualty insurance is **workers' compensation** insurance.

Insurance

category killer

A term used to describe a product, brand or service that dominates the market category. The term comes from the belief that other competitors will exit the market, leaving the category to the dominant entry.

Caterpillar Inc.

The manufacturer of mining and construction equipment is based in Peoria, Ill. Avoid the CAT abbreviation in all references.

Company Name, Manufacturing

CB Richard Ellis Group Inc.

The real estate company is based in Los Angeles.

Company Name, Real estate

CBS Corp.

A media company based in New York. When writing about the parent company and the television network of the same name in the same story, be sure to distinguish between the two.

Company Name

CC Media Holdings Inc.

The San Antonio-based company operates radio stations and owns billboards. Its radio subsidiary is Clear Channel Communications.

Company Name

Celanese Corp.

The chemicals manufacturer is based in Dallas.

Company Name, Manufacturing

Cemex S.A.B. de C.V.

Capitalize only the first letter in the name of the building materials company based in Mexico with large

operations in the United States. Cemex is acceptable in most first references.
Company Name

Centene Corp.
The Clayton, Mo.-based company provided managed care to people in the **Medicaid** program. Capitalize only the C in the name although the company logo uses all capital letters.
Company Name, Health care, Insurance

CenterPoint Energy Inc.
The Houston-based energy company spells CenterPoint as one word, with a capital P.
Company Name, Energy

cents
Always spell out and lowercase when writing about earnings below $1 per share. Write 31 cents per share, not $.31 per share.

CenturyLink Inc.
The telecommunications company is based in Monroe, La. Its name is one word with a capital L in all references.
Company Name

certificate of authority
A license from a state insurance department allowing an insurance or managed-care company to operate in the state. (**$$**)
Health care, Insurance

certificate of deposit
A savings certificate that pays interest during its term, which can be anywhere from several months to several years. *CD* is acceptable on second reference.
Finance

certificate of need
A regulatory process in many states that requires a health care facility such as a hospital or nursing home to apply for and receive approval to expand its services or to convert beds to other services. Avoid CON on all references. (**$$$**)
Health care

certificate of occupancy
A certificate issued by a local government agency that certifies that a building can be occupied.
Real estate

certified public accountant
A designation given by the American Institute of Certified Public Accountants for someone who has passed its exam and meets certain work requirements. *CPA* is acceptable on second reference.

CH2M Hill Cos.
The engineering and construction company is based in Meridian, Colo. Capitalize all of the letters in CH2M, but only the H in Hill.
Company Name

chairman of the board
The most senior executive, in terms of position, in an organization. The chair is responsible for running the annual meeting and the meetings

of the board of directors. He or she may be a figurehead, appointed for prestige, and may have no role in the day-to-day running of the organization. Sometimes the roles of chair and **chief executive officer** are combined. Chairwoman is acceptable if the person is female. Capitalize before a name.

channel stuffing

A term used to describe when a company induces suppliers and retailers to purchase more of its product near the end of a period to make its financial results look better. Channel stuffing can backfire on a company by reducing future sales and profits. **($$$$)**

Retail

Chap Stick

A trademarked product. Note that it is two words. The generic term is lip balm.

Trademark

Chapter 11

A **bankruptcy** court filing by a company or an individual where the debtor proposes paying off some, but not all, of its debt. The filing essentially asks the court to forgive some of the money owed. An overview of how a Chapter 11 filing works is on the U.S. Courts website.

Chapter 13

A **bankruptcy** court filing by an individual who proposes to repay all of his or her debt during an extended period of time. An overview of the Chapter 13 process is on the U.S. Courts website.

Chapter 7

A **bankruptcy** court filing by a company in which the business plans to liquidate its assets and close operations. Sometimes, a **Chapter 11** filing can be converted into a Chapter 7 by the court if a business can't come to a reorganization agreement with its creditors. Eligibility requirements for a Chapter 7 filing are on the U.S. Courts website.

charge

A one-time expense by a company that reduces earnings. There is no official accounting term. Bloomberg News asks that its reporters use a more specific term, such as cost, expense, **write-down**, investment loss or severance pay. **($$)**

charge-off (n., adj.), charge off (v.)

A debt that a lender can't collect and therefore is written off. When a bank's charge-offs decline, more of its loans are being paid on time.

Finance

Charles Schwab Corp.

The brokerage and banking company is based in San Francisco. Schwab is acceptable on second reference. Avoid capitalizing "the" before the name.

Company Name, Finance

Charter Communications Inc.

The cable, Internet and telephone provider is based in Town and Country, Mo.

Company Name

chartered financial analyst

A designation given by the *CFA* Institute to a financial analyst that measures his or her competency and integrity. CFA is acceptable on second reference.

Finance

Cheesecake Factory Inc.

Avoid capitalizing "the" before the company name of this Calabasas Hills, Calif.-based restaurant chain.

Company Name

cherry picking

Selecting a sample to show what you want to show rather than to show what's really happening. For example, a mutual fund may show in an advertisement its one-year performance because it beats the overall market rather than its 10-year performance, which underperforms the market. **($$)**

Chesapeake Energy Corp.

The natural gas company is based in Oklahoma City.

Company Name, Energy

Chevron Corp.

The San Ramon, Calif.-based company also owns the Texaco brand.

Company Name, Energy

Chicago Board of Trade

The world's oldest futures and commodities exchange. It merged with the Chicago Mercantile Exchange in 2007. Do not use CBOT on any reference.

Wall Street

Chicago Mercantile Exchange

A 1919 spinoff from the Chicago Board of Trade, the Chicago Mercantile Exchange trades financial and commodity derivatives. It merged with the Chicago Board of Trade in 2007 and the New York Mercantile Exchange in 2008. The terms Chicago Merc and Merc are acceptable on second reference. Do not use CME on any reference.

Wall Street

Chick-fil-A Inc.

Note the hyphens and capitalization of the privately held restaurant chain based in Atlanta.

Company Name, Restaurant

chief administrative officer

Oversees a company's daily operations, including its staff and services. Some companies have both a chief operating officer and a chief administrative officer. Avoid using CAO. **($)**

chief executive officer

The top management position at any company. The chief executive officer of a company typically sets the strategic direction of the business. CEO is acceptable on first reference.

chief financial officer

The person at a company who over-sees its financial statements and is also responsible for the financing, such as stock and bond offerings. The *CFO* is also typically the main point person at a company who deals with investors and analysts. CFO is acceptable on second reference.

Finance

chief information officer

A title often used for the person at a company in charge of information technology. This person typically re-ports to the chief operating officer or **president** of a company and has grown in importance in recent years. *CIO* is acceptable on second refer-ence. **($$$)**

Technology

chief marketing officer

An increasingly common title, especially in the food industry, for the executive in charge of a company's marketing operations. *CMO* is acceptable on second reference. **($)**

Restaurant

chief operating officer

The officer responsible for the day-to-day management of a company who usually reports to the chief executive officer. *COO* is acceptable on second reference. **($)**

chief risk officer

An executive responsible for ensuring that a company is in compliance with regulations and has minimized potential damage to its reputation, financial results and operations. Do not use CRO on any reference. **($$$)**

Chinese wall

A term used to describe the supposed separation between the investment banking and research operations of a brokerage house. Many firms were criticized for having little to no sepa-ration between the two areas in the 1990s and early part of the 21st cen-tury. Avoid using it.

Wall Street

chiropractor

A doctor who holds a doctor of chiro-practic degree and focuses treatments on the musculoskeletal system, often through spine manipulation. Chi-ropractors often treat patients with back problems. Chiropractors may be called chiropractic physicians.

Health care

Chubb Corp.

A **property and casualty insurance** company based in Edison, N.J.

Company Name, Insurance

churning

Unnecessary trading in accounts, solely to increase brokers' commis-sions. It's unethical. **($$)**

CiCi's Enterprises LP

Both Cs are capitalized in the name of the Coppell, Texas-based restaurant operator.

Company Name, Restaurant

Cigna Corp.

A health insurance and benefits company based in Philadelphia. Although the company spells its name with all capital letters, in stories it should be written as Cigna. The letters came from a combination of Connecticut General Corp. and INA Corp., which stood for Insurance Company of North America.

Company Name, Health care, Insurance

circuit breaker

A break in trading imposed by an exchange when the market falls by a certain percentage. A circuit breaker is designed to prevent panic selling. The New York Stock Exchange has posted information about its circuit breakers. (**$$**)

Wall Street

Cisco Systems Inc.

The San Jose, Calif.-based technology company can be referred to as Cisco on second reference.

Company Name, Technology

Citgo Petroleum Corp.

Lowercase the first name of the Houston-based gasoline retailer after the C.

Company Name, Energy

Citigroup Inc.

The New York-based financial services company has a bank subsidiary called Citibank. Distinguish between the two names when writing about the company.

claim

A statement of health care services submitted to a health insurer or managed-care plan. The patient or the health care provider can submit the claim.

Health care

claims administration

The process by which an insurer reviews and processes a claim.

Health care, Insurance

class action

A lawsuit filed by one or more people on behalf of many other people who may be in a similar situation. Class-action lawsuits may be difficult and are expensive, but they allow people who can't afford to file a lawsuit individually to band together.

classes of shares

Types of shares in a company that have different voting rights. For example, some companies may have Class A shares and Class B shares where Class A shares may have 10 votes each while Class B shares have only 1 vote each. Many companies set up the different classes when they go public to allow families to maintain control of the company. Note that Class is always capitalized.

clawback

A provision that allows a company to recapture money or benefits from executives if it restates its financial results. The term can also be used to describe a drop in a stock price or

the stock market.
Finance, Wall Street

clearing house

A third party that settles trades for futures and options contracts. Members of a commodity exchange, for example, are required to clear their trades through a clearing house. **($$$)**
Wall Street

Clif Bar & Co.

The Berkeley, Calif.-based natural energy bar company has just one f in its name.
Company Name

clinical trials

The **Food and Drug Administration** has three levels of trials for testing drugs. They are:

- Phase I trials, on a few dozen health volunteers, to determine the drug's safety;
- Phase II trials, on several hundred patients, to determine the drug's ability to combat the illness;
- Phase III trials, on several thousand people, to assess the drug's dosage and long-term safety.Because all of these levels involve humans, the phrase human trials is also acceptable.

Information about how clinical trials should be run is on the Food and Drug Administration website.
Health care, Real estate

Clorox Co.

A cleaning products company based in Oakland, Calif.
Company Name

closed shop

A business where union membership is a condition for employment.

closed-end fund

A publicly traded investment company that raises money in an initial public offering and has a fixed number of shares. Such funds trade like stocks and have little in common with mutual funds, which are also known as open-end funds. **($$)**
Wall Street

closely held

When there are a few shareholders controlling a company. It may still be publicly traded. **($$)**

closing bell

A term used to describe the close of the markets. In the United States, that time is 4 p.m. EST. It's also the name of a **CNBC** show.
Wall Street

closing costs

Expenses that are incurred in a real estate transaction. They include, but are not limited to, attorney's fees, the mortgage application fee, the appraisal fee, the home inspection fee, the agent's commission and the title fee. They can be paid for by the buyer or the seller.
Real estate

cloud computing

Internet-based computing that delivers shared resources, software and information to computers and other devices on demand. ($)

Technology

CMS Energy Corp.

The utility is based in Jackson, Mich. Use CMS Energy on second reference.

Company Name, Energy

CNA Financial Corp.

Because each letter is pronounced, capitalize CNA in all references to the Chicago-based insurer.

Company Name, Insurance

CNBC

A business news cable television network. As part of the National Broadcasting Co., it is based in Englewood Cliffs, N.J. The network went on the air in April 1989 and is now considered the primary business news venue on television. A competitor, **Fox Business Network**, started in October 2007. CNBC stands for Consumer News & Business Channel, but CNBC should be used on all references. CNBC is responsible for launching the careers of many business journalists, including Maria Bartiromo.

CNET.com

An online technology news service. It was acquired by CBS Corp. in 2008.

CNO Financial Group Inc.

The life and health insurer is based in Carmel, Ind. It was formerly known as Conseco Inc.

Company Name, Finance, Insurance

co-payment

A payment made by the health care consumer at the time services are provided. The health insurer determines the co-payment levels.

Health care, Insurance

coattail investing

A term used to describe when investors mimic the investment strategy of well-known investors, such as Warren Buffett. ($$)

Wall Street

COBRA

Stands for Consolidated Omnibus Budget Reconciliation Act. It is a federal law that allows employees to continue their health insurance after leaving a company's employment for between 18 and 36 months, depending on circumstances. Use COBRA on all references, but explain the law. For more on COBRA coverage, go to the Department of Labor's website. ($$$$)

Health care

Coca-Cola Co.

The Atlanta-based soft drinks company.

Company Name

Coca-Cola Enterprises Inc.

An Atlanta-based bottler of soft drinks and other beverages. It is separate from the Coca-Cola Co.

Company Name

code-sharing

When two or more airlines link their flights in reservation systems. It is used so that airlines can offer flights to destinations that they don't normally serve.

Coke

A trademarked product. Can also be referred to as Coca-Cola. The company, which is called Coca-Cola Co., recently dropped the word Classic from the end of the product.

cold calling

Making unsolicited phone calls in an attempt to drum up new business. Be careful using this term, as it sometimes has a negative connotation. **($$$)**

Colgate-Palmolive Co.

The New York-based consumer products company always uses a hyphen in its name.

Company Name

collar

A strategy that limits both the upside and the downside of an investment. A collar is also used in some acquisitions where stock is used as currency. **($$$$)**

collateral

A borrower's pledge to pay off a loan with a piece of property, such as a home. If the borrower defaults on the loan, then the collateral goes to the institution that made the loan.

Finance, Real estate

collateralized debt obligation

An investment security backed by a pool of bonds or loans. Do not use CDO on second reference. Do not hyphenate. **($$$$$)**

Wall Street

collateralized mortgage obligation

An investment security backed by mortgages that has different levels of when investors are repaid. Do not use CMO on second reference. Use *pool* or *investment*. Do not hyphenate. **($$$$$)**

Real estate, Wall Street

collective bargaining

Voluntary negotiations between an employer and a union aimed at reaching a new agreement.

combined ratio

A measure of profitability for a property and casualty insurance company. The combined ratio is the value of the claims paid plus the company's expenses divided by the dollar value of the premium collected. A combined ratio below 100 percent means that the company is making a profit from its insurance operations. An insurance company with a combined ratio of 105 percent is paying out $1.05 in claims and expenses for every $1 it collects in premiums. It may still be profitable, however, because of profits from investments. **($$)**

Insurance

Comcast Corp.

The Philadelphia-based company is the parent of CNBC, as well cable and Internet operations.

Company Name

commas

A common problem in business reporting. The tendency is to use commas in the wrong places. For example, there is no comma before a company's name and Co., Inc. or Corp. It should be written as Home Depot Inc. not Home Depot, Inc., even if the company places the comma there. Commas should also be used in numbers of 1,000 and above, including monetary amounts. Example: "The chief executive's salary rose to $450,000, up $50,000 from his salary in 2008."

Commercial Metals Co.

The Irving, Texas-based company manufactures steel and metal. Avoid using CMC in all references.

Manufacturing

commercial paper

Unsecured, short-term debt issued by a company. Such debt is typically used to finance **accounts receivable** and inventory at a company, and it is not registered with the **Securities and Exchange Commission**, like other debt issued by a company, because it is scheduled to be paid back in less than nine months. **($$$$)**

Wall Street

commission

A fee charged by a broker or an investment adviser, typically for services such as buying or selling stock for the customer.

committee names

Always lower case and never abbreviate. For example, "The executive compensation committee of the board decided to raise salaries in 2009."

commoditization

When a product that was previously identified by its brand name or another attribute becomes similar to competing products and is then sold based primarily on price, lowering the profit margin for the product. Avoid using the term in your own writing. If used in a quote, explain it later. **($$$$)**

Manufacturing

commodity

A good that is bought and sold by investors. Types of commodities include wheat, corn, beef, gold, silver and platinum. The term has recently also been used to refer to technology products that have become common.

Commodity Futures Trading Commission

A federal regulatory agency formed in 1974 that regulates the commodities and futures markets, much in the same way that the **Securities and Exchange Commission** regulates the stock market. Do not use CFTC on second reference. Use commission instead. **($)**

Finance, Wall Street

common area

An area in real estate that is available for use by anyone. An example would be a stairway or elevator in an apartment building, or a clubhouse in a subdivision.

common stock

The most common type of publicly traded shares. The common stock holders are the ones that vote on the board of directors and shareholder proposals. See **preferred stock**.

Wall Street

community development financial institution

A bank, credit union, venture capital fund or other financial source that provides loans to promote economic development in struggling areas, both urban and rural, underserved by traditional financial institutions. Often called microlenders, they can provide mortgage financing for homebuyers, financing for the rehabilitation of rental housing, financing for the building and rehabilitation of community facilities, commercial loans to small businesses, and financial services needed by low-income households and businesses. **($$$)**

Economy, Finance

Community Health Systems Inc.

The hospital operator is based in Franklin, Tenn. The *CHS* abbreviation is acceptable on second reference.

Company Name, Health care

community rating

A system used by a health insurer to set premiums based on an entire community rather than any subgroup. Community rating lumps low-risk and high-risk consumers into the same group. **($$$)**

Health care, Insurance

Community Reinvestment Act

A law that requires banks and credit unions to lend money to consumers in low-income neighborhoods where they have deposits. It was passed in 1977 in an attempt to eliminate discrimination in lending. Banks that don't meet the law are accused of **redlining**. For more on the Community Reinvestment Act, go to the Federal Financial Institutions Examination Council website.

Finance

company

Always abbreviate as Co. when used at the end of the company's name on first reference. Do not use at the end of the company's name on second reference. Spell out and lower case when it stands alone.

company names

The full company name should be used only on first reference, including Co., Inc., Corp. and Ltd. For example, Hewlett-Packard Co. on first reference, but Hewlett-Packard on second reference. Do not use all capital letters unless they are individually pronounced, such as BMW. Do not use symbols or exclamation points. Use an ampersand only if it is part of the company name. Do not capitalized the even if it is capitalized by the company. Company names in this stylebook are primarily listed because of capitalization and punctuation issues.

Company Name

company nicknames

IBM is often referred to as Big Blue after the first reference. However, please avoid using nicknames unless they will be familiar to the average reader. For example, the term Big Red might be acceptable to business news readers in Atlanta for a story about Coca-Cola Co., but note that there's a carbonated soft drink company, based in Waco, Texas, named Big Red Ltd.

Company Name

Computer Sciences Corp.

The information technology company is based in Falls Church, Va. Avoid using the CSC abbreviation.

Company Name, Technology

Con-way Inc.

The trucking company is based in San Mateo, Calif. Its name always uses a hyphen.

Company Name, Transportation

ConAgra Foods Inc.

The Omaha, Neb.-based food-processing company capitalizes the first A in its name.

Company Name

concept

The scheme or plan behind a restaurant or restaurant chain. Elements include its branding, decor, service style and menu. Don't call the restaurant or chain itself a concept. (**$**)

Restaurant

Conference Board

A nonprofit organization that makes economics-based forecasts and assesses trends in the marketplace that are useful to business reporters.

Economy

conference call

An event in which investors call a special phone number and hear the management of their company comment on the financial results of a recently completed quarter or another important event. Business journalists can listen to conference calls, but few companies allow them to ask questions.

conglomerate

A company that owns businesses in many different industries, including industries that may not be related. For example, **General Electric Co.** owns businesses that make airplane engines and dishwashers. **Walt Disney Co.** owns the ABC network and ESPN. (**$**)

ConocoPhillips Co.

The Houston-based oil and gasoline company spells its name as one word.

Company Name, Energy

consensus analyst estimate

The average earnings estimate for a company based on the predictions of all of the analysts covering the company. The estimate could be for an upcoming quarter or for a year. Business reporters often compare the consensus estimate with the actual results when writing earnings stories. **($$)**

Consol Energy Inc.

The coal-mining company is based in Cecil Township, Pa. Capitalize only the C in Consol.

Company Name, Energy

Consolidated Edison Inc.

An energy company based in New York. The abbreviations *Con Edison* and *ConEd* are acceptable on second reference.

Company Name, Energy

consolidated financial statement

A term used to describe the financial statements of a company and its subsidiaries. **($$)**

Constellation Energy Group Inc.

The Baltimore-based company operates power plants and distributes energy.

Energy

construction spending

Data that represent the expense by builders on residential and non-residential structures. Construction spending is compiled monthly by the Census Bureau and is split between private and public construction.

Economy, Real estate

consultant

A person who provides advice to a company on how its operations can be improved. The consultant can work for a consulting firm or can be an individual. Most consultants are experts in a specific field, such as management, manufacturing, sales or technology.

Company Name

Consumer Confidence Index

A measurement by the **Conference Board** on whether consumers are feeling optimistic or pessimistic about the economy. The University of Michigan and Thomson Reuters have a similar measurement called the Index of Consumer Sentiment. The Conference Board survey focuses on labor conditions, while the Michigan survey focuses on financial conditions. Use index for both on second reference. The latest index data from the Conference Board can be found on its website. The Thomson Reuters/Michigan index is also available online.

Economy

consumer credit

Debt used by consumers to purchase a good or service. Examples are credit card debt and auto loans. Consumer credit is also referred to as consumer debt. **($$)**

Finance

Consumer Financial Protection Bureau

A part of the Federal Reserve system created in 2010 by Congress that is designed to police consumer lending, protecting consumers from unethical mortgage, credit card and other financial products. Do not refer to it as an agency and avoid using the CFPB abbreviation. **($$$$)**

Finance, Real estate, Wall Street

consumer price index

A monthly measure of the price change of consumer goods such as gasoline, food and automobiles. It is compiled by the **Bureau of Labor Statistics** and released monthly. The story focuses on the change in the index for urban workers, or CPI-U, which covers about 87 percent of the population. *CPI* is acceptable on second reference. Answers to basic questions about the CPI can be found on the Bureau of Labor Statistics website. **($$)**

Economy

Consumer Product Safety Commission

The federal agency that protects consumers against faulty products. Its jurisdiction covers product safety for more than 15,000 products, and it can force a recall of a product. *CPSC* is acceptable on second reference. A list of product recalls from the agency is on its website.

consumer spending

The purchase of goods and services by consumers, also known as con-sumption and personal consumption expenditures. Consumer spending totals two-thirds of the U.S. gross domestic product. Consumer spending data can be found on the Bureau of Labor Statistics website.

Economy

continuing claims

A number compiled by the Department of Labor that measures the sum of all unemployed workers receiving benefits in a given week. **($$)**

Economy

contract

A binding agreement between two parties that is enforceable by law. One of the most common contracts is one where a buyer agrees to purchase a home from a seller.

Real estate

contractor

A person or business that provides goods or services to another business in accordance of the terms of a contract between the two parties. A subcontractor is someone hired by the contractor to provide all or part of those goods or services. A general contractor contracts with other businesses to construct a building, a road, or some other type of project.

Company Name, Real estate

contrarian

An investment strategy in which assets are purchased when most investors are selling and sold when

most investors are buying. **($$)**
Wall Street

convenience store

A small retail business that sells a wide array of products, but primarily groceries, gasoline and tobacco. Increasingly, convenience stores are offering prepared food items in competition with quick-service outlets, in part to make up for declining tobacco sales. *C-store* is acceptable on second reference.

Restaurant, Retail

conventional mortgage

A loan that is not insured or guaranteed by any government agency. It is typically a fixed-rate mortgage.

Real estate

conversion

The process in which a company changes its ownership structure, typically from one where the business is owned by its customers, such as a mutual insurance company, to one where the business is owned by stockholders. **($$$)**

convertible bond

A bond that can be converted to stock in the company, usually at the discretion of the investor. Convertible is acceptable on second reference. **($$$$)**

Wall Street

convexity

An adjustment to **duration**, which is an estimate of how much the price of a **bond** will change when interest rates rise or fall. The term is typically applied to callable bonds, whose prices tend to drop more for an increase in yield than rise for a decrease — a trait known as negative convexity. Positive convexity means a bond's price rises more for a drop in yield than it declines for the same increase in yield. **($$$$$)**

Finance, Wall Street

cook the books

A term used to describe when a company uses fraudulent accounting. Do not use this term unless charges have been filed against the company or its auditor.

cookie

Data sent to a website each time the site is accessed so that the site identifies the specific user.

Technology

core competency

A term used to describe the main strength of a company. **($$)**

core earnings

The profit derived from a company's main business. For example, the core earnings of an auto company would include its profits from making cars and trucks, but it would exclude profits or losses from a nonvehicle business such as the savings and loan that Ford once owned. **($$)**

Core-Mark Holding Co.

The San Francisco-based company provides food to convenience stores. Always use the hyphen.

cornering a market

When an investor purchases enough of the available supply of a stock or a commodity to manipulate its price. (**$**)

Wall Street

Corning Inc.

The glass and ceramics manufacturer is based in Corning, N.Y.

Company Name, Manufacturing

corporate America

Avoid this cliche, as most corporations based in the United States have large operations outside the country. In addition, all corporations do not act together or uniformly.

Company Name

Corporate Library LLC

An independent research firm based in Portland, Maine, that acts as a watchdog on behalf of shareholders.

corporation

The most common form of business organization. The organization is on-going, and the owners' liability is limited. Abbreviate as Corp. when used on first reference as part of a company's formal name. Do not use on the second reference of a company.

correction

A Wall Street euphemism for falling securities prices. Do not use this term as prices aren't mistakes. (**$$**)

Wall Street

correlation trade

A trading strategy based on the belief that debt of similar companies move in the same direction at the same time. The belief is that the higher the correlation, the lower the risk. (**$$**)

Wall Street

cost of capital

The necessary profit needed for a company project, such as the building of a new warehouse. (**$$**)

cost of goods sold

The cost required to make a product. It includes the cost of both the ingredients or parts and the labor but not the packaging and shipping. Do not abbreviate as COGS. Use cost on second reference. (**$$**)

cost of living

The amount of money needed to purchase housing and necessary goods. A cost of living adjustment increases or decreases someone's income to reflect changes caused by inflation or a contraction. Do not abbreviate as COL or COLA on second reference. (**$**)

Economy

Costco Wholesale Corp.

The Issaquah, Wash.-based company operates warehouse retail stores across the country.

Retail

counteroffer

A response to an acquisition offer when the company in play wants better terms before being acquired. Can also use counter as the verb.

counterparty

The other party in a financial transaction.

coupon

The interest rate on a bond when it's issued. **($$)**

Wall Street

courtesy titles

The New York Times business desk and The Wall Street Journal still use them, such as Mr., Ms. and Mrs., but virtually no other business media outlet does. Avoid unless you're writing for one of these.

covenants

A set of rules that often govern a neighborhood or subdivision. They define what a homeowner can do on his or her property, such as install a fence or a storage shed. Covenants are initially set in place by the developer, but later enforced by the homeowners association. A covenant is also a set of conditions in a loan agreement that the borrow must follow. When the borrower is in violation of the loan covenants, the lender can call for the loan to be repaid fully, or the borrower can negotiate with the lender to wave the covenants. At one time, covenants could place racial and religious restrictions on who could buy properties, but such covenants can no longer be enforced.

Finance, Real estate

Coventry Health Care Inc.

A health insurer based in Bethesda, Md.

Company Name, Insurance

coverage initiated

When a sell-side analyst begins coverage of a company's stock. Bank of America Merrill Lynch analyst Barney Google initiated coverage on Coca-Cola Co. on Thursday with a "buy" rating and a $50 price target.

Wall Street

CPM

Stands for cost per mille. It's a uniform rate for Internet advertising that specifies a rate to be paid for every 1,000 page views.

Technology

Cramer, Jim

The co-founder of **TheStreet.com** who also has a regular show on **CNBC** called "Mad Money." Cramer, a former professional investor, has been criticized for giving bad investment advice through the media. A jump in the stock price of a company mentioned on Cramer's show is known as the *Cramer effect.*

crash

A major, sudden decline in a market. The term crash is not used unless the market has fallen by at least 20 percent. **($$)**

Wall Street

Crayola

A trademarked product. The generic word is crayons.

Trademark

credentialing

A review process by a health insurer that determines the competence of a health care provider. **($$)**

Health care, Insurance

credit

When a borrower receives something of value now and agrees to repay the lender at a future date. The term can also refer to the borrowing capacity a person or company might have.

credit crunch

A time period when it becomes more difficult and costly for consumers or companies to borrow money. It usually follows a period in which consumers default on loans in higher-than-normal amounts, causing lenders to adjust their borrowing requirements. Credit crisis is not acceptable. A **credit** crisis means there's almost no borrowed money to be had.

Economy

credit default swap

A contract used to hedge or speculate on a company's ability to repay its debt. The contract pays the buyer should the company default. Give prices of credit default swaps in **basis points** rather than currency. **($$$$)**

Wall Street

credit enhancement

A strategy that attempts to reduce the risk of an investment by requiring a financial transaction on top of the investment. For example, the purchase of insurance that guarantees payments from a bond issue is a credit enhancement. Another type is **overcollateralization. ($$$)**

Finance, Wall Street

credit report

A record of an individual's history in terms of borrowing and paying off money. Lenders use a credit report to determine whether to give a person a credit card or lend money to a person who has applied for a loan.

Real estate

credit spread

The difference between the yields of a Treasury bill and company debt that have the same rating and the same maturity. The spread reflects the additional yield that an investor can earn by investing in a security with more risk.

credit union

A financial institution that competes with banks and **savings and loans** for consumer deposits and loans. Credit unions are cooperatives that are owned and controlled by members. They are regulated by the **National Credit Union Administration,** which has an online database of financial information about every credit union.

Finance

creditor
A person or company that is owed money.

creditworthiness
A creditor's measurement of a customer's ability and willingness to repay his or her debts.
Finance

Crispin Porter & Bogusky
Use the ampersand, not the plus sign, in the name of the Miami-based advertising agency.
Company Name

Crock-Pot
A trademarked product. Note the hyphen and capital P. The generic term is electric earthenware cooker.
Trademark

cross listing
When a company's stock is listed on a foreign exchange as well as a home country exchange. (**$**)
Wall Street

Crown Holdings Inc.
The packaging company is based in Philadelphia. Avoid using the old name of Crown Cork & Seal Co.
Company Name

CSX Corp.
The railroad operator is based in Jacksonville, Fla.
Transportation

Cuisinart
A trademarked product. The generic term is food processor.
Trademark

Cummins Inc.
The engine and machinery manufacturer is based in Columbus, Ind.
Company Name, Manufacturing

curb trading
Trading that occurs through computers or on the telephone after the market has closed. Also known as **after-hours trading**.
Wall Street

currency
A generally accepted form of money, usually referring to paper money but can also include coins. The currency market is the largest in the world in terms of the amount traded each day.

currency band
The range within which a government allows its currency to fluctuate in foreign exchange trading. If the currency trades outside that range, the government typically buys or sells the currency to bring it back within the range. (**$$$**)
Economy

CUSIP number
An identification number given to all stocks and bonds. Stands for Committee on Uniform Securities Identification Procedures. Capitalize CUSIP in all references. (**$$**)

custodial fee
A fee charged by an institution that holds securities for an investor. (**$**)

CVS Caremark Corp.
Use the full name when referring to the company. Use just CVS when referring to the drugstore operations or a specific store.
Company Name, Retail

Cyber Monday
A term used to describe the Internet-based Christmas shopping that occurs on the Monday after Thanksgiving. However, it is typically not the biggest Internet shopping day of the year. The phrase was coined by the National Retail Federation as a marketing gimmick. Avoid using it.
Retail

cyclical stock
A stock that is affected by the ups and downs of the economy more than other stocks. Examples are consumer goods companies. Cyclical stocks have a higher **beta** than non-cyclical stocks.
Wall Street

D

damp (adj.), dampen (v.)

Use dampen as the verb in instances such as, "The global recession continued to dampen sales of its products."

Dana Holding Corp.

The manufacturer of axles, transmissions and driveshafts is based in Maumee, Ohio.

Company Name, Manufacturing

Danaher Corp.

A tool manufacturer based in Washington, D.C.

Company Name, Manufacturing

Darden Restaurants Inc.

The Orlando, Fla.-based company is the parent of Olive Garden, LongHorn Steakhouse and Red Lobster.

Company Name, Restaurant

datelines

A dateline indicates where the reporter did the bulk of the reporting for his or her story, no matter where the major action in the story took place. If that location has little or no bearing on the story, use no dateline. For example, a story written from the South Korean capital on the North Korean economy should use a Seoul dateline because the reporting location is significant. A story being reported from Cleveland about the Cincinnati economy, however, should carry no dateline because the reporting location has no bearing on the story. If the bulk of the reporting took place in Cincinnati, then a Cincinnati dateline is appropriate.

DaVita Inc.

Capitalize the V in all references to the Denver-based kidney care company.

Company Name, Health care

day order

An order to buy or sell a security that expires if it cannot be executed on the day that it is placed. **($)**

Wall Street

day trading

When an investor holds positions for very short time periods, such as minutes or hours, and makes numerous trades during a day. Avoid using this term for traditional investors.

Wall Street

Day-Glo

A trademarked product. Note the hyphen and capital G. The generic name is fluorescent colors.

Trademark

daypart

The differing times of day for food service. In addition to breakfast, lunch and dinner, there are afternoon (snack) and evening dayparts.

TV and radio advertising sales periods are also broken into dayparts. **($$$)**

Restaurant

dead cat bounce

A temporary recovery in a market after a prolonged drop, typically followed by a continued decline. **($$$$)**

Economy, Wall Street

deal

A transaction such as a merger, acquisition or issuance of stock. Do not use on first reference.

Deal, The

A New York-based business publication that focuses on covering mergers and acquisitions.

dealer

A person or a firm willing to buy or sell investments for its own account. The term is not the same as **broker**. A broker is someone who buys and sells on behalf of clients.

Dean Foods Co.

A Dallas-based food and beverage company.

Company Name

death tax

Avoid this term because opponents of estate taxes have long used it to express their opposition. Use estate tax instead.

debenture

A type of debt that is not secured by **collateral** or an asset. **($$$)**

Wall Street

debt

Money owed by a person or a company.

debt-to-capital ratio

A measurement of a company's financial leverage, it is calculated by dividing a company's debt by its shareholder equity plus debt. When a company issues debt to make an acquisition, for example, it may then try to pay down that debt to lower its debt-to-capital ratio. **($$$$)**

debt-to-equity ratio

A company's total long-term debt expressed as a percentage of shareholders' equity. **($$$$)**

debtor

A person or company that owes money.

debtor-in-possession financing

Money that a company in bankruptcy court receives from lenders to continue operating its business. These lenders are first in line to repaid when the company reorganizes its debt. *DIP financing* is acceptable on second reference. **($$)**

deductible

The amount of a covered loss that an insurance customer pays before the insurer starts paying. The higher the deductible, the lower the premiums paid by the customer.

Insurance

deed

A legal document conveying title to a piece of property.

Real estate

DeepFreeze

A trademarked product. The F is capitalized although it's one word. The generic word is freezer.

Trademark

Deere & Co.

The Moline, Ill.-based manufacturer of agricultural equipment does not use John in its corporate name.

Company Name, Manufacturing

default

When a borrower fails to make payments on its debt when it comes due.

defensive stock

A stock that is typically immune to changes in the economy, such as a food company or a utility. Defensive stocks can also be called counter-cyclical stocks. Defensive stocks have a low **beta**.

Wall Street

deferred revenue

Revenue collected but not yet earned by a company. An example is subscriptions. Deferred revenue is also referred as unearned revenue by some companies.

deficit

When liabilities exceed assets, or expenses exceed profits. The term is also common to describe when a country's imports exceed its exports.

defined contribution plan

See **pension plan**. (**$$**)

Company Name

deflation

A general decline in prices. Long-term deflation can harm the economy. (**$$**)

Economy

delisting

When the shares of a company are removed from trading on a stock market because they no longer meet the market's requirements, such as an average minimum stock price. (**$$**)

Wall Street

Dell Inc.

The Round Rock, Texas, company makes computers. It was formerly known as Dell Computer Corp.

Company Name, Manufacturing

Deloitte & Touche LLP

The New York-based accounting firm's parent company is Deloitte LLP. The accounting firm and the parent company can be referred to as Deloitte on second reference.

Company Name

Delta Air Lines Inc.

The Atlanta-based company spells airline as two words in its name.

Company Name, Transportation

Department of Justice

A federal government department that, along with the Federal Trade Commission, reviews every merger and acquisition agreement. Use Justice Department or department on second reference.

Department of Labor

A federal government department that oversees business-related issues such as workplace safety and unemployment benefits. Many states also have a labor department. The terms Labor Department or department are acceptable on second reference.

departments

Companies often have departments. Lowercase them, such as information technology department, unless they have a formal name, such as the O'Neill Executive Department.

depreciation

A noncash accounting charge that reduces the value of an asset. If a company purchases a machine for $1 million, it may depreciate the value over 10 years, recording a noncash expense of $100,000 for each of those years. The term can also be used to describe the change in value of a currency compared to another currency. (**$$$**)

depression

A severe and prolonged recession in the economy marked by declining economic activity, high unemployment and sometimes falling prices. (**$$$$**)

Economy

deregulation

When the government relaxes its regulation of an industry, typically to create more competition.

derivative

An investment whose price is determined by an underlying asset. Futures contracts and swaps are types of derivatives. (**$$$$**)

Wall Street

dermatologist

A doctor who specializes in treating skin, hair and nail conditions.

Health care

devaluation

A downward adjustment in a country's currency exchange rate in relation to other currencies. It is always expressed as a percent.

Economy, Finance, Wall Street

Devon Energy Corp.

The oil and natural gas producer is based in Oklahoma City, Okla.

Company Name, Energy

DHL

Acceptable on all references for the delivery company. The Bonn, Germany-based parent company's formal name is Deutsche Post DHL.

Company Name

diagnostic and treatment codes

Codes used by health care providers and health insurers to indicate specific diagnosis and treatments. Unethical medical providers have been known to change codes in documentation to receive higher payments from health insurers. Employees called insurance coders or medical records coders often do the coding.

Health care, Insurance

Dick's Sporting Goods Inc.

The sporting goods retailer is based in Findlay Township, Pa.

Company Name, Retail

Dictaphone

A trademarked product. The generic term is dictation machine.

Trademark

dietitian

Not "dietician."

Restaurant

Dillard's Inc.

The department store chain is based in Little Rock, Ark.

Company Name, Retail

diluted earnings per share

Earnings per share calculated by including the number of shares that would be outstanding if all of the stock options and warrants were exercised. For companies that have issued millions of stock options to executives, the diluted EPS number is lower than or equal to the basic EPS number. See **basic earnings per share**.

Finance, Wall Street

dilutive (n.)

An acquisition that will decrease the acquiring company's earnings per share. As a general rule, a dilutive **merger** or **acquisition** occurs when the **price-to-earnings ratio** paid for the target firm is less than that of the acquiring firm. (**$$**)

director

A member of the board of a company.

directors and officers insurance

A policy that protects the **board of directors** and officers of a company should they be sued. The company typically buys the policy. Without it, a company might find it hard to attract board members and executives. *D&O insurance* is acceptable on second reference.

Company Name, Insurance

DirecTV Group Inc.

Only one T in the El Segundo, Calif.-based direct broadcast satellite service.

Company Name

disability insurance

Coverage that pays benefits if an employee is injured and can't continue to work.

Insurance

disclosure statement

A document that outlines the terms of a loan, including the interest rate, fees and amount borrowed.

discount

When the price of a bond is lower than the **par** value. If a **bond** with a par value of $1,000 is selling at $990, it is selling at a discount. **($$)**

Wall Street

discount broker

A stockbroker who carries out buy and sell orders at a reduced commission rate but provides no investment advice.

Wall Street

discount point

A fee paid to a lender to lower the interest rate on a mortgage. The fee is typically paid during the closing. One point equals 1 percent on the loan.

Finance, Real estate

discount rate

The interest rate that financial institutions are charged when borrowing short term from the **Federal Reserve**. It can also be referred to as a rediscount rate. **($$$$)**

discouraged workers

A person who is eligible to work but is not seeking a job. The number of discouraged workers typically increases when the unemployment rate is high. However, discouraged workers are not counted in the unemployment rate, which is the total number of people working divided by the total number of people working plus the total number of people seeking employment. Information and data about discouraged workers can be found on the Bureau of Labor Statistics website. **($$)**

Economy

Discover Financial Services

The Riverwoods, Ill.-based financial services company is best known for its Discover credit card.

Company Name, Finance

discretionary income, disposable income

These two terms are often used wrongly, or for each other. Disposable income is gross income minus the taxes paid on that income. Discretionary income is the gross income minus taxes paid and minus expenses such as housing, food and transportation needed to maintain a normal lifestyle. The Bureau of Economic Analysis measures disposable income and releases the data monthly. **($$)**

Economy

disease management

A system designed to provide the most cost-effective and quality health care for a patient. The strategy has been criticized by some for not providing the care that a patient needs. **($$)**

Health care

Dish Network Corp.

Capitalize only the first letter in the first name of the Englewood, Colo.-based direct satellite provider.

Company Name

disinflation

A decrease in the rate of **inflation**. Prices are not declining. Disinflation simply means that prices are not rising as fast as they were in the past. **($$$$)**

Economy

Disposall

A trademarked product. The generic term is garbage disposer.

Trademark

distressed borrower

A consumer who does not have the financial means to repay what he or she owes. The term is commonly used to refer to credit card debtors. **($$$$)**

Finance

distressed debt

Debt where the borrower has defaulted on its payments or is highly likely to default. Distressed debt has seen its rating lowered by credit agencies, and it's often seen a decline in price. **($$)**

Wall Street

distressed sale

When a company is sold to another company because it is in financial trouble and might go under without becoming part of another entity. Can also refer to the sale of stock. The acquirer typically receives the assets at a low price.

divest

To sell an operation.

dividend

A payment distributed to stockholders. Dividends may be in the form of cash, stock or property. All dividends are declared by the board of directors. When writing about dividends, specify the time period.

dividend reinvestment plan

An option that allows investors to purchase additional shares of stock in a company by using their **dividend** payments, usually without broker's fees. Do not use DRIP on any reference. Plan is acceptable on second reference. **($)**

division

Companies often have divisions. Lowercase unless they have a proper name, such as the Chevrolet Division of General Motors.

doctor's hospital

Some local hospitals, such as the one in Augusta, Ga., that use this name have an apostrophe, while others, such as the one in Shreveport, La., don't. Check and use the local preference.

Health care

Dodd-Frank Wall Street Reform and Consumer Protection Act of 2010

A wide-ranging law that went into effect in 2010 designed to overhaul the financial system in the United States as a result of the economic recession. The law created a number of new agencies designed to prevent the economy from suffering from another crisis involving banks and real estate. On second reference, Dodd-Frank Act is acceptable. Information about the law can be found on the Govtrack.us website. **($$$$)**

Economy, Finance, Real estate

dog-and-pony show

When investment banks and executives of a company selling securities visit potential investors in an attempt to persuade them to invest in the offering. The term **road show** is preferred, as dog-and-pony show is considered pejorative.

Wall Street

Dolan Co.

A company based in Minneapolis that is the parent of weekly business newspapers, including the Long Island Business News, Mississippi Business Journal, Colorado Springs Business Journal, Idaho Business Review and the Daily Journal of Commerce in Portland, Ore. Its primary business, however, is in providing business data to lawyers and other professionals.

Dole Food Co.

The food company is based in Westlake Village, Calif.

Company Name

dollar

The official name of the currency in many countries, including the United States, Canada, Australia, New Zealand and Singapore.

Dollar General Corp.

A discount retailer based in Goodlettsville, Tenn. Do not confuse it with competitors **Dollar Tree Inc.** and **Family Dollar Stores Inc..**

Company Name, Retail

Dollar Tree Inc.

A discount retailer based in Chesapeake, Va. Do not confuse it with competitors **Dollar General Corp.** and **Family Dollar Stores Inc.**

Company Name, Retail

dollar-cost averaging

An investment technique where the investor purchases a specific dollar amount of a security at regular intervals, regardless of the price. Do not use DCA on any reference. **($$$$)**

Wall Street

domain name

An Internet website address. http://www.chrisroush.com is the domain name of one of the authors of this stylebook.

Technology

Dominion Resources Inc.

The utility company is based in Richmond, Va.

Company Name, Energy

Domino's Pizza Inc.

The Ann Arbor, Mich.-based pizza chain operates 9,000 stores in more than 60 countries.

Domtar Corp.

The paper company's head office is in Montreal, but its operating headquarters are in Fort Mill, S.C., and it is considered an American company.

Company Name

dot-com

A term used to describe the technology industry, particularly companies that operate primarily on the Internet. The hyphen is per AP style.

Technology

Dover Corp.

The industrial **conglomerate** is based in Downers Grove, Ill.

Company Name, Manufacturing

Dow Chemical Co.

The Midland, Mich.-based chemical manufacturer's name should be Dow Chemical on second reference to distinguish it from Dow Jones & Co.

Company Name, Manufacturing

Dow Jones & Co.

The parent company of **The Wall Street Journal, Marketwatch.com, Dow Jones Newswires** and **Barron's**. It is currently owned by News Corp. The ampersand is used on first reference. Dow Jones is acceptable on second reference.

Dow Jones Industrial Average

A popular indicator that tracks the price average of 30 stocks. Operated by **The Wall Street Journal** and **Dow Jones & Co.**, the index started in May 1896 with 12 stocks. In 2009, the average replaced **General Motors Corp.** and Citigroup Inc. with Travelers Cos. and Cisco Systems Inc. The stock that has been in the index the longest is **General Electric Co.**, which has been there since 1907. On second reference, use average or Dow. DJIA is not acceptable on any reference.

Wall Street

Dow Jones Newswires

The newswire subsidiary of **Dow Jones & Co.** It competes with Bloomberg, **Reuters** and the **Associated Press**. The full name should be used on all references to distinguish it from the parent company.

down payment

The initial payment made when a consumer makes a large purchase, such as a home or car. The lender requires a down payment to determine whether the consumer has the financial wherewithal to raise the money needed to pay off the loan. If the consumer defaults on the loan, he loses his down payment.

Real estate

down zoning

Avoid this term. It can refer to the act of limiting development on a piece of property to certain types of construction. For example, a government entity may prohibit high-rise apartments on a piece of property but allow low-rise apartments. But that kind of action can also be regarded as up zoning because it is more restrictive. **($$$$)**

Real estate

downgrade (v.)

A term used to describe when an analyst lowers his or her rating on a stock. To downgrade a stock would mean to lower a rating from "strong buy" to "buy" or from "buy" to "hold," for example. Do not use as a noun.

Wall Street

download

The transfer of data from a server or the Internet to a personal computer hard drive.

Technology

downsize

A euphemistic term often used by companies to describe layoffs or the elimination of specific jobs or lines of business. It should be avoided in all cases, except in quotes. Also known as rightsizing.

downturn (n.)

A negative change.

DPI

Stands for dots per inch. It measures the resolution of a photo or a scanner.

Technology

Dr Pepper Snapple Group Inc.

As with the soft drink, there is no period in the Plano, Texas-based company's name.

Company Name

drive-through (adj.)

Use this spelling in general-interest media. Specialty publications may prefer drive-thru.

Restaurant

Droid

A **smartphone** designed by Motorola that uses Google's Android software. It should be lowercase after the D in all references.

Technology, Trademark

DTE Energy Co.

The Detroit-based utility takes its name from the former stock ticker of its subsidiary Detroit Edison.

Company Name, Energy

due diligence

An investigation of a potential investment or acquisition. In some cases, performing due diligence is a legal obligation.

Duke Energy Corp.

An energy company based in Charlotte, N.C. It is in the process of acquiring another North Carolina energy company, **Progress Energy Inc.**

Company Name, Energy

dumping

An action in international trade where a manufacturer in one country sends a large amount of a good into another country at a price below the manufacturer's domestic price. **($$$)**

Economy

Dumpster

A trademarked brand. The generic term is trash bin.

Trademark

Dunkin' Donuts

The Canton, Mass.-based parent company is Dunkin' Brands Inc., which also owns the Baskin-Robbins brand. It spells doughnuts differently from **Krispy Kreme Doughnuts Inc.**

Company Name, Restaurant

DuPont

Although the formal name of the Wilmington, Del.-based chemical company is E. I. du Pont de Nemours and Co., DuPont is acceptable in all references.

Company Name, Manufacturing

durable goods

Products with a life span of more than three years, such as refrigerators, televisions, microwaves, automobiles and furniture. The opposite is **soft goods**.

Economy

durable goods orders

An economic indicator compiled by the Census Bureau that tracks new orders with manufacturers for goods in the near term. In addition to **durable goods** orders, the government also measures shipments and inventory. The data is released about the fourth week of the following month, and the story focus is on total orders, nontransportation orders, nondefense orders and inventories. This data can be found on the Census Bureau website. **($$)**

Economy

duration

An estimate of how much the price of a bond will change when **interest rates** rise or fall. Bonds with longer maturities, such as 10 years or 30 years, have greater duration than short-term debt of two or five years. See **convexity**. **($$$)**

Finance, Wall Street

Dutch auction

A public offering in which the price of the offering is set after taking in bids and determining the highest price at which the entire offering can be sold back to a company. For example, let's say that 200 shares are to be sold. If one investor offers to buy 100 shares at $20, but another investor offers to sell 100 shares at $18, then all of the shares will be sold at $20. The name comes from the traditional form of auction in the Netherlands, where products are sold simultaneously to equal high bidders. **($$$$$)**

Wall Street

E-commerce

Sales of goods and services where an order is placed by the buyer or price and terms are negotiated by the Internet. Payment may or may not be made online. E-commerce sales data is collected by the Census Bureau and released quarterly.

Economy, Retail

E-Trade Financial Corp.

The New York-based online broker capitalizes all of the letters in "Trade" and a star symbol between the E and Trade. Avoid and use an en dash or hyphen and lowercase letters.

Company Name

E.I. du Pont de Nemours & Co.

The formal name of the Wilmington, Del.-based chemical company. DuPont is acceptable on all references. **($$)**

Company Name

early withdrawal

The removal of money from an investment or a retirement account before its term has expired. Early withdrawal typically results in the investor paying a penalty. **($$)**

Finance, Wall Street

earnest payment

Money the buyers offer as a deposit on a house, to show that they are truly interested in buying. If the buyers back out of the deal, this money may be forfeited to the seller. Earnest money is also acceptable.

Real estate

earnings

A word commonly used to describe a company's net income, or its total earnings. Profit is an acceptable synonym for both words after earnings or net income has been used first. When reporting about earnings, use net income first. Otherwise, the reader or viewer might infer that the earnings are a different type of earnings, such as operating earnings or EBITDA. **($)**

earnings guidance

A term used when a company provides analysts and investors with a range of expected earnings. For example, a company could issue a press release saying it expects its first-quarter earnings to be between 18 cents per share and 22 cents per share. That would be earnings guidance. **($$)**

earnings momentum

When a company's earnings per share is increasing or decreasing from previous quarters. Positive earnings momentum typically occurs when a company's revenue is rising or when it has cut its costs. For earnings to have momentum, the trend needs to occur for at least three consecutive quarters. **($$)**

earnings per share

A company's profits divided by the number of outstanding shares. Company earnings are typically reported by business journalists in terms of net income first, and then earnings per share. Do not use EPS on any reference. See **basic earnings per share** and **diluted earnings per share**.

earnings story guidelines

Nearly every business journalist at some time will write a story about a public company's earnings. Some will even write a story about a private company's results. The following guidelines are important to consider in such stories:

- When calculating the earnings growth or decline, focus on the net income or net loss, not the earnings per share. Companies can manipulate their earnings per share growth by decreasing the number of shares outstanding through share repurchase programs.

- Leads need to emphasize why a company's earnings rose or fell during the quarter. Don't just tell the reader that the earnings rose or fell by a certain percentage. They'll want to know the reason.

- Context, context, context. If a company's earnings have fallen after quarters of increases, then you'll need to tell the reader the last quarter in which earnings fell. Was there a loss in the quarter? Then tell the reader when the last quarterly loss occurred. Net income rose 49 percent? When was

the last quarter that profits rose faster?

- Listen to the conference call. Sometimes, the story is not the press release with the numbers, but what the executives say to the analysts and investors later in the day. One telltale sign is to watch how the stock price reacts while you're listening to the call. If the price begins to move up or down dramatically, then something newsworthy was said.

- Compare a company's quarterly earnings with the same quarter from the previous year, not the previous quarter. Many businesses are cyclical, making the better comparison the same time a year ago. You can't compare, for example, Coke's second-quarter earnings with the first quarter because it's hotter in the second quarter and more people are thirsty.

- When writing about earnings, focus on the most-recent earnings first before mentioning the same quarter a year earlier. For example, write "Earnings rose 25 percent to $4.5 billion from $3.6 billion in the same time period a year ago, not Earnings rose 25 percent from $3.6 billion in the time period a year ago to $4.5 billion."

- Whom are you going to quote? Increasingly, investors in the stock are being quoted in stories about the earnings, not buy-side analysts. While both have a bias, the investors have less of a conflict of interest.

earnings warning

When a company announces that its earnings will be lower than Wall Street projections. The phrase earnings surprise is also acceptable, particularly when a company announces that its earnings will be better than expected.

Company Name, Wall Street

earnout

Money paid by the buyer of a company to the seller of a company if the business's financial results exceed expectations after the deal closes. (**$$**)

Company Name

earthquake insurance

Specific property insurance that protects a home against damage from an earthquake, which is not covered under a traditional homeowners insurance policy.

Insurance, Real estate

easement

The right to use another person's property. The most typical easements are those granted to utilities for electrical or telephone lines.

Real estate

Eastman Chemical Co.

The chemical manufacturer is based in Kingsport, Tenn. It was founded in 1920 by George Eastman, the founder of Eastman Kodak, to supply chemicals for photographic processes.

Company Name, Manufacturing

Eastman Kodak Co.

The photography and imaging company is based in Rochester, N.Y. Kodak is acceptable on second reference. The company filed for bankruptcy court protection in January 2012 and said it would stop making cameras.

Company Name

eatery

An acceptable term for any restaurant.

Restaurant

Eaton Corp.

An electrical components manufacturer based in Cleveland.

Company Name, Manufacturing

eBay Inc.

Lowercase the first letter in the name of the San Jose, Calif.-based online reseller unless it begins a sentence. Capitalize the B in all references.

Company Name, Retail, Technology

EBIT

Earnings before interest and taxes. The preferred term is **operating income**.

EBITDA

A company's earnings before interest, taxes, depreciation and amortization. Because EBITDA is not specified by **generally accepted accounting principles**, or GAAP, a company can change what is included in these earnings from quarter to quarter. When writing about a company's earnings, it's OK to mention EBITDA, but make sure that the company's net income or loss is also reported. That's the more conservative reflection of its performance. **($$$)**

Ecolab Inc.

The cleaning and pest control services company is based in St. Paul, Minn.

Company Name

economic indicator

Data typically collected by the federal government that tells investors or consumers which way the economy might be moving. An economic indicator could be the unemployment rate, the **consumer price index**, the **gross domestic product** or retail sales, among many examples.

Economy

economic stimulus

An attempt by the federal government to improve the economy by pumping money into the economy. For example, in 2009, the government gave people $75 billion to purchase new homes or to stay in homes where the mortgage is **under water**.

Economy, Real estate

Economist, The

A weekly magazine based in England that covers international issues and the world economy. Founded in 1843, it has gained a wider following in the United States in the past decade. The is always capitalized in the magazine's name. Although it is printed on glossy paper, the publication considers itself a newspaper, a throwback to a former version.

Economy

economy

The production and consumption of goods and services in a geographic area. Economies can be entire countries, states, counties or a **metropolitan statistical area**.

EDGAR

Stands for Electronic Data Gathering, Analysis and Retrieval. It's the system used by the **Securities and Exchange Commission** to compile documents from publicly traded companies. EDGAR is acceptable in all references. **($$$)**

Edison International

There is no Inc., Co. or Corp. after the name of the Rosemead, Calif.-based utility.

Company Name, Energy

effective date

The date at which securities can start trading, as determined by the **Securities and Exchange Commission**. The effective date is typically used when referring to an initial public offering.

Wall Street

efficiency ratio

A ratio used to calculate a bank's efficiency. It's typically calculated by dividing noninterest expenses by revenue, although some banks calculate it differently. **($$)**

Finance

84 Lumber Co.

The privately held retailer always uses the number 84 in its name. Its headquarters, however, is in Eighty Four, Pa.

Company Name, Retail

El Paso Corp.

The natural gas producer is based in Houston. The company is in the process of being sold to Kinder Morgan Inc., and El Paso is selling its exploration and production business to investors.

Company Name, Energy

Electronic Arts Inc.

The Redwood City, Calif.-based video game manufacturer can be referred to as EA on second reference.

Company Name, Technology

elevator pitch

A short sales effort of a product, service or company that would take the time of a short elevator ride. It is concise and to the point and is often used to refer to an entrepreneur asking for money from investors.

Finance, Technology

Eli Lilly and Co.

The Indianapolis, Ind.-based pharmaceutical company is known as Lilly on second reference.

Company Name, Health care

eligible list

A list of securities that a financial firm can purchase based on its rules and policies.

Wall Street

embargo

When a country, or a group of countries, halts trading with another country. The embargo can be for a specific good or service, or for an entire country's products.

Economy

EMC Corp.

An information storage company based in Hopkinton, Mass. Its name came from the initials of its founders.

Company Name

Emcor Group Inc.

The engineering and construction company is based in Norwalk, Conn. Capitalize only the first letter of its name although the company spells it with all capital letters.

Company Name

emerging markets

The term has become outdated as many of the countries to which it has referred now exceed Western countries in measurements such as per capita income. It's also considered patronizing. Avoid using it. Stacy-Marie Ishmael of the Financial Times suggests replacing "emerging" with "tilt" because it reflects that economic and financial power is tilting away from the United States and Europe and toward Latin America, Asia and the Middle East.

Economy

Emerson Electric Co.

The engineering services company is based in Ferguson, Mo.

Company Name

eminent domain

A situation in which a government agency purchases real estate from a consumer or business — without the owner's consent — for the good of the community. The government may want the land to build a road, for example.
Real estate

employee stock ownership plan

A plan where a company allows its employees to buy shares of the business. These plans are increasing in popularity with small and private businesses. Do not use ESOP on any reference. **($$)**

Enbridge Energy Partners LP

The Houston-based energy company operates liquid petroleum and natural gas businesses. Do not confuse with Enbridge Inc., the Canada-based company that owns 26 percent of Enbridge Energy.
Company Name, Energy

end user

The person or persons who actually use the software or website.
Technology

endocrinologist

A doctor who cares for thyroid disease and diabetes and other conditions affecting the endocrine system such as hypertension. **($$$)**
Health care

energy company

Use this term only to describe companies that produce energy. Others in the energy industry that do not manufacture energy should be described as a distributor, broker or retailer. In general specify what types of energy (natural gas, electricity, wind energy) an energy company produces.
Energy

Energy Future Holdings Corp.

The utility based in Dallas was known as TXU until it was sold in 2009 in a leveraged buyout.
Company Name, Energy

Energy Transfer Equity LP

The Dallas-based limited partnership operates is one of the country's largest propane distributors. It is the parent company of Energy Transfer Partners LP.
Company Name, Energy

enplanements

The number of people getting on a plane, whether to start or continue a journey. Use passenger boardings, or some other simple phrase, when possible. **Entrainments** is a parallel term. **($$)**
Transportation

Enron Corp.

A former Houston-based energy company that collapsed and filed for bankruptcy in late 2001 after one of the largest financial and accounting frauds in history was uncovered. Be cautious when comparing a company to Enron.
Company Name, Energy

ensure, insure

To ensure means to make sure something happens. To insure means to issue an insurance policy. The words are not interchangeable.

Insurance

Entergy Corp.

The energy company is based in New Orleans.

Company Name, Energy

Enterprise Rent-A-Car Co.

The St. Louis-based car rental company is the only one in the industry that hyphenates rent-a-car in its name. **($$$$)**

Company Name

enterprise value

A measure of a company's value. It is calculated by adding stock market capitalization, debt and preferred shares.

entrainments

See **enplanements**. **($$)**

Transportation

Entrepreneur

A monthly business magazine that caters to small companies.

Environmental Protection Agency

The federal agency whose job is to protect the environment and human health by preventing the release of harmful items into the environment. The agency can ban the use of certain products, and it can fine companies for violating environmental laws.

The use of *EPA* is acceptable on second reference. The EPA has an online database where pollutants can be searched by ZIP code.

EOG Resources Inc.

The oil and natural gas company is based in Houston. EOG stands for Enron Oil and Gas. Use EOG in all references.

Company Name, Energy

Equal Employment Opportunity Commission

The federal agency created in 1964 to investigate claims of employment discrimination on the basis of race, color, sex, age, natural origin and religion. Its jurisdiction has since been expanded to include discrimination based on disability. The abbreviation *EEOC* is acceptable on second reference.

equity

A synonym for a stock or another investment that conveys ownership. Stock is the preferred term. In terms of real estate, it's the difference between the market value of a home or a commercial property and the amount owed on the mortgage. **($)**

Wall Street

equity fund

A mutual fund that invests primarily in stocks. *Stock fund* is the preferred term. **($$)**

Wall Street

ergonomics

The science of designing a workplace that produces the best conditions for employees. The object of ergonomics is to avoid injuries and make the workers as productive as possible. **($)**

Company Name

Erie Indemnity Co.

The Erie, Pa.-based company provides **property and casualty** insurance and life insurance. It operates using the name Erie Insurance Group.

Company Name, Insurance

ERISA

Stands for Employee Retirement Income Security Act. It's a federal law that provides rights for pension plan participants and standards for pension plan investments. Use the acronym on all references, but explain the law. More information about ERISA can be found on the Department of Labor website. **($$$)**

Health care

errors and omissions insurance

A liability policy that covers professionals should they be sued by a client for failure to perform the duties described in a contract. Professionals who purchase errors and omissions insurance include real estate agents, insurance agents and architects. *E&O insurance* is acceptable on second reference.

Insurance

escalator clause

A part of a contract that allows one party to pass along the increasing cost to the other party. Escalator clauses typically come into play when **inflation** increases costs. **($$$$$)**

escrow

Money held by a third party in a transaction that is not released until one of the other parties satisfies prearranged conditions. For example, a home seller may not receive money from the sale until he makes repairs on the home that the buyer wants.

Real estate

establishment survey

One of the ways in which the unemployment rate is determined by the U.S. Department of Labor. The establishment survey questions 350,000 businesses with 39 million workers about the number of workers they have employed in the past month.

Economy

Estée Lauder Cos.

The cosmetics and perfume company is based in New York.

Company Name

euro

The official currency of the **European Union**. It was introduced in 1999, though euro banknotes and coins didn't enter use till 2002. Not all countries in Europe use the euro as their currency. Great Britain still uses the pound.

Eurodollars

Dollars held in banks outside of the United States that are typically used for international transactions. **($$)**

Economy

European Union

A group of European countries that participate in the world economy as one. The theory behind the European Union is to create a trade zone with no barriers. There are 27 countries in the union. They are Austria, Belgium, Bulgaria, Cyprus, Czech Republic, Denmark, Estonia, Finland, France, Germany, Greece, Hungary, Ireland, Italy, Latvia, Lithuania, Luxembourg, Malta, the Netherlands, Poland, Portugal, Romania, Slovakia, Slovenia, Spain, Sweden and United Kingdom. *EU* is acceptable on second reference.

ex-dividend

The date on which stock buyers will not receive a dividend that has been declared by a company. If a company announces a dividend on Oct. 15, and says its ex-dividend date is Oct. 25, then investors who purchase the stock on Oct. 25 will not receive the dividend when it is paid. **($$$$)**

excess and surplus lines

A segment of the property and casualty insurance market that allows customers to buy coverage from insurance companies even if there aren't any licensed to sell the policy in that jurisdiction. For example, an insurer may withdraw from selling a specific line of property and casualty insurance, such as medical malpractice, in a state but would still offer the coverage as an excess and surplus line. **($$$)**

Insurance

exchange

A market where securities, commodities, options or futures are traded.

Wall Street

exchange rate

The number of shares of the acquiring company that shareholders will receive for one share of the acquired company that they hold. This rate is typically reported high in an **acquisition** story. The exchange rate is also the measurement of a currency in terms of other currencies. **($$)**

exchange-traded funds

An investment that trades on an exchange. The value of the fund is based on the assets it holds, such as stocks or bonds. Many exchange-traded funds track an index, such as the Standard & Poor's 500. Use *ETF* on second reference. **($$$)**

executive compensation

The amount of money and other compensation that an executive receives for working at a company, including the value of items such as country club memberships and stock options. The executive's compensation can be found in the company's **proxy statement**, also known as a DEF 14A filing with the **Securities and Exchange Commission**. When writing about an executive's compensation, use the total compensation amount in the proxy, and compare it with the total compensation amount from the previous year.

This differs from AP Stylebook policy in writing about executive compensation. The AP guidelines for executive compensation stories state that the number in the proxy statement should not be used, and the AP has its own formula for executive compensation.

Here are some other potential newsworthy items to look for when writing about executive compensation:

- The perks given to executives, such as country club memberships and personal use of corporate jets and cars. These sometimes are worth more than the salary or bonus given to an executive.

- The compensation committee report. This often discloses how the company determined the **CEO's** pay, and whether he or she is in line for a pay increase.

- Outside shareholder proposals. In recent years, these proposals, which are voted on by all stockowners, have increasingly focused on limiting huge compensation packages.

- The stock option chart. Given the increased focus on the timing of grants, reporters should be looking at when companies gave options.

- Relationships between board members and the company. This

is where you find out whether a board member's company has been doing business with the company whose board he or she sits on. Examine whether the amount of that business has increased or decreased in the past year.

Exelon Corp.
The electrical utility is based in Chicago.

exercise price
The price at which the underlying security can be bought or sold. For example, stock options given to an executive of a company have a price at which the executive can purchase the shares. That price is the exercise price.

Company Name, Wall Street

existing home sales
The resale of existing homes by current owners to new owners. Existing home sales are a majority of home sales in the United States. The term is not to be confused with **new-home sales**. These data are compiled by the National Association of Realtors on a monthly basis and are released in the last week of the following month. The story focuses on the level and the monthly change in total sales.

Economy, Real estate

exit strategy
How a major investor plans to sell its stake in a company. A hedge fund or venture capital fund that has acquired a major stake in a company

may implement its exit strategy by selling the company to another company or have that company hold an **initial public offering**.

exotic instrument

An option with a nonstandard feature, such as an option that allows an investor to select the exercise price. **($$)**

Wall Street

expectations index

Part of the **Consumer Confidence Index** that measures how consumers think the economy will be in six months.

Economy

Expedia Inc.

Write as Expedia.com when referring to the Bellevue, Wash.-based company's online travel service site.

Company Name

expense ratio

The cost, as a percent of assets, that investors pay for a mutual fund's expenses. **($$)**

Finance

expiration date

The last day in which an option can be exercised. In terms of stock options, it's the last day that an executive can purchase those shares at the predetermined price.

Wall Street

Express Scripts Inc.

The Cool Valley, Mo.-based company is a pharmacy benefit manager. It was once a subsidiary of **New York Life Insurance Co.**

Company Name, Health care

extraordinary item

Gains or losses in a company's financial statement that are unusual in nature. For example, losses resulting from a hurricane or tornado would be listed as an extraordinary item in an insurance company's financial statement. See **nonrecurring charge**. **($$)**

Exxon Mobil Corp.

An Irving, Texas-based company formed by a 1999 takeover. Exxon-Mobil is acceptable on second reference.

Company Name, Energy

F

face value

The dollar value of a security when issued. It's also called the **par value** or **par**. (**$$**)

Wall Street

Facebook Inc.

Use Facebook.com when writing about the Palo Alto, Calif.-based company's social networking site.

Company Name, Technology

fair market value

The price that an asset would bring in the marketplace, assuming that the market is acting normally.

fairness opinion

A professional evaluation by an investment bank or other party as to whether the terms of a merger, acquisition, spin-off or other transaction are fair. Details of a fairness opinion are often included in a **Form S-4**. (**$$$**)

falling knife

A phrase used to describe a stock or industry where the value has dropped dramatically in a short period of time. Avoid using in all but the most extreme cases, such as a company that has unexpectedly filed for bankruptcy court protection. For example, real estate prices fell in the latter part of the first decade of the 21st century, but at nowhere near falling knife levels. (**$$$$**)

Real estate, Wall Street

Family Dollar Stores Inc.

A discount retailer based in Matthews, N.C. Do not confuse it with competitors **Dollar Tree Inc.** and **Dollar General Corp.**

Company Name, Retail

Fannie Mae

The shortened name for the Federal National Mortgage Association, a government-sponsored entity created to expand the mortgage market. It purchases loans from lenders and then packages those loans into pools that are sold to investors. Fannie Mae is acceptable in all references.

Company Name, Real estate

Fannie May Confections Inc.

Note the May spelling in the name of the Chicago-based candy company, which also owns a number of other consumer brands.

Company Name

Farmers Group Inc.

A property and casualty insurance company based in Los Angeles. It is owned by Zurich Financial Services. Its main business is actually in managing insurance exchanges such as the Farmers Insurance Exchange that maintain the risk, while Farmers Group receives management fees for

running the exchanges.
Company Name, Insurance

Fast Company

A business magazine started in 1995 by two former Harvard Business Review editors, Fast Company focuses on innovation. It is now owned by Mansueto Ventures, which also owns Inc. The magazine publishes 10 issues a year.

fast food (n.) fast-food (adj.)

A fast-food restaurant offers basic, low-cost food that is prepared and sold quickly.
Restaurant

fast-casual (adj.)

A restaurant or restaurant chain offering somewhat-upscale food items but not providing table service. Panera Bread and Chipotle Mexican Grill are common examples.
Restaurant

featherbedding

The practice of a union requiring a company to hire more workers than necessary to complete the work. **($$)**

Federal Aviation Administration

A branch of the Department of Transportation that regulates the airline industry and airplane manufacturers. *FAA* is acceptable on second reference. The FAA maintains an online database of accident reports.

Federal Communications Commission

The federal regulatory agency charged with overseeing interstate and international communications by radio, television, wire, satellite and cable. *FCC* is acceptable on second reference.

Federal Deposit Insurance Corp.

The government arm that attempts to maintain stability in the financial market by insuring most bank deposits and examining financial institutions. *FDIC* is acceptable on second reference. Note that the FDIC prefers the word "chairman" before its head, Sheila Bair. The FDIC maintains a financial database of all banks that it regulates.
Finance

Federal Energy Regulatory Commission

The agency that regulates natural gas and electricity transactions. FERC is acceptable on second reference.The agency maintains an online database of all of its decisions.
Energy

federal funds rate

The interest rate at which financial institutions borrow very short-term money from each other through the **Federal Reserve Board. The Federal Open Market Committee** sets a target for this rate, but the actual rate is determined in the open market. **($$$$)**
Economy

Federal Highway Administration

A federal government agency that is part of the Department of Transportation and oversees the country's highways and roads. Do not use FHA on second reference.

Federal Home Loan Bank system

A dozen regional banks throughout the country from which local lenders borrow money to fuel economic development and housing construction. It essentially brings the debt market to **Main Street**. The Home Loan Bank system is a government-sponsored enterprise chartered by Congress in 1932. Do not use FHLB on second reference. Refer to it as the system on second reference.

Finance

Federal Housing Administration

A government entity that provides mortgage insurance to lenders it approves. FHA is acceptable on second reference.

Real estate

Federal Insurance Office

Part of the U.S. Treasury Department created in 2010 to monitor the insurance industry. The office has no regulatory authority, however. State insurance departments regulate the insurance industry. The office was created by the **Dodd-Frank Wall Street Reform and Consumer Protection Act of 2010**. Avoid using the FIO abbreviation. **($$$$)**

Insurance

Federal Open Market Committee

The 12-person board that sets the country's monetary policy. It includes the seven members of the **Fed-eral Reserve Board** and five presidents of regional reserve banks, one of whom is always the president of the Federal Reserve Bank of New York. Do not use FOMC on any reference. The board's most-recent statements can be found online at the Federal Reserve website. **($$)**

Economy

Federal Reserve Board

The federal government agency that makes key decisions about short-term interest rates. The chairman is considered one of the most powerful people in the United States. On second reference, use the Fed or the board. Do not lowercase Fed on second reference.

Economy

Federal Trade Commission

The federal agency that works to ensure the nation's markets are efficient and free of restrictions that harm consumers. The commission enforces federal consumer protection laws that prevent fraud, deception and unfair business practices. The commission also enforces federal antitrust laws that prohibit anticompetitive mergers and acquisitions and other business practices that restrict competition and harm consumers. FTC is acceptable on second reference. The agency maintains an online database of its decisions.

FedEx Corp.

Do not spell out Federal Express on any reference to the Memphis, Tenn.-based delivery service company.

Company Name

fee schedule

A list of acceptable charges for a health care procedure or service, determined by a managed-care operator.

Health care

Fiberglas

A trademarked product. The generic term is fiberglass.

Trademark

FICO score

An individual's credit score that is used by lenders to determine whether to give the person a loan. It stands for Fair Isaac Corp., which created the system. FICO score is acceptable in all references. **($$)**

Finance, Real estate

Fidelity National Financial Inc.

The title insurer is based in Jacksonville, Fla. Avoid the FNF abbreviation in all references.

Company Name, Finance, Real estate

FIFO

An accounting method that assumes for purposes of calculating cost of goods sold that the first inventory in a warehouse is the first shipped out when orders are placed. It does not have to correspond with the actual physical flow of inventory. When materials prices are rising, FIFO makes earnings higher but also increases income taxes. The term FIFO stands for first in, first out and should be explained on first reference. **($$)**

Manufacturing

Fifth Third Bancorp

The Cincinnati-based bank holding company's main subsidiary is Fifth Third Bank. Do not use numerals for the company name or the bank name.

Company Name, Finance

fighting the tape

When an **investor** is taking an action — buying or selling — that is contrary to the rest of the market. It is similar to **contrarian** investing. **($$$)**

fill

The price at which an order is executed.

Financial Accounting Standards Board

A seven-person board that is independent of the federal government and sets the accounting standards used by companies in reporting their financial performance. *FASB* is acceptable on second reference. When referring to one of the board's rules, use the abbreviation and the number, such as FASB 157 requires companies to report the value of their assets at fair value. **($$)**

financial adviser

A person who offers financial advice and planning to individuals. Financial advisers are typically are paid via commissions, although some are paid fees.

Finance

financial analyst

A person who performs financial analysis on investments for internal or external clients as part of his or her job. This person can also be called an equity analyst, investment analyst, research analyst or securities analyst. See **buy-side analyst** and **sell-side analyst**. **($$$)**

Finance, Wall Street

financial derivative

An investment whose value depends on the value of the underlying assets. See **derivative**. **($$)**

Wall Street

Financial Industry Regulatory Authority

A regulatory body that oversees brokers and dealers and their interaction with the investing public. It was created in 2007 by the merger of the New York Stock Exchange regulatory committee and the National Association of Securities Dealers regulatory apparatus. *FINRA* is acceptable on second reference.

Finance, Wall Street

financial landscape

A phrase used in business journalism, often to describe a change, as in the changing financial landscape. This phrase has become overused and should be avoided because the world of finance and business rarely involves trees, bushes and shrubs.

financial planner

A person who provides advice to individuals for situations such as funding for retirement and how to ensure descendants pay smaller estate taxes. This person differs from a **financial adviser**, who focuses on investing an individual's money. Should not be confused with a stock broker, who is sometimes called a financial adviser.

Finance

financial porn

A term first used by personal finance writer Jane Bryant Quinn in 1998 to describe articles that encourage readers to make investment decisions that may not be wise, but will sell magazines or newspapers.

financial ratio

A number of mathematical measures that help investors evaluate a company. These include everything from **return on equity** and **debt-to-capital ratio** to a **price-to-earnings** and **price-to-book ratio**. When writing about a financial ratio, refer to the specific one being used.

Finance, Wall Street

Financial Stability Oversight Council

A new council of regulators created to monitor risk in the U.S. financial system. The council is charged with identifying threats to the financial stability of the United States, promoting market discipline and responding to emerging risks. It is part of the U.S. Treasury Department and was created by the **Dodd-Frank Wall Street**

Reform and Consumer Protection Act of 2010. Avoid using the FSOC abbreviation and refer to it as the council on second reference. **($$$$)**

Finance, Wall Street

financial supermarket

A financial services company that provides a wide range of the services an individual might need, from a checking account at a bank to a stock brokerage and insurance agency.

Finance

Financial Times, The

A British-based business newspaper launched in 1888. It is considered a competitor to **The Wall Street Journal**, primarily in Europe, where it dominates.

fire

To discharge or terminate someone from his or her job. In some instances, the employee has been fired for cause, meaning the employer believes the employee hasn't met required standards. Dismissed is also acceptable.

firm

Popularly, it can be used for any company. Technically, it applies to businesses of two or more people that are not legally recognized as a separate person, as is the case with corporations. It's commonly used when referring to law firms or accounting firms. The term firm is also used when a company is the subject of an acquisition, i.e. target firm.

firmware

The programs that control an electronic device.

Technology

First American Financial Corp.

The title insurance company is based in Santa Ana, Calif.

Company Name, Finance, Real estate

First Data Corp.

The Atlanta-based company processes electronic payments.

Company Name

first mortgage

The mortgage that has priority over all other liens or claims on a property if the homeowner defaults. If the first mortgage is for greater than 80 percent of the value of the home, then the lender may require mortgage insurance.

Real estate

first-quarter, first quarter

Hyphenate when used as a compound modifier, such as a company's first-quarter earnings rose 23 percent. No hyphen when it stands alone, such as profits also rose in the first quarter. In earnings stories, avoid using the term quarter repeatedly. Other acceptable terms are in the last three months or period.

first-time defaulter

A consumer who had a strong credit rating but ran into financial difficulties after losing a job, not from taking on too much debt. Creditors look more favorably at such consumers when determining whether to give them future credit. (**$$$$**)

Economy

FirstEnergy Corp.

The Akron, Ohio-based energy company's name is one word with the first E capitalized.

Company Name, Energy

fiscal policy

Government spending or taxing policies that influence the broad economy.

Economy

fiscal quarter, fiscal year

The term fiscal is not necessary except on first reference when referring to a fiscal year that does not coincide with the calendar year. Simply use quarter and year instead. It is acceptable to write in stories when the quarter or year ended if it is not the calendar year, such as the fourth quarter ended Jan. 31.

fiscal year

The term fiscal is not necessary except on first reference when referring to a fiscal year that does not coincide with the calendar year. Simply use quarter and year instead.

Fiserv Inc.

The Brookfield, Wis.-based company sells information management systems to financial services and insurance companies.

Company Name, Technology

Fitch Ratings

A credit rating agency based in New York and London, although its parent company is based in Paris. Its competitors are **Moody's** and **Standard & Poor's**. Fitch is acceptable on first reference.

Company Name

501(c)(3)

A provision of the U.S. **Internal Revenue Service** code that exempts certain types of organizations, such as charities, churches and universities, from paying federal taxes. These organizations are called nonprofits. Note that both the c and the 3 are in parentheses. The IRS has information about the exemption requirements for these organizations on its site. (**$$**)

fixed annuity

An insurance contract in which the insurer makes a regular payment into the contract for its term. It's considered a safer investment than a **variable annuity**. (**$$$**)

Finance, Insurance

fixed income

A type of investing or budgeting strategy in which income is received at a regular rate. A fixed-income strategy is typically used by retirees or risk-averse investors. (**$$**)

fixed-rate mortgage

A mortgage where the interest rate will not change during the course of the mortgage. When writing about mortgages, distinguish between fixed-rate and adjustable-rate. (**$**)

Real estate

flack
Derogatory term for public relations professionals. Do not use in print. **Spokesman, spokeswoman** or representative is preferable.

flak
Slang for strong criticism. The term comes from anti-aircraft fire.

flash drive
A portable storage device that plugs into a computer **USB** port.
Technology

flash price
The price of a stock that shows when trading is extremely heavy. The ticker will "flash" forward to the current price instead of reporting the incremental changes. **($$$)**
Wall Street

flash trading
Where traders use computers to examine investors' orders for milliseconds before publishing them to the rest of the market, having bought or sold the shares first after analyzing the trade. The **Securities and Exchange Commission** moved in 2009 to ban such trading.
Wall Street

flat tax
A tax system where the same tax rate is applied to all consumers and businesses, no matter their income or profits. Critics say that a flat tax is unfair to the poor. Supporters say it would encourage economic growth because it doesn't penalize a person making more money with higher taxes. **($$)**
Economy

Fleishman-Hillard Co.
Hyphenate the name of the St. Louis-based public relations agency.
Company Name

flexible spending account
A type of savings account in the United States where workers can set aside pre-tax money to pay for expenses such as health care or dependent care. Do not use FSA on any reference. **($$)**
Health care, Insurance

flexible work schedule
An alternative to the traditional 9 a.m. to 5 p.m., 40-hour work week, it's a policy at many companies that allows employees to adjust their work schedules, particularly their arrival and/or departure times. It's also known as an alternative work arrangement.

flipping
An investing strategy where the individual buys an investment in the hope that it can be sold quickly at a higher price. Flipping became common in many real estate markets in the first decade of the 21st century. **($$)**
Wall Street

float

The amount of stock available for trade in a company on a regular basis. The float is less than the total number of outstanding shares because of **restricted stock** given to executives and in some cases large blocks of stock held by holders who don't plan to sell. **($$$)**

Wall Street

flood insurance

Specific property insurance that protects a home against damage from flooding, which is not covered under a traditional homeowners insurance policy.

Insurance, Real estate

flow of funds

Data collected by the **Federal Reserve Board** that shows the flow of money in certain sectors of the economy, such as the lending of money by banks and investing in businesses. Flow of funds can also be used to refer to the movement of money into or out of a mutual fund or a specific stock. The data is released quarterly, typically on the first Thursday of the final month of the following quarter. The story focuses on domestic nonfinancial debt. **($$$$)**

Economy

Flowserve Corp.

The manufacturer of pumps, seals and valves is based in Irving, Texas.

Company Name, Manufacturing

Fluor Corp.

The engineering, construction and maintenance services company is based in Irving, Texas.

Company Name

FMC Technologies Inc.

An oil and gas equipment company based in Houston. Do not confuse with FMC Corp., a chemical company based in Philadelphia.

Company Name, Energy

FNB Bancorp

A bank holding company based in San Francisco, but F.N.B. Corp. is a bank based in Hermitage, Pa.

Company Name, Finance

Food and Drug Administration

A federal government agency that regulates the safety of food and pharmaceuticals, certifying when drugs can be sold to the public. It also regulates animal food, cosmetics and medical devices, among other products. *FDA* is acceptable on second reference. Sometimes wrongly called the "Federal Drug Administration," which doesn't exist.

food service (n.) food-service (adj.)

An umbrella term for all businesses involved in providing food outside the home. Included are restaurants and caterers. In general, use a more specific term.

Restaurant

food-service distributor
A company that supplies food products to restaurants, schools, hospitals and other groups that serve meals outside the home. **($$)**
Restaurant

Foot Locker Inc.
The sporting goods retailer is based in New York. It has about 3,500 stores in 21 countries.

Forbes
A business magazine started in 1917 by Bertie Charles Forbes, Forbes remains primarily in the hands of the Forbes family, although a minority stake was sold in 2006. Forbes is best known for its lists, including the Forbes 400 list of the richest people in the United States. It is the longest-running business magazine in the United States.
Company Name

force majeure
A clause in a contract that removes liability for natural events such as catastrophes. A company can also declare force majeure andsuspend delivery of a productbecause of circumstances beyond its control. **($$)**

Ford Motor Co.
The automobile manufacturer is based in Dearborn, Mich., not Detroit.
Company Name, Manufacturing, Transportation

forecast
A term used to describe when a company predicts future earnings or other financial performance. Avoid using when describing an analyst's prediction for a company's financial performance. Estimate is preferable when referring to an analyst.

foreclosure
A legal process where the mortgage lender obtains the ownership of a piece of property because of the borrower's inability to pay off the loan. There are fewer foreclosures than foreclosure filings, so be careful when using these two terms in the same story.
Real estate

foreclosure sale
The sale of a mortgaged property where the proceeds go first to the lender, then second to any lien holders and finally to the borrower. The process is faster than a foreclosure sale by court order.
Finance, Real estate

foreign exchange trading
The buying and selling of various currencies. The foreign currency market is the largest in terms of value traded daily. When writing about foreign exchange trading, the values of currencies should always be paired. For example, the value of the U.S. dollar should be compared with the British pound, or the Japanese yen should be compared with the **euro**. In general, stronger-than-expected U.S. economic data is positive for the U.S. dollar in foreign exchange trading, and vice versa.
Wall Street

forensic accounting

A term to describe using auditing and investigative tactics to examine a company's financial statements. Some business journalists turn to forensic accounting experts to help them determine the true finances of a company. **($$$)**

Form 10-K

An annual document filed by all public companies and some private companies with the **Securities and Exchange Commission** at the end of their fiscal years. Companies must file this document within 60 to 90 days after the end of the fiscal year, depending on the size of the company. The 10-K includes the company's financial performance for the year as well as management's discussion of that performance.The SEC explains information about the filing on its website.

Form 10-Q

A quarterly document filed by all public companies and some private companies with the **Securities and Exchange Commission** at the end of each of their first three fiscal quarters. It is filed within 40 to 45 days after the end of the fiscal quarter and includes the most-recent quarter's financial performance. The company has typically already released this financial information in the form of an earnings release, but the 10-Q should still be reviewed to see if the company has added other information.

Form 13-F

A form filed with the Securities and Exchange Commission by institutional money managers with more than $100 million in investments. As a business journalist, what you want to do is compare the current 13-F to the one right before it to see what investments the money manager sold and what investments it added to its portfolio. The investment that changed the most is the lead of a story about the 13-F.

Wall Street

Form 3

A document filed with the **Securities and Exchange Commission** by an insider of a company or someone who owns more than 10 percent of the company's stock. It must be filed within 10 days of the person becoming an insider or the investor passing the 10 percent threshold. See **insider**.

Form 4

A document filed with the **Securities and Exchange Commission** by a company insider or an investor with more than 10 percent of the company stock when the amount of stock he or she owns changes, either through a purchase or a sale. The document must be filed before the end of the second business day after the trade.

Form 8-K

A document filed by public companies with the **Securities and Exchange Commission** when they have a materially important event occur. The

SEC has a number of incidents that require the filing of an 8-K, including change of control, the resignation of a board member, the change in a fiscal year and change in auditors. Some companies include important earnings supplements in 8-Ks.

Form 990

A public document filed by non-profit organizations with the **Internal Revenue Service**. A Form 990 must be filed within six months after the end of the fiscal year, and it includes how the nonprofit spent its money as well as the salaries for the top five employees. The Form 990 of a religious organization is exempt from public records requirements.The IRS has background on the Form 990 on its website.

Form NT

A document filed by a company when it is unable to file its **Form 10-K**, **Form 10-Q** or other filing with the **Securities and Exchange Commission** before the prescribed deadline. The Form NT is often, but not always, a sign that a company faces financial issues.

Form S-1

A document filed by a company with the **Securities and Exchange Commission** when it intends to sell shares to public investors. The S-1 is often amended with additional information before the shares are actually sold.

Form S-4

A document filed by a public company with the **Securities and Exchange Commission** in the event of an acquisition or merger. As a result, Form S-4s often have useful information about the deal, such as behind-the-scenes negotiations between the two companies, whether the price was raised or lowered, and whether there were competing bids.

Formica

A trademarked product. The generic term is laminated plastic.
Trademark

Fortune

A business magazine started in February 1930 by Time magazine founder Henry Luce. It was published monthly until January 1978, when it became an every-other-week publication. The magazine spells its names with all capital letters, but lowercase all except the F.
Company Name

Fortune 500

Commonly used to refer to a company that is listed in **Fortune** magazine's annual list of the largest companies in the United States. The list is based on the previous year's revenue.

Fortune Brands Home & Security Inc.

The manufacturer based in Deerfield, Ill., spun off its liquor business, Beam Inc., in 2011 and can be called Fortune Brands on second reference.
Company Name, Manufacturing

forward-looking statement

A statement made by a company that predicts or projects its future performance, such as earnings or revenue for the next fiscal year. A public company puts a forward-looking statement warning on its website and in its news releases so it won't get sued for making such statements if they later prove false. (**$**)
Company Name

forward

An agreement to buy or sell assets such as a currency or a metal at a set price and date. A forward is different from a **future** in that it isn't traded on an exchange. (**$$$$**)

foundation

A nonprofit organization that donates funds to support other organizations. Foundations are required to spend at least 5 percent of their assets annually. Many of the largest U.S. companies — or their founders — have affiliated foundations. An example is the Bill and Melinda Gates Foundation, run by the co-founder of Microsoft and his wife.

401(k) plan

A retirement plan available in the United States where workers can deduct a portion of their pay and have that money placed in a retirement savings plan. With a 401(k) plan, the worker then chooses how that money will be invested — mutual funds, company stock, money market accounts, etc. Note

that the k is lowercase and always in parentheses. (**$**)
Finance

Fox Business Network

A cable business news television network started by News Corp. in October 2007 as a competitor to **CNBC**. Acceptable to use Fox Business on second reference. Lowercase the letters in Fox although the network spells it with all capital letters.

FPL Group Inc.

The Juno Beach, Fla.-based utility company is the parent of Florida Power & Light Co.
Company Name, Energy

fracking

The term is acceptable on first reference for hydraulic fracturing, but it must be quickly defined. It involves pumping water, sand and chemicals under pressure through a well to fracture underground shale formations, releasing petroleum and natural gas.

fractions

When used, they should be spelled out, such as three-fourths or four-fifths. Decimals, however, are preferred in many business references, particularly stock prices.

franchise

A license agreement between a company and a party that gives the party access to the company's operating techniques and trademarks in return for a start-up cost and an annual fee. Many restaurant companies, such as McDonald's and Burger King, operate using the franchise system.

Restaurant, Retail

Franchise Disclosure Document

It's the document that franchisers must supply to prospective franchisees at least 14 days before any contract is signed. The document covers items including initial and ongoing costs, restrictions on the franchisees and earnings information. Sometimes referred to as the FDD, but disclosure document makes a better second reference. The Federal Trade Commission provides suggestions on how to obtain copies of these documents. **($$$)**

Restaurant, Retail

franchisee

The holder of a franchise from a franchiser.

Restaurant, Retail

franchiser

A company offering franchises. Also spelled "franchisor," but the "er" spelling conforms to AP style.

Restaurant, Retail

fraud

Do not write that someone was arrested "for fraud." Write that they were charged with fraud or arrested on suspicion of fraud.

Freddie Mac

A shortened name for the Federal Home Loan Mortgage Corp., a government-sponsored enterprise that purchases and securitizes home loans. Freddie Mac is acceptable in all references.

Company Name, Real estate

free cash flow

A measure of operating performance of a company. It is calculated by subtracting capital expenditures from a company's operating cash flow, which is net income adjusted for noncash items that affect income such as amortization and depreciation. Some companies create their version of free cash flow that differs from the customary definition. Always ask for how it is determined. **($$$)**

free market

An economic market that is based on supply and demand, not government intervention such as tariffs and regulation. The opposite is controlled market. There are few free markets remaining today, so use this term sparingly. It can be used to refer to an economist's thinking.

Economy

Freeport-McMoRan Copper & Gold Inc.

Maintain the capitalization in McMoRan for the Phoenix-based mining company.

Company Name

Freon

A trademarked type of refrigerant whose use is being phased out because of concerns of its effect on the ozone layer. The generic term is refrigerant.

Trademark

friendly takeover

When a company's executives and board agree to sell the operation to another company. It's in contrast to a **hostile takeover**, which is when a company makes an offer to buy another company after the target rebuffs an acquisition offer. **($$)**

Frisbee

A trademarked product. The generic term is flying disk.

Trademark

front of house

The dining room of a restaurant and its other public areas, including restrooms. **($$$)**

Restaurant, Retail

front running (n.)

An unethical practice in which a broker trades in a stock based on information from his firm's research department or trading desk before it is given to clients. For example, a broker might acquire 100 shares of a company just before the research department issues a "buy" rating on the stock, which would result in the firm's clients also buying the stock, sending the price higher. **($$$$$)**

Wall Street

front-end

The application that allows a user to access a database.

Technology

HollyFrontier Corp.

An oil and gas refiner based in Dallas ceated by the 2011 merger of Holly and Frontier Corps.

Company Name, Energy

FSBO

For sale by owner. Always spell out and lower case. Also see **principals only**.

Real estate

FTSE 100

The benchmark index of the London Stock Exchange. It's the British equivalent of the **Dow Jones Industrial Average** or the **Standard & Poor's 500 Index**. Some people call it the Footsie, but we'd avoid that term. **($$)**

Wall Street

Fudgsicle

A trademarked product. The generic term is fudge ice-cream bar.

Trademark

fully funded plan

A health care plan where the insurer or managed care operator takes responsibility for guaranteeing all claims payments and paying all benefits and administrative costs. **($$$)**

Health care, Insurance

fund

A collection of money from various investors into a large pool, which then invests that money uniformly, such as a mutual fund or a hedge fund.

Wall Street

fund of funds

A mutual fund or hedge fund that invests its money by investing in other mutual funds or hedge funds. Do not use an s after the first fund. **($$)**

Wall Street

fundamentals

Qualitative and quantitative information that contributes to the value of a company or an investment.

funds from operations

A measurement of cash flow from trust operations used by **real estate investment trusts**. It is earnings with amortization and depreciation added back in. Funds from operations is used to measure a REIT's financial performance.

Real estate

futures

A contract that requires the buyer to purchase an asset at a predetermined future price and date. A futures contract can be purchased for a stock or a commodity. Such contracts lock in the price for the investor, minimizing the risk of the price going up or down. **($$$)**

G

G-2

Term used to describe the economic relationship between the United States and China, the two largest economies in the world. Group of Two is acceptable on first reference, while G-2 is accceptable on second reference. (**$$$$**)

Economy

G-20

A group of finance ministers and central bank governors from 20 economies — 19 countries and the European Union. It replaced the G-8 as the main economic council of wealthy countries in 2009. The countries are South Africa, Canada, Mexico, the United States, Argentina, Brazil, China, Japan, South Korea, India, Indonesia, Saudi Arabia, Russia, Turkey, France, Germany, Italy, the United Kingdom and Australia. Group of Twenty is acceptable on first reference. Use G-20 on second reference.

Economy

G-5

Otherwise known as the Group of Five, the top five industrialized countries in the world that meet regularly to discuss economic and monetary issues. The countries are France, Germany, Japan, the United Kingdom and the United States. Group of Five is acceptable on first reference, while G-5 is acceptable on second reference. (**$$$$**)

Economy

G-7

Otherwise known as the Group of Seven, it includes the Group of Five countries plus Canada and Italy. It deals primarily with economic issues. Group of Seven is acceptable on first reference, while G-7 is acceptable on second reference. (**$$$$**)

Economy

G-8

Otherwise known as the Group of Eight, it includes the Group of Seven countries plus Russia. Group of Eight is acceptable on first reference, while G-8 is acceptable on second reference. Reuters refers to these countries as the world's richest countries on second reference. That's acceptable as well. (**$$$$**)

Economy

gadfly

An investor who attends a company's annual meeting and often asks embarrassing questions to its management. The term is acceptable, as many gadflies revel in their role. The most famous is Evelyn Y. Davis.

GameStop Corp.

The video game retailer is based in Grapevine, Texas. Its name is one word with a capital S.

Company Name, Retail

gaming vs. gambling

The gambling industry would prefer business journalists use the term "gaming" because it does not have a negative connotation. The more common phrase, however, is gambling, and is the one we suggest you use.

Gannett Co.

The newspaper owner is based in Tysons Corner, Va.

Company Name

Gap Inc.

Avoid using "the" before the name of the San Francisco-based clothing retailer.

Company Name, Retail

gas vs. gasoline

While it may be OK to use gas on second reference as a synonym for gasoline (what most of us use to fuel our cars), make sure there's no confusion with other fuel gases, such as natural gas or propane, which also can power vehicles and are becoming more commonly used. Best practice is to use gasoline on first reference except in casual uses: He ran out of gas. Never refer to diesel fuel as gas.

Energy

gas, natural

The common home-heating fuel, delivered by pipelines. Always use nat-ural gas on first reference. See also, **Natural gas pricing**.

Energy

GDP deflator

A measure of the shift in prices of goods and services produced in a specific economy. It is used by economists to determine the strength of the economy. **($$$$)**

Economy

Geico

Capitalize only the first letter in the name of the auto insurer, in contrast to the all caps that the company uses. Geico is now a subsidiary of **Berkshire Hathaway Inc**. Its headquarters is in Chevy Chase, Md., although its corporate address is Washington, D.C.

Company Name, Insurance

General Cable Corp.

The provider of copper, aluminum, and fiber optic wire and cable products is based in Highland Heights, Ky.

Company Name

General Dynamics Corp.

The defense contractor is based in Falls Church, Va. Avoid the GD abbreviation in all references.

General Electric Co.

A conglomerate based in Fairfield, Conn. GE is acceptable on second reference.

Company Name

General Mills Inc.

Do not use the GM abbreviation for the Minneapolis-based food company. GM more commonly refers to **General Motors Co.**

General Motors Co.

An automaker based in Detroit. *GM* is acceptable on second reference. General Motors Corp. was the name of the company before filing for bankruptcy court protection in 2009.

Company   Name,   Manufacturing, Transportation

general obligation bond

A municipal bond issued based on the credit rating and taxing power of the government entity rather than just the revenue that would be generated from the project that will be constructed from the money raised by the bond issue. General obligation bonds are usually used to fund projects such as roads and parks that don't produce revenues. Do not use GO bond on second reference. **($$$$)**

Wall Street

general practitioner

Also known as a family doctor. While these doctors are considered to be able to perform any and all types of medicine and surgical procedures, few doctors remain today that can deliver a baby, remove your tonsils and set a broken arm.

Health care

generally accepted accounting principles

A common set of accounting standards and procedures used by companies to compile their financial statements. Reporters should always be leery of management that responds, "It's GAAP." Some managements are more aggressive than others in their interpretation. *GAAP* is acceptable on second reference. The Financial Accounting Standards Advisory Board explains GAAP on its website.

generic substitution

The dispensing of a drug that is the generic equivalent of a brand name drug.

Health care

Genuine Parts Co.

The auto parts retailer and distributor is based in Atlanta.

Genworth Financial Inc.

The financial services company is based in Richmond, Va.

Company Name, Finance

Genzyme Corp.

The biotechnology company is based in Cambridge, Mass. InApril 2011, it was acquired by Sanofi-Aventis Group.

Company Name, Technology

Georgia-Pacific LLC

The Atlanta-based paper and pulp company uses a hyphen on all references. It was acquired by Koch

Industries, one of the largest private companies in the world, in 2005.
Company Name, Manufacturing

Gilead Sciences Inc.
The biopharmaceutical company is Foster City, Calif.
Company Name, Health care

Glass-Steagall Act
The act passed by Congress in 1933 that prevented commercial banks from owning brokerage firms or investment banks. It was repealed in 1999. As a result, it is rarely mentioned in current business news stories.

GlaxoSmithKline PLC
The name of the London-based pharmaceutical company is all one word. *GSK* is acceptable on second reference.
Company Name, Health care

glide path
1. The formula used to determine asset allocation in a target date fund. The glide path creates an investment portfolio that becomes more conservative the closer the fund gets to its target date. 2. In aviation, the path a plane follows as it descends to land, marked by a radio beam that helps guide the pilot. It is also called a guide slope. Both terms may also be applied to the radio beam. **($$$$)**
Finance, Wall Street

Global Partners LP
The Waltham, Mass.-based company distributes and markets oil and gas products.
Company Name, Energy

going concern
A description used for a company that has the financial resources to continue operating indefinitely. **($$)**

golden handcuffs
Long-term incentives promised to employees or executives so that they will remain with the company. The employee often forfeits the incentive if he or she leaves the company. **($$$)**

golden parachute
Lucrative benefits given to top executives in the event their company is taken over by another firm, resulting in the loss of a job. These benefits could include **stock** options, bonuses and severance pay. **($$$)**

Goldman Sachs
The parent company is Goldman Sachs Group Inc., while the brokerage unit is Goldman Sachs & Co. Distinguish between the two when writing about the company.
Company Name, Finance

Goodrich Corp.
The Charlotte, N.C., company has not made tires since 1988. It's primarily in the aerospace industry now. BFGoodrich tires are now made by Michelin.
Company Name

goodwill

When one company is purchased for another company above the value of its tangible assets, the difference is called goodwill. Goodwill comes from intangible assets such as the value of a company's brand names or its customer list. **($$$)**

Goodyear Tire & Rubber Co.

The Akron, Ohio-based company can be referred to as simply Goodyear on second reference.

Company Name, Manufacturing

Google Inc.

The formal name of the Internet-search company includes Inc. When referring to its search function, do not use Google as a verb.

Company Name

Government National Mortgage Association

Otherwise known as Ginnie Mae, it's a federal entity that guarantees the payment of loans backed by the Federal Housing Administration, the Veterans Administration and Rural Housing Service. Ginnie Mae is acceptable on first reference.

Company Name, Real estate

government-sponsored enterprise

A privately held corporation created to lower the cost of lending and capital in the economy. Examples are **Freddie Mac** and **Fannie Mae**. Do not use GSE on any reference. **($$$)**

grantor trust

A trust where its maker retains control of the management of the trust and the distribution of its assets. **($$$)**

Graybar Electric Co.

The electronics company is based in St. Louis. It spells its name with a capital R, but lowercase when writing in a story or headline.

Company Name

Great Atlantic & Pacific Tea Co.

The grocery store chain based in Montvale, N.J. can be referred to as A&P on second reference.

Company Name, Retail

Great Depression

The decade-long recession that began in October 1929 with the crash of the U.S. stock market. The Depression is acceptable on second reference.

Economy

greenmail

A strategy where an unfriendly investor purchases a large amount of stock in a company, forcing the company to buy back the stock at a higher-than-market price to prevent a takeover. **($$$)**

Greenspan, Alan

Chairman of the Federal Reserve Board from 1987 to 2006. Greenspan oversaw the longest economic expansion in U.S. history, but some of his policies are being criticized as leading to the recession that began in

2008. Greenspan's relationship with the business media was characterized by giving off-the-record interviews and being the subject of a number of laudatory articles.

Economy

greenwashing

The act of promoting environmentally friendly measures or images but actually operating in a way that harms the environment. **($$$)**

gross domestic income

The sum of all income in the production of goods and services in an economy. It differs slightly from **gross domestic product**. *GDI* is acceptable on second reference. **($$)**

Economy

gross domestic product

The value of all goods, services and products by an economy during a certain time period. It includes purchases, investments and exports minus imports. Stories about the gross domestic product focus on the annualized quarterly percentage change in the GDP. *GDP* is acceptable on second reference. The latest GDP data can be found on the Bureau of Economic Analysis website. **($$)**

Economy

gross income

Income before expenses.

Company Name

gross margin

Revenue minus cost of goods sold divided by revenue. It measures the money a company makes on its product or service before paying for other expenses. Gross margins can vary by industry. **($$)**

gross national product

The measure of all output produced by a country's residents and resident-owned capital, regardless of where that output is produced. For the United States, it would include output produced by residents and capital abroad, but exclude output produced by foreign-owned capital and foreign residents produced in the United States. The difference between gross domestic product and gross national product in the United States is small, but it can be large in other countries. *GNP* is acceptable on second reference. **($$)**

Economy

gross profit

Revenue minus cost of goods sold for a company. It can also be called gross income. **($$)**

Group 1 Automotive Inc.

The auto dealership operator is based in Houston. Use the numeral 1 in all references.

Company Name, Retail

growth fund

A mutual fund that attempts to invest in stocks of companies that are growing rapidly. **($$)**

Wall Street

growth stock

A stock where the company's revenues and profits are expected to grow at a faster rate than competitors'.

Wall Street

guaranteed investment contract

An insurance contract that promises the holder the repayment of the principal plus interest for a predetermined time period. **($$$$)**

Insurance

Guardian Life Insurance Co. of America

The mutual life insurance company is based in New York. Guardian Life is acceptable on second reference.

Company Name, Insurance

Guess Inc.

Do not use the question mark in the name of the Los Angeles-based company.

Company Name, Retail

gynecologist

A doctor who treats the female reproductive system. Many gynecologists are also **obstetricians**.

Health care

H&R Block Inc.
Use the ampersand in the name of the Kansas City, Mo.-based tax preparer.
Company Name, Finance

H.J. Heinz Co.
The Pittsburgh-based food company is known as Heinz on second reference.
Company Name

hacker
A person who breaks into a computer network without authorization.

haircut
The reduction in value of a security. It's commonly used when securities are used as collateral in a **margin call**.
Finance, Wall Street

Halliburton Co.
The Houston-based oil and gas company also has an office in Dubai, United Arab Emirates, where its CEO works and resides.
Company Name, Energy

hard money
Money borrowed from a nonregulated lender. Hard money loans are typically for higher interest rates and for shorter time periods than traditional loans.

Harley-Davidson Inc.
The motorcycle manufacturer is based in Milwaukee, Wis. A hyphen is used in all references.
Company Name, Manufacturing, Transportation

HarperCollins Publishers Inc.
The name of the publisher, a subsidiary of News Corp., is one word with a capital C.
Company Name

Harris Corp.
The communications equipment company is based in Melbourne, Fla.
Company Name

Hartford Financial Services Group Inc.
The insurance and financial services company can be referred to as Hartford Financial on second reference. Yes, it is based in Hartford, Conn.

HCA Inc.
Use capital letters for the name of the country's largest hospital operator, formerly known as Hospital Corporation of America.
Company Name, Health care

headquarters
The location where a company's executives and many other employees reside. Some companies call their headquarters by another name.

Home Depot refers to it as a "store support center." However, headquarters should be used in all references as it means that the company has other operating locations. Do not use as a verb. We prefer it being followed with a singular verb.

health care

The treatment and management of an illness or injury. It's always two words except when spelled as one word as part of the name of a company. Do not use the term health care to describe health insurance, and vice versa.

Health care

health insurance

Coverage that helps pay for the treatment and management of an illness or an injury. Many consumers receive health insurance through their employer.

Health care, Insurance

Health Insurance Portability and Accountability Act

A federal law that outlines the requirements for insurance companies and managed-care organizations to provide health insurance. *HIPAA* is acceptable on second reference. The U.S. Department of Health and Human Services maintains information about HIPAA on its website. **($$)**

Health care

health maintenance organization

A managed-care form of health insurance where the insurer has contracts with physicians and other medical care providers, guaranteeing them a certain number of patients. In return, the health care providers charge a flat rate to patients. *HMO* is acceptable on second reference. **($$)**

Health care, Insurance

Health Management Associates Inc.

The hospital operator is based in Pelican Bay, Fla. Avoid the HMA abbreviation in all references.

Company Name, Health care

Health Net Inc.

The health insurance company is based in Woodland Hills, Calif. Its name is two words.

hedge funds

An investment vehicle typically offered to institutional investors and individuals with high net worths. Do not use interchangeably with **mutual funds**. Although both pool investments into one fund, hedge funds differ from mutual funds in that they do not advertise publicly for investors, and the manager typically gets a share of investors' profits, a share known as the carried interest, or carry. Frequently funds hedge their investment bets by buying some investments they believe will rise in value and buying some investments they believe will decline, but trying to make money off both. See **short selling**.

However, many hedge funds no longer split their investments this way, so the term "hedge" is actually a misnomer. When writing about hedge funds, avoid using adjectives such as "risky," "hazardous" or "unsafe." **($$$$)**

Wall Street

hedging

Making an investment to decrease the risk of the change in value of an asset.

Wall Street

held at the opening

When a stock cannot be traded when the market opens. This occurs for two reasons: 1. The company might be about to release major news, or 2. An imbalance exists between buy and sell orders. **($$$)**

Wall Street

hematologist

A doctor who specializes in treating and preventing medical illnesses related to blood and bone marrow. **($$$)**

Health care

Henry Schein Inc.

The distributor of health care products is based in Melville, N.Y.

Company Name, Health care

herd mentality

Refers to when a large group of investors moves the market up or down by following the crowd. The opposite would be **contrarian** investing.

Wall Street

Hershey Co.

The chocolate and candy manufacturer is based in Hershey, Pa.

Company Name, Manufacturing

Hertz Global Holdings Inc.

The Park Ridge, N.J.-based company does not hyphenate the name of its Hertz Rent a Car subsidiary. It is also the parent of Advantage Rent A Car.

Company Name

Hess Corp.

The New York-based petroleum company was formerly known as Amerada Hess.

Company Name, Energy

Hewlett-Packard Co.

The Palo Alto, Calif.-based computer maker can be referred to as *HP* on second reference.

Company Name, Technology

HHGregg Inc.

Capitalize the first two letters of the name of the Indianapolis-based electronics retailer, although the company uses lowercase letters.

Company Name, Retail

Hi-Liter

A trademarked product. The generic term is highlighting marker.

Trademark

high-yield bonds

See **junk bonds**.

hit

When writing about the stock market, don't use this word because there is no physical hitting when a stock reaches a new high or new low. See more detail at **stock market stories**.

hold

A rating given a stock by a sell-side analyst who doesn't think the shares will underperform or outperform the overall market. The analyst is telling investors not to sell the stock, but also not to purchase any additional shares. The **neutral** rating means the same thing.

Wall Street

holding company

A holding company holds controlling interests in stock of other companies. It usually exists for that purpose alone. See **parent company**.

holding period

The time during which an investment is held by an investor. A holding period is used to determine the investment's performance. An investment that rose 10 percent that was held for three months would have an annual return of 40 percent. **($$)**

Home Affordable Modification Program

A Treasury Department program designed to provide eligible homeowners the opportunity to reduce their monthly mortgage payments. *HAMP* is acceptable on second reference. **($$$$)**

Economy, Real estate

Home Depot Inc.

Avoid capitalizing "the" before the Atlanta-based company's name.

Company Name, Retail

home equity line of credit

A loan from a lender where the home serves as the collateral. The homeowner is essentially borrowing against the value of the home.

Finance, Real estate

home inspection

An inspection of a home's condition, generally as a precursor to its sale. The buyer may require the seller to make repairs or improvements to the home based on what is discovered during the home inspection.

Real estate

homeowners association

An organization that loosely governs a neighborhood or subdivision and manages its common property, such as a clubhouse or swimming pool. The president and other officers of the homeowners association are property owners in the neighborhood or subdivision, and can often be good sources for stories about issues affecting their area.

Real estate

homeowners insurance

Insurance purchased by the owner of a home to protect against loss or damage to the house and its contents, along with liability coverage. Two of the largest home insurers in the country are State Farm and Allstate.

Insurance, Real estate

Honeywell International Inc.
The conglomerate is based in Morristown, N.J.
Company Name

Hormel Foods Corp.
The food manufacturer is based in Austin, Minn. One of its products is **Spam** meat.
Company Name

hospice care
Health care provided to a patient who is terminally ill. **($)**
Health care

Hospital Corp. of America
The Nashville, Tenn.-based company is the largest private hospital company in the world. HCA is acceptable on second reference.
Company Name, Health care

Host Hotels & Resorts Inc.
The **real estate investment trust** is based in Bethesda, Md. The company's logo capitalizes all of the letters in Host, but capitalize just the H in writing.
Company Name, Real estate

hostile takeover
An acquisition that occurs when the target company does not want to be sold. In some cases, the company making the offer will bypass the company's board and its management and make a pitch to shareholders. **($$)**

hot issue
An **initial public offering** that trades well above the offering price on the first day of trading.
Wall Street

household survey
One of the ways in which the unemployment rate is determined. Monthly interviews are conducted by the U.S. Department of Labor with 60,000 households.
Economy

housing starts
The number of residential buildings that have begun construction in any month. The data includes construction starts and permits and is compiled by the Department of Housing and Urban Development. It is released around the middle of the following month. It does not include mobile homes, dorms, rooming houses or long-term hotels.
Economy, Real estate

HQSC
Hospitality, quality, service and cleanliness — what every restaurant should offer. **($$$)**
Restaurant

HSN Inc.
The St. Petersburg, Fla.-based parent company of the Home Shopping Network.
Company Name, Retail

HTML

Stands for Hypertext Markup Language. It is programming language used to create documents for display on the Internet.

Technology

hull and machinery insurance

A policy that covers damage to a boat, ship or barge caused by collisions, storms and shipwrecks. It also covers fires, explosions and thefts. H&M insurance is acceptable on second reference. **($$)**

Insurance

Humana Inc.

The Louisville, Ky.-based company no longer owns hospitals and is strictly a health insurance company.

Company Name, Insurance

Huntsman Corp.

A chemicals manufacturer based in The Woodlands, Texas.

Company Name, Manufacturing

HVAC

An abbreviation that stands for heating, ventilation and air conditioning. A poor HVAC system in a house or office building can lead to **sick building syndrome**. The abbreviation is acceptable in all references. **($$)**

Real estate

hybrid fund

A mutual fund that uses multiple investment strategies. **($$)**

Wall Street

hyperinflation

Extremely high, out-of-control **inflation**. There is no quantitative measure for hyperinflation, so use the term carefully. **($$$$)**

Economy

hyperlink

A connection between websites. It can also be called a link.

Technology

IBM

Acceptable on all references for International Business Machines Corp., which is based in Armonk, N.Y. (**$$**)

Company Name, Technology

Icahn Enterprises LP

The New York-based holding company owns the Fountainbleau Resort in Las Vegas, among other businesses.

Company Name

ICE Futures

The current name of the **New York Board of Trade**.

Company Name, Wall Street

Ikea

Capitalize only the first letter in the name of the Swedish retailer instead of the all-capital spelling that the company prefers. The parent company is Inter Ikea Systems B.V.

Company Name, Retail

Illinois Tool Works Inc.

A manufacturer based in Glenview, Ill. ITW is acceptable on second reference.

Company Name, Manufacturing

illiquid

An asset that can't easily be bought or sold at its current market price. (**$$$**)

Imax Corp.

Capitalize only the first letter in the name of the Toronto-based operator of large-screen movie theaters.

Company Name

imbalance of orders

Occurs when there are too many types of orders — buy or sell — for a specific stock to allow it to trade. Order imbalance is also accepted. (**$$$**)

Wall Street

impairment

When a company reduces the value of its capital because its assets are worth less than they are carried for on its financial statements. An impairment charge is generally not good news. (**$$$**)

Economy

import and export prices

A monthly index that measures the prices of goods imported into the United States and exported to other countries. It is measured by the Bureau of Labor Statistics and released monthly about the second week of the following month. The story focuses on import prices, particularly the monthly change in total and nonoil commodity prices.

in the money

When a **put option** has a strike price higher than the underlying futures

price, or when a **call option** has a strike price lower than the underlying futures price.
Wall Street

In-N-Out Burger

Note the hyphenation and capitalization for the Irvine, Calif.-based restaurant company.
Company Name, Restaurant

Inc.

A monthly business magazine founded in 1979 in Boston and now published in New York. The magazine owned by Mansueto Ventures is a sister publication to Fast Company. Inc. and is known for its list of the fastest-growing private companies in the United States, called the Inc. 5,000. Note that the period is always used in the magazine's name.
Company Name

incentivize

Nearly all ize verbs are suspect; in this case say offer incentives when describing contracts or pay plans that offer bonuses for performance.

income

Equals revenues less expenses. Earnings and profit are acceptable synonyms, but operating profit and operating income are not.

income statement

The accounting of sales, expenses and net profit for a given period, such as a quarter or year.

income tax

A tax levied by the government on the income of an individual, company or other organization.

incorporated

An adjective indicating that a company or nonprofit organization is a corporation. Abbreviate as Inc. when used on first reference after the full company name.

incurred but not reported

An accounting rule used by the insurance industry in which the cost of claims is estimated, but the actual claims have not yet been reported. This happens often after major hurricanes because insurance companies are unable to perfectly predict the value of their damage liabilities until all repairs have been made, which sometimes can take months or years. Do not use IBNR on any reference. (**$$$$$**)
Insurance

independent agent

An insurance agent who sells policies from a variety of companies. This person is in contrast to a captive agent, who sells policies for only one company.
Health care, Insurance

independent auditor

An outside accountant with the certified public accountant designation who inspects a company's financial statements.

independent practice association

An organization of physicians who contract with a managed care organization to provide health care. **($$)**

Health care

index

A collection of stocks or other securities that measures a change in a specific market. Examples of indexes are the **Standard & Poor's 500** and the **Dow Jones Industrial Average**.

Wall Street

index fund

A mutual fund that buys investments used in a specific index and tries to mimic the index's performance. It's considered a passive form of investing. **($$)**

Wall Street

individual retirement account

A retirement account where people can invest money on a pre-tax basis and let it compound tax-free. Withdrawals from the account are taxable. *IRA* is acceptable on second reference.

Finance

inflation

The increase in the prices of goods and services. When inflation rises, purchasing power falls. Inflation is measured by the **consumer price index**. **($$)**

Economy

informal inquiry

A term used by the Securities and Exchange Commission when it collects information from a company to determine whether it should launch a formal investigation of potential wrongdoing. A company will often disclose an "informal inquiry" in its SEC filings. **($$)**

Ingram Micro Inc.

The Santa Ana, Calif.-based technology company was formerly known as Micro D.

Technology

initial claims

A number compiled by the Department of Labor that measures newly unemployed individuals who filed for unemployment insurance benefits in a given week.

Economy

initial public offering

When a private company sells shares to the public for the first time and becomes a public company. Companies typically try to make their initial public offering when the market is receptive to investing in stocks of similar companies. *IPO* is acceptable on second reference.

Wall Street

insider

A person with knowledge or non-public information about a company. The word can be used to describe executives, employees, managers, board members and investors.

insider information

Information about a company that has not been disclosed to the general public. If insider information is used to buy and sell the company's stock, the executive or employee could be charged with illegal **insider trading**.

Company Name, Wall Street

insider trading

The buying and selling of a company's shares by board members, executives and others within the company. Despite the term's negative connotation, nearly all trading by insiders is perfectly legal. When the trader has inside information that's not disclosed to the general public, insider trading is illegal. **($$$)**

Wall Street

insolvent

When an individual or a company can no longer meet its obligations or when liabilities exceed assets.

Institute for Supply Management

A U.S. organization that releases two monthly purchasing manager's indices. If the indices are above 50, it likely means that the economy is expanding. If the indices are below 50, it likely means that the economy is contracting. The data can be found on its site. *ISM* is acceptable on second reference.

Economy

institutional investor

An investor such as a mutual fund company or money manager. Institu-tional investors are considered long-term holders of the shares, so com-panies try to cultivate relationships with institutional investors. **($$)**

Wall Street

intangible asset

A company asset that is not physical, such as trademarks, patents and brand names. The iPod brand name is an intangible asset for Apple. **($$$)**

Integrys Energy Group Inc.

An energy company based in Chicago that owns gas and electric utilities and also supplies compressed natural gas for transportation.

Company Name, Energy

Intel Corp.

The Santa Clara, Calif.-based tech-nology company is the world's larg-est semiconductor manufacturer.

Company Name, Technology

interbank rates

The interest rate charged on short-term loans between banks. The **LIBOR** is the most common interbank rate. **($$$)**

Economy

interest

The fee that an individual or company must pay when it borrows money. The interest rate is usually expressed as an annual number.

Finance

interest expense

The amount a borrower has paid for borrowed money during a specific time period.

Finance

interest income

The amount of money that an individual or a company receives from others that it has lent money to. It can also be used to describe interest received on accounts such as certificates of deposits or savings accounts.

Finance

interest rate

The rate paid on money borrowed, or received on money lent if you are the lender. It is typically expressed as a percent. A $1,000 loan borrowed at a 6 percent annual interest rate means the person pays $60 a year in interest.

Finance, Real estate

interest rate swap

An agreement between two parties where one stream of future interest payments is swapped for another. A company will use an interest rate swap to lower its exposure to potential fluctuations in interest rates. The first interest rate swap occurred between IBM and the World Bank in 1981. **($$)**

interest-only loan

A loan in which the borrower pays only the interest for a set period of time, typically five or 10 years, leaving the principal unpaid. After the set period, the borrower must pay off the loan or convert the loan into another format. A homeowner may be able to get more money with such a loan, but these loans are considered risky, and some banks issued such loans to consumers during the real estate boom in the first part of the 21st century who were then unable to repay them. See also **negative amortization mortgage. ($$$)**

Finance, Real estate

interim financing

A loan made during the construction of a building or a project. It's commonly used in commercial real estate transactions. When writing about such a loan, please specify its length.

Finance, Real estate

internal audit

When a company conducts an internal investigation of its operations, its processes and its procedures to determine how it can improve itself. Internal audits are also conducted to ensure that a company is following government rules and regulations, as well as its own procedures. **($$)**

Internal Revenue Service

The federal regulatory agency that collects taxes from businesses and individuals. The IRS also determines the tax status of a business and reviews documents to determine if a company such as a nonprofit is in compliance with federal laws. *IRS* is acceptable on second reference.

international fund

A mutual fund that invests primarily in non-U.S.-based companies. **($$)**
Wall Street

International Monetary Fund

An organization of 185 countries that promotes the stability of currency exchanges, trade and payment for goods and services. It often lends money to countries in need. *IMF* is acceptable on second reference. **($$)**

International Paper Co.

The paper and pulp company is based in Memphis.
Company Name, Manufacturing

Internet

The short term for the World Wide Web. It's always capitalized.
Technology

Interpublic Group of Cos.

The holding company for advertising agencies can be referred to as Interpublic Group on all references.
Company Name

INTL FCStone Inc.

The company specializes in corporate risk management. It was created by the 2009 merger of FCStone Group and International Assets Holding Corp., and moved its headquarters to New York from Kansas City.
Company Name

intraday trading

The buying and selling of shares within the same day. An investment can be described as reaching a new high or low in intraday trading if it does not close at that high or low during the end of the day. **($$$)**
Wall Street

Intranet

A private, internal Internet connection for an organization or company.
Technology

inventory

The materials and goods that a company holds that are ready for sale to customers. A company's inventory is recorded on its financial statement. If the inventory level is rising, it could be a sign that the company is having trouble selling its products, or that it is getting ready to expand its operations.
Manufacturing, Retail

inverted yield curve

When the interest rates of long-term debt are lower than the interest rates of short-term debt of the same quality. **($$$$$)**
Finance

investment banker

A person working for a financial institution that is in the business of raising capital for corporations and municipalities. Investment bankers do the grunt work behind IPOs and debt offerings.

investment banking vs. retail banking

Do not use these terms interchangeably. An investment banker provides services to large companies, such as selling stock to investors in an initial or secondary offering or negotiating terms in a merger or acquisition. A retail banker offers services such as checking and savings accounts to consumers.

Finance

investment grade

A bond with one of the four highest ratings.

Finance, Wall Street

investment income

The money that a company makes from its investment portfolio. An insurance company often takes the premiums it receives from customers and invests that money. It then reports income from its insurance operations and income from its investment operations.

Finance, Insurance, Wall Street

investor

A person or company that owns an investment.

Wall Street

Investor's Business Daily

A Monday through Friday business newspaper based in Los Angeles that was started in 1984 by investor William O'Neil. It was called Investor's Daily until 1991. Avoid using the IBD abbreviation.

Company Name

involuntary bankruptcy

When creditors file a plan to force a debtor into bankruptcy court protection. The debtor can protest and argue against the involuntary bankruptcy before the court. **($$)**

iPhone

A trademarked product from Apple. The generic term is **smartphone**.

Technology

iPod

A trademarked product from Apple. The generic term is digital music player.

Technology

irrational exuberance

A term used by former Federal Reserve Chairman **Alan Greenspan** in 1996 to warn that the stock market might be overvalued. It has since become a common term used to describe people, companies or other investments that have gotten ahead of themselves in terms of growth, expansion or value.

Economy

ISP

Stands for Internet Service Provider. An example is AOL.

Technology

ITT Corp.

The manufacturing conglomerate is based in White Plains, N.Y. ITT stands for International Telephone & Telegraph, but the company's telecommunications operation was divested in 1986. Use ITT in all instances.

Company Name, Manufacturing

J.C. Penney Co. Inc.
The retailer is based in Plano, Texas.
Company Name, Retail

Jabil Circuit Inc.
The St. Petersburg, Fla.-based company manufactures circuit boards.
Company Name, Manufacturing

Jack in the Box Inc.
The San Diego-based hamburger restaurant company operates and franchises more than 2,200 restaurants in 19 states. The company also operates and franchises the **Qdoba Mexican Grill.**

Jacobs Engineering Group Inc.
The Pasadena, Calif.-based company provides engineering and construction services.
Company Name

Jacuzzi
A trademarked product. The generic term is whirlpool bath.
Trademark

January effect
Describes a general increase in stock prices in the first month of the year, generally attributed to selling in December by investors who want to create tax losses to offset capital gains. **($$)**
Wall Street

Jarden Corp.
The consumer products company is based in Rye, N.Y. Its brand names include Crock-Pot and Sunbeam.
Company Name

Javascript
A trademarked product. The generic term is scripting software. It's a programming language primarily used to build websites.
Technology, Trademark

Jeep
Use when referring to the Chrysler-made vehicle. Use jeep for military vehicles. Otherwise, use sport utility vehicle.
Trademark

Jell-O
A trademarked product. The generic term is gelatin dessert.
Trademark

Jet Ski
A trademarked product from Kawasaki. The generic term is personal watercraft.
Trademark

JetBlue Airways Corp.
An airline based in New York. The B is always capitalized.
Company Name

job polarization

A trend in the U.S. economy in which job opportunities are increasing in high- and low-skill jobs but disappearing in middle-skill (sales, clerical, administrative) positions and in blue-collar craft jobs. Job polarization has been seen as pushing workers without a four-year college degree into lower-paying work. (**$$$$**)

Economy, Manufacturing, Retail

jobless claims

A number reported weekly by the U.S. Labor Department to track how many people are filing for unemployment benefits. There are two numbers reported. The first is **initial jobless claims**, which tracks the number of people filing for unemployment benefits for the first time. The second is **continuing jobless claims**, which tracks people who have previously filed for benefits. When writing about these data, please distinguish between the two numbers. Jobless claims are reported by the Department of Labor weekly on Thursdays, with a five-day lag for initial claims and a 12-day lag for continuing claims. The current data can be found on the Labor Department's website.

Economy

Jockey shorts

A trademarked product. The generic term is boxer shorts.

Trademark

Johnson & Johnson

The New Brunswick, N.J.-based pharmaceutical, medical device and consumer product company has no Co., Inc., or Corp. before its name. Avoid the J&J abbreviation.

Health care

Johnson Controls Inc.

The Milwaukee-based company was founded by the man who invented the first electric room thermostat.

Company Name, Manufacturing

joint venture

When two companies create a separate, new company and agree to share its profits, expenses and control. The new company must have equal ownership between the two companies, otherwise it cannot be called a joint venture.

Jos. A. Bank Clothiers Inc.

The Hampstead, Md.-based men's clothing retailer abbreviates Joseph.

Company Name, Retail

JPEG

Stands for Joint Photographic Experts Group. It is a compressed graphics format for photos and graphics.

Technology

JPMorgan Chase & Co.

No periods or spaces in JPMorgan, but the securities division is *J.P. Morgan Securities Inc.* The company is headquartered in New York.

Company Name, Finance

jumbo loan

A mortgage that exceeds the limit set by the Federal Housing Finance Agency, meaning it can not be guaranteed by **Fannie Mae** or **Freddie Mac**. As of 2012, the limit is $417,000 for most of the United States. Such loans have higher interest rates than typical mortgages. Read more about them on the Federal Housing Finance Agency's site.

Finance, Real estate

junk bonds, high-yield bonds

The term junk bonds is more commonly used and is preferable when referring to bonds issued by a company that has a low rating from a rating agency. Junk bonds are typically rated below BBB- by **Standard & Poor's** and below Baa3 by **Moody's**. Because they are rated lower, they offer a higher interest rate, or yield, to investors, but more risk as well. Wall Street uses the term "high-yield bonds" as a euphemism to give the issues a more positive connotation. **($$$)**

Wall Street

just in time

An inventory strategy where the materials needed to produce a finished good are delivered just as they're needed. A just-in-time inventory cuts down on the amount of goods stored in warehouses. Many companies shift to just in time during an economic slowdown. The shift trickles through to suppliers, often causing their inventories to swell. **($$)**

Manufacturing

K&W Cafeterias Inc.

There are no spaces between the letters and the ampersand of the Winston-Salem, N.C.-based cafeteria chain.

Company Name, Restaurant

K-Swiss Inc.

The Westlake Village, Calif.-based shoe company's name has a hyphen.

Company Name

KBR Inc.

A Houston-based engineering, construction and military contracting company. It formerly was a subsidiary of **Halliburton Co.** The company was previously known as Kellogg Brown & Root. However, the KBR abbreviation is now acceptable in all references.

Company Name

Kellogg Co.

The cereal manufacturer is based in Battle Creek, Mich. Note that the brand name of its cereals, however, is Kellogg's.

Company Name

Kelly Services Inc.

The staffing company is based in Troy, Mich.

Company Name

Keogh plan

A tax-deferred pension plan available to self-employed individuals or unincorporated businesses. There is no u in Keogh.

Finance

KeyCorp

The Cleveland-based bank spells its name as one word with a capital C.

Company Name, Finance

KFC Corp.

Use all capital letters for the chicken restaurant chain, formerly Kentucky Fried Chicken, based in Louisville, Ky. The parent company is named Yum! Brands Inc., but drop the exclamation point in writing.

Company Name, Restaurant

kickback

A form of payment made to persuade an individual or company to make a decision. For example, a stock broker might provide a kickback of his or her commissions to an investor who frequently trades stocks with the brokerage. Kickbacks are sometimes illegal, so be wary of using this term. **($$$$)**

kicker

A feature added, such as a **warrant**, to a debt offering to make it more attractive to investors. **($$)**

Wall Street

kicking the tires

A slang term used to describe when one company does preliminary research about buying another company. It should be avoided.

kidnap and ransom insurance

A policy purchased by companies to protect employees working in high-risk areas of the world. If an employee is kidnapped, the company pays the ransom and then files a claim with the insurance company that sold them the coverage to get repaid. *K&R insurance* is acceptable on second reference.

Company Name, Insurance

kids' meal

A meal package designed for children, often including a toy.

Restaurant

Kiewit Corp.

The employee-owned construction and mining company is based in Omaha, Neb. It is sometimes referred to as Peter Kiewit Sons' Inc.

Company Name, Manufacturing

Kimberly-Clark Corp.

Note the hyphen in the name of the Irving, Texas paper-based consumer products company.

Company Name, Manufacturing

Kinder Morgan Inc.

A pipeline and energy storage company based in Houston.

Company Name, Energy

Kindred Healthcare Inc.

The operator of hospitals, nursing homes and long-term care facilities is based in Louisville, Ky. It spells Healthcare as one word.

Company Name, Health care

Kiplinger's Personal Finance

A personal finance magazine started in 1947 and called Changing Times until 1991. It bought Individual Investor magazine in 2001, folding that magazine's subscriber list into its own. As with other family-controlled media companies, ensure your writing distinguishes between the publication and the family member. On second reference, this publication can be referred to as Kiplinger's.

Company Name

Kitty Litter

A trademarked product. The generic term is cat-box filler.

Trademark

KKR & Co.

The New York buyout firm is no longer called Kohlberg Kravis Roberts & Co.

Company Name, Finance

Kleenex

A trademarked product. The generic term is tissue.

Trademark

Kmart

No hyphen or space in the name of the retailer now part of Sears Holdings Corp.

Company Name, Retail

Koch Industries Inc.

The privately held conglomerate is based in Wichita, Kan. Its subsidiaries include Georgia-Pacific LLC, Flint Hills Resources and Invista.

Company Name, Manufacturing

Kohl's Corp.

The department store chain is based in Menomonee Falls, Wis.

Company Name, Retail

Kool-Aid

A trademarked product. The generic term is soft-drink mix.

Trademark

Kraft Foods Inc.

The Northfield, Ill.-based food company has numerous well-known brands, including Oscar Mayer, Maxwell House, Nabisco and Oreo.

Company Name

Krazy Glue

A trademark for a series of extra-strong glues. The generic term is super adhesive.

Trademark

Krispy Kreme Doughnuts Inc.

The Winston-Salem, N.C.-based company spells doughnuts differently from rival **Dunkin' Donuts** in its name. Krispy Kreme is acceptable on second reference. Doughnut is the correct spelling for the deep-fried cake treat.

Company Name, Restaurant

Kroger Co.

Delete "the" before the name of this supermarket chain based in Cincinnati.

Retail

L

L-3 Communications Holdings Inc.
The New York-based defense contractor uses a hyphen between the L and the 3 in all references.
Company Name, Manufacturing

La-Z-Boy Inc.
Hyphenate the name of the Monroe, Mich.-based furniture manufacturer.
Company Name, Manufacturing

labor force
The total number of people, 16 and older, employed and unemployed in an economy. Labor force statistics can be found on the Census Bureau website.
Economy

Laboratory Corporation of America Holdings
LabCorp is acceptable on second reference for the Burlington, N.C.-based medical testing company.
Company Name, Health care

lagging indicators
An economic measurement that begins to change after the economy has already moved in that direction. **($$)**
Economy

Land O'Lakes Inc.
The agriculture cooperative is based in Arden Hills, Minn. There are no spaces between the O, the apostrophe and Lakes. The O is capitalized in all references.
Company Name

Land Rover
A trademarked product. The generic term is sport utility vehicle.
Trademark

landlord
The owner of an apartment, house, condominium or other real estate who rents or leases it to an individual or business. Landlord and lessor are often interchangeable, although landlord is more commonly used for residential real estate stories.
Real estate

large cap
A term used to describe a company with a market capitalization of more than $10 billion. Big cap is also acceptable.
Wall Street

large group
A term used by a health insurer to describe a large pool of individuals. It can be a minimum of 250, 500 or 1,000 members. **($)**
Health care, Insurance

Las Vegas Sands Corp.
The casino operator is based in Paradise, Nev.

later stage

A new company that has reached the stage of producing revenue and growing. It is more advanced than a **startup.**

Laundromat

A trademarked name. The generic term is coin-operated laundry.

layoff

When a company eliminates jobs because of economic downturns or corporate restructurings. Companies use many other terms to describe layoffs, including "reduction in force," "rightsizing," "downsizing," "eliminations," "workforce moderations" and "streamlining the workforce ." All of these should be avoided. Layoffs usually don't reflect on an employee's job performance. Firing, however, has a different connotation and should be used carefully. Both layoffs and firings are terminations. Challenger, Gray and Christmas Inc., a Chicago-based firm, issues a monthly report on corporate layoffs. It comes out the second or third business day of the following month at 7:30 a.m. EST. The story focuses on changes from the previous month and the same month a year ago.

Economy

LCD

Stands for liquid crystal display. It is a flat, electronic display that does not emit light directly and is used in video games, computer monitors, watches and televisions.

Technology

lead underwriter

The managing underwriter who maintains the books of securities sold for a new issue. The firm is also commonly known as the **book runner. ($$)**

Wall Street

leading indicators

An economic measurement that begins to change before the economy moves in that direction. The Conference Board compiles a leading economic index, a composite of 10 economic indicators. It is released on the third week of each month. **($$)**

Economy

Lear Corp.

The manufacturer of automobile interiors is based in Southfield, Mich. It is not to be confused with the Bombardier subsidiary Learjet, which makes airplanes.

Company Name, Manufacturing

LED

Stands for light-emitting diode. LEDs are used as indicator lights in many devices, doing such things as telling the user whether a device is on or off. They are also used for aviation, signage and street lighting, and, increasingly, in household lighting.

Technology

LEED

A registered trademark of the U.S. Green Building Council for its certification program. The acronym stands for Leadership in Energy and Environmental Design. Acceptable on first reference. The council describes the program as "the nationally accepted benchmark for the design, construction, and operation of green buildings." **($$$$)**

Lego Group

Capitalize only the L in the name of the Denmark-based manufacturer of children's toys, as well as the name of its stores.
Company Name, Manufacturing

lemon

A bad investment or a new vehicle with multiple defects that were not apparent when purchased. Many states have lemon laws that allow consumers to return faulty vehicles to a dealership within a certain time period.

lender

A financial institution that makes loans.
Finance, Real estate

lessee

The person who rents land or property from another person. Tenant is also acceptable.
Real estate

lessor

The owner of land or property who rents it to another person. **($)**
Real estate

letter of credit

A letter from a bank that guarantees that a buyer's payment to a seller will be received on time and for the correct amount. It's often used in international transactions. **($$)**

levels of real estate agents

In most states, there are two levels of real estate agent, the salesperson and the broker. In most states, a broker must have a license if he or she is to be paid commissions from a real estate transaction. When writing about real estate, please distinguish between a salesperson and a broker.
Real estate

leverage

The use of borrowed money to increase the potential return on an investment, or the use of debt to finance a company's assets. **($$)**

leveraged buyout

A strategy involving the acquisition of a company using borrowed money. The acquirer uses the acquired's assets as collateral for borrowing in hopes that the future cash flow of the acquired company will cover the loan payments and produce a healthy profit. *LBO* is acceptable on second reference. **($$$$)**

leveraged portfolio

A portfolio that includes risky assets such as junk bonds purchased with borrowed money.
Wall Street

Levi's

A trademarked product. The generic term is jeans.
Trademark

liability

A legal debt or obligation, including accrual obligations such as pension liabilities. Recorded on the balance sheet, current liabilities are debts payable within one year, while long-term liabilities are debts payable over a longer period.

Liberty Global Inc.

The Englewood, Colo.-based company is one of the largest broadband providers in the world.

Liberty Media Corp.

A cable and broadcast company based in Meridian, Colo.

Company Name

Liberty Mutual Group Inc.

The Boston-based insurance company no longer uses the word insurance in its name. However, it does have a subsidiary named Liberty Mutual Insurance Co.

Company Name, Insurance

LIBOR

The London interbank offered rate; it's the rate at which banks in London can borrow money from other banks on a short-term basis. LIBOR is acceptable on second reference. **($$$$)**

Economy

lien

A legal claim or hold on a piece of property.

Real estate

life insurance

A policy purchased by an individual or company that promises a payment if the person dies.

Insurance

LIFO

The last-in, first-out accounting method for inventory. The assets produced or acquired last will be treated as if they are sold first. LIFO is acceptable on all references. **($$$)**

Manufacturing, Retail

limit order

An order placed with a brokerage firm to purchase or sell a certain amount of shares at a certain price or better. Limit orders are often used with low-volume or highly volatile stocks. **($$$)**

Wall Street

limited

A form of company where the equity put into the business has limited uses based on its charter. When used on first reference at the end of the company's name, it's abbreviated Ltd. This is the equivalent of Inc. for some non-U.S. companies.

Limited Brands Inc.

The Columbus, Ohio-based retailer operates chains such as Bath & Body Works and Victoria's Secret. It does not own the Limited retail store chain.

Company Name, Retail

limited liability company

A business structure with corporation and partnership aspects. Often a business will become a limited liability company to receive the tax advantages of a partnership and the liability advantages of a corporation. LLC is acceptable at the end of a company name on first reference only.

limited liability limited partnership

A modified version of a limited partnership where the general partners manage the partnership and the limited partners have only an investment interest. The difference from a limited partnership is that in a limited liability limited partnership the partners are not liable for damages arising from the acts of other partners. LLLP is acceptable at the end of a company name. **($$)**
Company Name, Finance, Real estate

limited partnership

A business organization in which one more more general partners manage the business and assume responsibility for the debts and obligations, and limited partners are only liable to the extent of their investment. The limited partners have no management control. LP is acceptable at the end of a company name. **($)**
Company Name

Lincoln National Corp.

The Philadelphia-based company has insurance and asset management operations. Its marketing name is Lincoln Financial Group.
Company Name, Finance, Insurance

LinkedIn Corp.

The Mountain View, Calif.-based company that operates a social networking site for professionals spells its name as one word.
Company Name, Technology

liquidate

To convert an investment or asset into cash by selling it, or the process of a company selling some or all of its assets to pay off creditors.

liquidity

The ease with which an asset can be bought or sold. An asset with high liquidity is being frequently traded at a stable price.

listed security

Securities that have been approved for trading on a specific exchange.
Wall Street

Little League Baseball

A trademarked name. The generic term is youth baseball.
Trademark

Live Nation Entertainment Inc.

The concert promoter, ticketing agent and artist management company is based in Beverly Hills, Calif.
Company Name

LLC

Stands for **limited liability company**, not limited liability corporation. It's a form of a business that limits the liability of the partners.
Company Name

Lloyd's of London

A London-based insurance and reinsurance market. It works like a mutual fund in that financial backers join Lloyd's as members and spread the risk of the insurance that they're funding among the members. Lloyd's is acceptable on second reference.

Company Name, Insurance

LLP

An abbreviation for limited liability partnership. Acceptable on all references. Limited liability partnerships differ from limited partnerships.

Company Name

load fund

A mutual fund that charges consumers a commission or a sales charge. The money goes primarily to pay the **broker** or investment adviser for his or her expertise in selecting the fund. See **no-load fund**. **($$)**

Wall Street

loan

When an individual or a company borrows money from a financial institution. The borrower agrees to repay the money, plus interest, over a certain time period.

Real estate

loan (n., v.), lend (v.)

Although historically the word loan has been used only as a noun, it is increasingly being used as a verb. The Associated Press Stylebook says to use loan only as a noun, but we think it's acceptable as a verb as well. The Chicago Manual of Style states that lend should be used only when something nonfinancial changes hands, but we think that loan or lend can be used no matter what is being borrowed.

Finance, Real estate

loan loss provision

When a bank sets aside money for loans that it believes might default. An increase in a loan loss provisions means that a bank's loan portfolio is decreasing in quality. **($$$)**

Finance

lock-in period

The time period that a mortgage lender agrees to hold steady the mortgage rate and discount points to be paid by the borrower. The period is typically 30 days or 60 days.

Finance, Real estate

lockup agreement

An agreement between the underwriters of a company's initial public offering and the executives and board members of that company that prevents those insiders from selling the stock for a certain amount of time — as short as four months or as long as a year — after the **IPO**. When the lockup agreement expires and those insiders sell their shares, the stock price typically falls because of the increase in available shares in the market. **($$$$)**

Lockheed Martin Corp.

The Bethesda, Md.-based company is the largest U.S. federal government contractor, providing primarily aerospace and defense manufacturing.

Manufacturing

Loews Corp.

A New York-based company that operates hotels, a property and casualty insurance company, oil and gas rigs, and an interstate gas pipeline.

Company Name, Energy, Insurance

LoJack Corp.

The name of the Westwood, Mass.-based company is one word with a capital J. When referring to its LoJack car security product, maintain the same capitalization.

Company Name

long position

Owning an investment with the expectation that it will rise in value. The opposite is a short position. The phrases buying long or going long can also be used. **($$)**

long-term debt

Loans and other obligations that are due to be repaid in more than a year. Can also be called *long-term liabilities.*

loose credit

The act of making credit easy to obtain. The real estate market in the United States in the early 21st century was marked by loose credit

terms from lenders.

Finance, Real estate

loss

When expenses total more than revenue or sales. Losses widen and narrow. Do not use the terms rise and fall.

loss portfolio transfer

An insurance transaction in which a **reinsurer** assumes, for a fee, the potential losses from policies written by an insurance company. An insurance company that wants to stop writing a specific line of policies may use a loss portfolio transfer to exit that market immediately. **($$$)**

Insurance

Lowe's Cos.

The home improvement chain and Home Depot competitor is based in Mooresville, N.C. The name of its stores is Lowe's Home Improvement Warehouse, but Lowe's is acceptable when referring to its locations. Avoid confusing with Lowe's Food Stores Inc., the Winston-Salem, N.C.-based grocery store chain.

Company Name, Retail

Ltd. Co.

A business structure used in Canada and England in which shareholder responsibility for company debt is limited, usually to the amount that the shareholder has invested in the company.

LTO

Limited-time offer. Spell out on first reference.

Manufacturing, Restaurant, Retail

Lubrizol Corp.

The chemicals company is based in Wickliffe, Ohio. In September 2011, Berkshire Hathaway Inc. acquired the company for $9.2 billion.

Company Name

Lucite paint

A trademarked product. The generic term is acrylic paint.

Trademark

M

M&A

An abbreviation for mergers and acquisitions. Acceptable on first reference.

Mace

A trademarked product. The generic term is tear-gas spray.

Trademark

Macy's Inc.

The department store company has headquarters in Cincinnati and New York and changed its name from Federated Department Stores Inc. in 2007. It is also the parent company of Bloomingdale's.

Company Name, Retail

Magic Marker

A trademarked product. The generic term is felt-tip marking pen.

Trademark

Main Street

A term used to describe the investing public. It's often used in contrast to **Wall Street**, which is used to describe the collection of professional investment and financial experts who primarily work in New York.

management

The people at a company who are in charge. They organize, plan and direct the company's operations.

management buyout

When the executives of a company purchase a controlling interest from shareholders. The management often teams up with an outside investor, such as a leveraged buyout house, to complete such an acquisition. Do not use MBO on any reference. **($$$)**

management fee

A fee paid by the investors in a fund to its financial adviser.

Finance, Wall Street

manager

The term can be used to describe someone who oversees an investment portfolio or someone who oversees a department within a company. When using this term, state in the story specifically what the person is managing.

Manpower Inc.

The employment agency company is based in Milwaukee, Wis.

Company Name

maquiladora

A manufacturing plant in Mexico near the Mexican-U.S. border that is exempt from tariffs on raw materials and components as long as the final product is exported. **($$$)**

Manufacturing

Marathon Oil Corp.
The Houston-based oil and gas company spun off its refining business, Marathon Petroleum Corp., in June 2011.
Company Name, Energy

margin
In business terms, the difference between a product's selling price and the cost to produce the product. Margin can also refer to money borrowed to purchase an investment.

margin call
A demand made by a broker that an investor using margin place more money or securities into his or her account. This typically occurs when the account decreases in value. (**$$$**)
Wall Street

market capitalization
A company's stock market value. It is calculated by multiplying the number of outstanding common shares by the current market price of a share. The term market cap is acceptable on second reference. (**$$**)

market maker
A broker-dealer that holds an amount of shares in a company to make it easier for investors to buy or sell the stock. The term is often used as a firm making a market in a stock. (**$$**)
Wall Street

market share
The percentage of a specific business or product line that a company controls with its offerings. Coca-Cola and PepsiCo controlled more than 70 percent of the carbonated soft drink market in 2008. Coca-Cola had a 42.8 percent market share, while PepsiCo had a 31.1 percent market share, according to industry newsletter Beverage Digest.

market timer
An investor who believes that he or she can forecast the ups and downs of the market.
Wall Street

MarketWatch.com
A business news website founded in 1994 and acquired by Dow Jones & Co. in 2005. The W is capitalized in the name although it's spelled as one word. Since its content is exclusively online, use the .com as part of the name in all references.
Company Name

markup
The difference between the lowest offering price for a security and the price that a dealer charges a customer. The term can also be used as the difference in price of a product sold by a retailer from the retailer's cost to purchase the product.
Retail, Wall Street

Marriott International Inc.
The hotel operator is based in Bethesda, Md.
Company Name

Marsh & McLennan Cos.

The New York-based insurance brokerage uses an ampersand in all references.

Company Name, Insurance

Masco Corp.

The Taylor, Mich.-based company manufactures and distributes building materials.

Company Name, Manufacturing

Massachusetts Mutual Life Insurance Co.

The Springfield, Mass.-based insurance and financial services company refers to itself as MassMutual. It uses the name MassMutual Financial Group in marketing. We'd prefer Mass Mutual as two words on second reference.

Company Name, Finance, Insurance

Master of Business Administration

An advanced degree offered by a university's business school. *MBA* is acceptable in all references.

MasterCard Inc.

The financial services company based in Purchase, N.Y., capitalizes the C in all references.

material event

An occurrence at a public company that would require it to file a **Form 8-K** with the Securities and Exchange Commission. **($$$)**

material weakness

A phrase used by an auditor to indicate that the company's controls in reporting its financials are defective and could result in a misstatement of its performance. **($$$)**

Mattel Inc.

The toy manufacturer is based in El Segundo, Calif. Lowercase the letters in the name after the M even though its logo uses all capital letters.

Company Name, Manufacturing

maturity date

The date the borrower has to pay back the money it has borrowed through a bond issue or loan. **($$)**

Wall Street

McDonald's Corp.

Distinguish between the Oak Brook, Ill.-based company and its restaurants when writing about the two in the same story.

Company Name, Restaurant

McGraw-Hill Cos.

The publisher is based in New York. It is no longer the owner of Business-Week magazine. Use a hyphen in all references.

Company Name

McKesson Corp.

The largest pharmaceutical distributor in North America is based in San Francisco. A scandal at the company in 1938 led to the Securities and Exchange Commission requiring public companies to have audit committees of **outside directors** and that shareholders approve outside auditors.

Health care

McMoRan Exploration Co.

Retain the capitalization on the R for the New Orleans-based oil and gas company.

Company Name, Energy

MDU Resources Group Inc.

The electric and natural gas utility is based in Bismarck, N.D.

Company Name, Energy

MeadWestvaco Corp.

The packaging company based in Richmond, Va. spells its name as one word, with a capital W.

Company Name

mechanic's lien

A **lien** filed by a **contractor** or supplier against a piece of property to recover the value of its work.

Medco Health Solutions Inc.

The prescription plan manager is based in Franklin Lakes, N.J. Lowercase the C.

Medicaid

The federal and state health insurance program that provides medical care for low-income families.

Health care, Insurance

medical director

The executive of a health care plan who is responsible for the quality and cost effectiveness of the care provided. *Chief medical officer* is also an acceptable term.

Health care

medical underwriting

The evaluation of health insurance applications submitted by potential group members to determine the insurability of the group. An underwriter also decides on premiums to be charged. (**$$**)

Health care, Insurance

Medicare

The federal health insurance program that subsidizes health care for those 65 and older and those who are disabled and have been on Social Security for two years.

Health care, Insurance

Medicare supplement

An insurance plan purchased by a consumer to provide reimbursement of benefits, deductibles and coinsurance payments excluded from Medicare. Medigap is also acceptable. (**$**)

Health care, Insurance

Medtronic Inc.

The medical technology company is based in Minneapolis.

Meijer

The retailer is based in Grand Rapids, Mich. Its name does not include an Inc., Co. or other corporate designation. It operates 195 "supercenters" and grocery stores in Illinois, Indiana, Kentucky, Michigan and Ohio.

Company Name, Retail

memory

The amount of computer data storage available.

Technology

Memory Stick

A trademarked name from Sony. The generic term is flash memory storage device or flash drive.

menu board

A sign displaying the restaurant's offerings, ranging from a chalkboard to digital electronic displays.

Restaurant

Men's Wearhouse Inc.

Avoid capitalizing "the" before the name of the Houston-based men's clothing store chain, and note the spelling of Wearhouse.

Company Name, Retail

merchant cash advance

The purchase of future credit card receivables. It is also called future credit card receivable funding or forward credit card factoring. (**$$**)

Finance, Restaurant

Merck & Co.

The Whitehouse Station, N.J.-based pharmaceutical company is known as Merck Sharp & Dohme outside of the United States and Canada.

Company Name, Health care

merger

When two companies combine to form a new company, and the shareholders of each company own about 50 percent of the new company. Rarely, if ever, are there true mergers, although companies will announce takeovers as "mergers." Be careful when using this word. The more appropriate word often is **acquisition** or **takeover**.

Meritor Inc.

The name of the truck parts manufacturer based in Troy, Mich., was changed back from ArvinMeritor Inc. in 2011.

Company Name, Manufacturing

MetLife Inc.

The New York-based company is the parent company of Metropolitan Life Insurance Co. Refer to either the parent company or the life insurer as MetLife.

MetroPCS Communications Inc.

The wireless provider based in Richardson, Texas, spells its name as two words, with PCS capitalized.

Company Name, Technology

metropolitan statistical area

A formal metropolitan area as determined by the U.S. Office of Management and Budget. It is used to compile census and economic data on a regular basis. *MSA* is acceptable on second reference. A list of such areas can be found on the Census Bureau website.

Economy

mezzanine financing

A hybrid combination of debt and equity financing. The lender can convert the debt to an ownership position in the company if the loan is not repaid in time or in full. The origin of the term comes from Italian architecture, where a mezzanine floor is built between two main floors. **($$$$$)**

Retail

MGM Resorts International

The gambling and hotel operator is based in Las Vegas. MGM Resorts is acceptable on second reference.

Company Name

Michaels Stores Inc.

No apostrophe in the name of the Irving, Texas-based crafts retailer.

Company Name, Retail

microbusiness

A business with fewer than 10 employees. The definition is the same in the United States and the European Union. Microbusinesses often operate out of the owner's house.

microcap

A company with a market capitalization between $50 million and $300 million.

microlender

See **community development financial institution**.

Economy, Finance

Micron Technology Inc.

The semiconductor manufacturer is based in Boise, Idaho.

Company Name, Manufacturing, Technology

Microsoft Corp.

The computer software company is based in Redmond, Wash. Cofounder Bill Gates is no longer the chief executive officer.

Company Name

midcap

A company with a market capitalization between $2 billion and $10 billion.

middle class

A term loosely used to describe the population between the working class and the upper class. There is no specific quantitative measure, so use sparingly as many blue-collar workers actually make as much, if not more, than some who consider themselves middle class.

Economy

midsized business

A business that has between 100 and 500 employees in the United States and between 100 and 250 employees in the European Union.

millage

The amount per $1,000 of assessed value used to determine taxes on a piece of property. **($$$)**

Real estate

MillerCoors LLC

The Chicago-based joint venture between SAB Miller and Molson Coors is one word.

Company Name

Mohawk Industries Inc.

The carpet manufacturer is based in Calhoun, Ga.

Company Name, Manufacturing

momentum investing

An investment strategy that relies on current trends in the market to continue. An investor buys into stocks and commodities that have risen in price, believing that they will continue to keep rising. **($$)**

Wall Street

monetary policy

The regulation of money supply and interest rates by a central bank. In the United States, the Federal Reserve regulates money supply. The Fed submits a monetary policy report to Congress twice a year, and the Fed chairman testifies to the House and Senate in conjunction with the report's submission.

Economy

Money magazine

A monthly publication from Time Inc. started in 1972 to complement Fortune, another Time business magazine. It focuses primarily on personal finance. The word magazine is lowercased.

Company Name

money market

The market where investments with high liquidity and short maturities are traded. They include Treasury bills, certificates of deposits and municipal notes.

money market funds

Mutual funds that invest in short-term debt instruments. A money market account from a bank is different. It's a savings account in which banks pay the lowest interest rate they can get by with.

Wall Street

money supply

The entire quantity of currency, loans and credit in an economy. Data about the U.S. money supply can be found on the Federal Reserve website. **($$)**

Economy

monopoly

A situation in which a single company controls a large portion of a market for a product or a service, often resulting in higher prices.

Monsanto Co.

An agricultural biotechnology company based in Creve Coeur, Mo.

Company Name

monthly Treasury statement

A report from the U.S. Treasury Department that totals the revenues collected and the payments made by the federal government each month. It comes out about two weeks after the end of each month, and the story focus is on the overall surplus or deficit. The latest report can be found online.

Economy

Moody's Corp.

The New York-based parent company of Moody's Investors Service, which rates credit issues and provides financial research. Use Moody's on second reference for both.

Company Name, Finance

Moon Pie

A trademarked name. It should be capitalized. The generic term is marshmallow sandwich.

Trademark

Morgan Stanley

The New York-based financial services company no longer uses the "& Co." after its name in all references. Morgan Stanley Smith Barney is a retail brokerage joint venture with Citigroup.

Company Name, Finance

Morningstar Inc.

A Chicago-based independent investment research company best known for providing information about mutual funds.

Company Name, Finance

mortgage

A loan used by an individual or company to purchase real estate. The loan is secured by the real estate purchased. The lender can take ownership of the real estate if the buyer fails to repay the loan.

Real estate

mortgage application

An application to borrow money to purchase property. Mortgage application data is released weekly on Wednesdays by the Mortgage Bankers Association of America. The story on the data focuses on changes in the purchase index, the refinancing index and the four-week moving average.

Economy, Real estate

mortgage bank

A financial institution that originates loans for real estate, funding them through its own funds or a **warehouse lender**.

Finance, Real estate

mortgage insurance

An insurance policy that protects the lender against a mortgage default. Lenders often require mortgage insurance if the lender is putting up less than 20 percent of the value of the home at the time of closing.

Insurance, Real estate

mortgage servicer

A company to which some borrowers make their mortgage payments even though the company may not be the actual lender. Mortgage servicers have been criticized for holding up refinancing so they can collect big fees on foreclosed mortgages. (**$**)

Real estate

Mosaic Co.

The fertilizer manufacturer is based in Plymouth, Minn.

Company Name, Manufacturing

most-favored nation

A designation given by one country to another in which the two governments agree to lower tariffs for trade. Members of the **World Trade Organization** have agreed to most-favored nation status with one another.

Economy

motor vehicle sales

The number of domestically produced cars, SUVs, vans and light trucks sold during a monthly time period. Car manufacturers report their sales on the first business day of the following month. Motor vehicle sales are less than 5 percent of the gross domestic product, but they are important because they are highly discretionary purchases and are looked at to see whether consumer spending behavior is changing. The latest data on new car sales is available here. The term new car sales is also acceptable.

Economy

Motorola Mobility Holdings Inc.

The former mobile devices unit of Motorola Inc. was acquired by Google Inc. in 2012.

Technology

Motorola Solutions Inc.

The data and telecommunications equipment company is based in Schaumburg, Ill. that succeeded Motorola Inc. after its mobile operation, Motorola Mobility Holdings Inc., was spun off in 2011.

Motors Liquidation Co.

The name of the old General Motors Corp., which entered into bankruptcy court protection.

Company Name, Manufacturing

MP3

A common format for storing audio such as songs on digital audio players.

Technology

MP4

A method of storing audio and video content.

Technology

MPEG

Stands for Moving Pictures Experts Group. It is the name of an audio/video file format.

Technology

multiple

A term used to describe a measure of a company's stock price. Both **price-to-book ratio** and **price-to-earnings ratio** can be referred to as a multiple after first reference. **($$)**

municipal bond

Debt issued by a state, county or municipality to fund capital expenditures, such as roads and schools. Avoid using the term "muni." Municipal bonds can be both **general obligation bonds** and **revenue bonds**. **($$)**

Wall Street

municipal note

A short-term municipal borrowing that matures in one year or less. **($$)**

Murphy Oil Corp.

The El Dorado, Ark.-based petroleum company owns the Murphy USA gasoline stations.

Company Name, Energy

mutual fund

Fund operated by an investment company that raises money from shareholders and invests it in stocks, bonds, options, commodities or money market securities. Mutual funds are seen as a less-risky way for small investors to invest in the market. **($$)**

Wall Street

Mutual of Omaha Insurance Co.

The insurance and financial services company is based in Omaha, Neb.

Company Name, Finance, Insurance

mutual ownership

An ownership structure commonly found in the insurance and thrift industries where the company is owned by the policyholders and depositors. **($)**

Finance, Insurance

Mylan Inc.

The pharmaceutical company is based in Canonsburg, Pa.

Company Name, Health care

MySpace.com

Note the capitalization for the News Corp. division.

Company Name, Technology

naked shorting
The illegal practice of shorting a stock without actually having the stock to short. Short selling requires that the shares be borrowed before they are shorted. In naked shorting, the shares are not borrowed. **($$$$$)**

Nasdaq
Created in 1971 as the world's first electronic stock market, the Nasdaq — which stands for National Association of Securities Dealers Automated Quotations — is a computerized system that facilitates trading and provides price quotations on about 5,000 of the more actively traded over-the-counter stocks. Its largest stocks include Microsoft, Dell and Cisco. Do not use all caps.
Company Name, Wall Street

Nash Finch Co.
The food distributor based in Edina, Minn., uses no hyphen in any reference.
Company Name

Nathan's Famous Inc.
The name of the Jericho, N.Y.-based restaurant chain does not include hot dog.
Company Name, Restaurant

national account
A large health insurance account that has members in multiple geographic areas covered through one contract.

Employees of retailers such as Wal-Mart and Home Depot are covered by a national account.
Health care, Insurance

National Association of Convenience Stores
An international trade group, it claims to represent more than 2,100 retail outlets and 1,500 supplier companies. In general, the trade group is a better second reference than NACS. **($$$)**
Restaurant, Retail

National Association of Securities Dealers
The former self-regulatory agency of the securities industry that also oversaw the Nasdaq exchange. In 2007, it merged with the New York Stock Exchange's regulation committee to form the **Financial Industry Regulatory Authority**, or FINRA.
Finance, Wall Street

National Bureau of Economic Research
A private, nonprofit, nonpartisan research organization. *NBER* is acceptable on second reference.
Economy, Finance

National Credit Union Administration
The federal agency that regulates credit unions in the country. *NCUA* is acceptable on second reference.

national deficit vs. national debt

Do not confuse these terms. The national deficit is the annual budget deficit of the federal government. The national debt is the total amount of money owed to creditors of the federal government. These creditors own Treasury bills, notes and bonds.

Economy

National Labor Relations Board

A federal agency created in 1935 to enforce the National Labor Relations Act. It conducts secret-ballot elections to determine whether employees want union representation and investigates unfair labor practices by employers and unions. *NLRB* is acceptable on second reference. The agency maintains an online database of its decisions.

National Oilwell Varco Inc.

An oil well drilling rig manufacturer based in Houston.

Company Name, Energy

National Restaurant Association

The Washington-based trade group representing the restaurant industry. It claims about 380,000 members. Avoid NRA on second reference except in an industry-specific publication.

Restaurant

Nationwide Mutual Insurance Co.

The Columbus, Ohio-based insurance and financial services company previously had a publicly traded company known as Nationwide Financial Services, but that was acquired by Nationwide Mutual in 2009.

Company Name, Finance, Insurance

natural gas pricing

Remember that mcf stands for 1,000 cubic feet, not a million (think Roman numerals). Gas sales can be in those units or in BTUs — British Thermal Units — a measure of the gas's heat content. BTU can be used on first reference, but usually explained elsewhere in the story; substitute 1,000 cubic feet for mcf in all references, except publications serving the energy industry. Additional terms: A therm is 100,000 BTUs and a dekatherm is 10 therms. Use per million cubic feet, not dekatherm, when natural gas is priced that way.

Energy

Naugahyde

A trademarked product. The generic term is simulated leather.

Trademark

Navistar International Corp.

The Warrenville, Ill.-based manufacturer of trucks, engines and buses was previously known as International Harvester Co.

Company Name, Transportation

NCR Corp.

The Dayton, Ohio-based company's name is all capital letters.

Company Name

negative equity

When the value of an asset falls below the balance of the loan used to purchase the asset. The term upside down is also acceptable. The term can also refer to a situation where a company's liabilities exceed its assets. (**$$**)

negative growth

Companies like to use this term to sugarcoat when revenue or profits decline. Avoid using it.

negative-amortization mortgage

A loan in which the amount of money owed actually grows during the first five or so years of the mortgage, allowing for initially lower monthly payments but increased risk. Such mortgages are typically no longer available.

Real estate

negotiated sale

A municipal bond sale in which the government entity and an underwriter work together to set the terms of the sale rather than having underwriters bid on the offering to set the terms. It often results in a better rate for the issuer. (**$$$$$**)

Wall Street

Neiman Marcus Group Inc.

No hyphen in the name of the Dallas-based upscale retailer, and note the spelling of Neiman.

Company Name, Retail

nephrologist

A doctor who can treat and diagnose illnesses related to the nervous system. These can also include diseases that affect the brain, the spinal cord and muscles.

Health care

Nerf

A trademarked product. The generic term is foam toy.

Trademark

net asset value

A mutual fund's assets per share or an exchange-traded fund's net assets divided by the number of outstanding shares. NAV is acceptable on second reference. (**$$$**)

Wall Street

net income

A company's total earnings, after subtracting costs of doing business, depreciation, interest, taxes and other expenses. Do not confuse net income with **net operating income**. When a company loses money, it's called a net loss. This is the most important number in any earnings story.

net interest income

For financial companies, the difference between the interest received on loans and the interest it pays on deposits and other borrowed funds. (**$$**)

Finance

net interest margin

The difference between what a bank pays in interest on deposits and receives on loans and investments. (**$**)

Finance

net operating income

A company's profits after operating expenses are subtracted, but before subtracting depreciation, income taxes and interest. The term is commonly used by banks, insurance companies and other financial institutions and is not part of **the generally accepted accounting principles**. Operating income is also common, as is operating profit. **($$)**

net proceeds

The amount of money left over after all costs are deducted from the sale of an asset or securities, such as stock. In an initial public offering, the net proceeds are the money that a company raises after paying its underwriters and other expenses. **($$$)**

net worth

The amount by which the value of an individual's or a company's assets exceeds liabilities.

Netflix Inc.

Use the full name for the Los Gatos, Calif.-based Internet entertainment company only on first reference. When referring specifically to its service, Netflix can be used on first reference.

network

A group of physicians, hospitals and other health care providers that have contracted with a managed care organization to provide services in a geographic area.

Health care

neutral

A rating given to a stock by a sell-side analyst. A "neutral" rating means that the analyst doesn't believe that the stock will outperform the overall market, nor will it underperform the overall market. The rating **hold** is synonymous.

Wall Street

new home sales

The sale of newly built homes to buyers from builders. An increase in new home sales can be a sign of a growing economy. Compiled monthly by the Census Bureau, the data is released in the last week of the following month. The story focuses on the level and the monthly change in total sales. Revisions to the data can be extensive.

Economy, Real estate

New York Board of Trade

A commodities exchange that trades futures and options on products such as sugar, cotton, coffee and orange juice. It was renamed ICE Futures US in 2007 after it was acquired by the Intercontinental Exchange, or ICE. The name New York Board of Trade is still used by some media outlets, but **ICE Futures** is the preferred name. Avoid NYBOT.

Wall Street

New York Life Insurance Co.

The New York company is the largest mutual life insurance company in the country. Avoid the NYLIC abbreviation.

Insurance

New York Mercantile Exchange

The largest commodity exchange in the world. There are two divisions. One primarily trades contracts for oil, propane, natural gas, platinum and palladium. The other primarily trades contracts for gold, silver, copper and the Eurotop 100 Index. Avoid NYMEX and COMEX in all references. The exchange is acceptable on second reference.

Wall Street

New York Stock Exchange

The largest stock exchange in the country. It is responsible for setting policies and supervising the stock exchange and its member activities. The NYSE also oversees the transfer of members' seats on the exchange and judging whether a potential applicant is qualified to be a specialist. *NYSE*, the *stock exchange* or *exchange* is acceptable on second reference. In February 2012, the exchange's parent, NYSE Euronext, called off a deal where it would be acquired by Deutsche Boerse AG, the German exchange, because of regulatory concerns.

Wall Street

Newell Rubbermaid Inc.

The commercial products company is based in Sandy Springs, Ga. Its products include Sharpie pens and Levolor blinds.

Company Name, Manufacturing

Newmont Mining Corp.

The gold-mining company is based in Denver.

Company Name

News Corp.

The New York-based media company is the parent of The **Wall Street Journal, Barron's, Marketwatch.com** and **Dow Jones Newswires**.

Company Name

next level

A term used by many companies when discussing where they would like their financial results to be. Avoid using it because often the "next level" cannot be quantified. If a company talks about its "next level," ask for specific measurements, such as exactly how much it would like to increase its profits.

NII Holdings Inc.

The mobile phone company formerly known as Nextel International is based in Reston, Va.

Company Name

Nike Inc.

Lowercase the name of the Beaverton, Ore.-based sporting goods company after the N.

Company Name, Manufacturing, Retail

NiSource Inc.

Always capitalize the S in the name of the Merrillville, Ind.-based gas and electrical utility.

Company Name, Energy

no-cost loan

A type of loan that requires no cash at the time of closing, but does come with a higher interest loan. Zero-cost loan is also acceptable. **($$)**

Real estate

no-load fund
A mutual fund without a commission or a sales charge. No-load funds make money from management fees. **($$)**
Wall Street

nobody knows/no one knows
These terms are often used in sentences such as "Nobody knows where the equity markets are headed." Avoid using either term when discussing future business or market prospects. While no one likely knows where the markets are headed, there are plenty of professional investors or other business experts who can give their opinion.
Wall Street

noninterest income
Income that a bank receives from fees on checking accounts and credit cards, service charges and the sales of securities or mutual funds. **($)**
Finance

noncore
A part of a company no longer considered part of its main strategy.

nonperforming asset
A loan, held by a financial institution, that isn't paying interest. Such loans have typically not had a payment in the past 90 days. Avoid NPA in all references. Also called a nonperforming loan. **($$$)**

nonprofit organization
An organization created to provide a good or service to the community without a profit motive. Also called a **501(c)(3)**, many nonprofit organizations receive more in donations and other revenues than they pay out in expenses. Also referred to as a not-for-profit organization. **($$$)**

nonrecurring charge
An expense that only occurs once on a company's financial statement. Can also be called a nonrecurring item but not always an **extraordinary item**. Extraordinary items are a subset of nonrecurring items. **($$$)**

Nordstrom Inc.
The department store chain is based in Seattle. There is no apostrophe or S in the name of the company or its stores.
Company Name, Retail

Norfolk Southern Corp.
The Norfolk, Va.-based company operates the Norfolk Southern Railway.
Company Name, Transportation

North American Free Trade Agreement
A 1994 agreement among the United States, Canada and Mexico that eliminated a number of tariffs and charges to encourage free trade on the North American continent. *NAFTA* is acceptable on second reference.
Economy

Northeast Utilities
The electrical and natural-gas utility is based in Hartford, Conn. Avoid the NU abbreviation in all references.
Company Name, Energy

Northern Trust Corp.

The financial services company is based in Chicago.

Company Name, Finance

Northrop Grumman Corp.

The aerospace and defense company recently moved its headquarters from Los Angeles to Falls Church, Va. The first name is spelled without a U.

Company Name

Northwestern Mutual Life Insurance Co.

The **life insurance** and financial services company is based in Milwaukee.

Company Name, Finance, Insurance

not a going concern

A statement made by independent auditors that raises doubts about the company's ability to function in the future. **($$$$$)**

not-for-profit

Another way to describe a **nonprofit organization**. The term also is used by the **Internal Revenue Service** to describe activities that it regards as hobbies or sporting or recreational activities, rather than businesses. Losses from those activities cannot be used to offset other income.

notary public

A person authorized to certify documents and signatures.

note

A short-term debt issue, usually with a maturity of five years or less.

Novocain

A trademarked product. Use the term local anesthetic.

Trademark

NRG Energy Inc.

Use all capital letters for the first name of the Princeton, N.J.-based power-generation company.

Company Name, Energy

Nucor Corp.

The Charlotte, N.C.-based company operates steel manufacturing plants. The name comes from an old nuclear services operation that is no longer in business.

Company Name, Manufacturing

numbers

In general, follow the Associated Press rule and spell out numbers below 10 and use the numerals for 10 and higher. Some exceptions would be stock prices, which are always numerals, and interest rates or yields, which are always numbers. Monetary amounts are always numbers. Also, spell out numbers that begin a sentence, and when numbers are included in a company name, follow the company's style, such as 3M and 20th Century Fox.

nursing home

A place for people who require constant medical care because of age or a disability. A skilled nursing home is where residents may receive physical, occupational or rehabilitative therapy. Nursing homes are regulated by both state and federal government agencies. The term nursing home is preferred to convalescent home.

Health care

NYSE Euronext

The parent company of the **New York Stock Exchange** is based in New York.

Company Name, Wall Street

Obamanomics

A word used to describe the economic policy of U.S. President Barack Obama. Avoid using unless it's in a quote.

Economy

obligation bond

A municipal bond used to secure a mortgage on a piece of property that can be liquidated. The face value of the bond exceeds the value of the property. The difference is often used to compensate the lender for closing and transaction costs. Schools, public parks and streetlights are often paid for using obligation bonds. **($$$$$)**

Wall Street

obstetrician

A doctor whose specialty is taking care of woman during pregnancy, childbirth and the postnatal period. Almost all obstetricians are also **gynecologists**.

Health care

Occidental Petroleum Corp.

The Los Angeles-based oil and gas company is sometimes referred to as Oxy on second reference, but we'd prefer that Occidental be used on subsequent references.

Company Name, Energy

Occupational Safety and Health Administration

A federal agency whose job it is to enforce laws to ensure a safe and healthy workplace. *OSHA* is acceptable on second reference. The agency maintains an online database where inspection reports and other records can be accessed for any company.

occupational titles

Follow the AP Stylebook and lowercase them. They include stockbroker, dealer, broker, lender, financial adviser, analyst, manager and financial planner.

odd lot

A trade order for less than 100 shares. **($)**

Wall Street

off-balance-sheet financing

The way a company raises money that does not appear on the balance sheet, unlike loans, debt or equity that do appear on the balance sheet. Examples are **joint ventures**, research and development partnerships and leases rather than purchases of capital equipment. **($$$$$)**

offer

When a company offers to buy another company, the target may receive another offer, so do not use the terms "agreed to buy" or "agreed to purchase." The targeted company needs to agree to a deal before buy or purchase can be used.

offering price
The price at which an offering is sold to investors by the underwriters. With initial public offerings, the **opening price** may be different from the offering price. **($$)**
Wall Street

Office Depot Inc.
The office products retailer is based in Boca Raton, Fla.
Company Name, Retail

Office of Credit Ratings
A part of the Securities and Exchange Commission designed to oversee credit rating companies. It was created by the Dodd-Frank Wall Street Reform and Consumer Protection Act of 2010. Avoid using the OCR abbreviation. **($$$$)**
Finance

Office of Federal Housing Enterprise Oversight
An agency inside the Department of Housing and Urban Development that previously regulated Fannie Mae and Freddie Mac. In 2008, it was combined with the Federal Housing Finance Board to create the Federal Housing Finance Agency. Because it no longer exists, use only in historical contexts. **($$$)**
Real estate

Office of Financial Research
An office within the U.S. Treasury Department designed to improve the quality of financial data available to policymakers and to support more robust and sophisticated analysis of the financial system. Avoid the OFR abbreviation and use office on second reference. **($$$$)**
Finance

Office of Thrift Supervision
The part of the U.S. Treasury Department that is in charge of regulating savings banks and savings and loans. *OTS* is acceptable on second reference. Please note that this government agency was eliminated by the Dodd-Frank Wall Street Reform and Consumer Protection Act of 2010.
Finance

OfficeMax Inc.
The Naperville, Ill.-based office supplies retailer spells its name as one word with a capital M.
Company Name, Retail

offshore
Used to describe bank accounts, investments or company operations located outside a country's boundaries, often for tax purposes.
Finance

Omnicom Group Inc.
The New York-based company is the largest owner of advertising agencies, including BBDO and DDB Worldwide. It also owns public relations

firms such as **Fleishman-Hillard Co.**
Company Name

omnibus account

An account held by two futures brokers. It is the combination of individual client accounts into one account, allowing the brokers to trade more easily. Unlike a street account, there is no access to the individual account information by a third-party money manager in an omnibus account. **($$$)**
Finance, Wall Street

Omnicare Inc.

The pharmaceutical company is based in Covington, Ky. It also operates nursing home pharmacies.

oncologist

A physician who studies, diagnoses and treats cancerous tumors. A medical oncologist treats cancer with the use of medicine, while a surgical oncologist treats cancer through surgery. A radiation oncologist treats cancer through radiation treatments. **($$)**
Health care

one-time charge

An expense that a company says won't be repeated.

Oneok Inc.

Capitalize only the first letter in the name of the Tulsa, Okla.-based natural gas distributor.
Company Name, Energy

open shop

A place of employment where a prospective employee does not have to join a union or pay union dues to keep a job. See **closed shop** and **union shop**.

open source

Software where the coding is provided to the users under a licensing agreement, allowing users to make modifications to fit their needs.
Technology

open-end fund

A mutual fund that has no restrictions on how many shares it will issue. Most mutual funds are open-ended. **($$)**
Wall Street

opening bell

The beginning of trading in a market. In the United States, that occurs at 9:30 a.m. EST.
Wall Street

opening price

The price at which an offering begins trading on the first day. The opening price is not always the **offering price**. **($$$)**
Wall Street

operating expenses

Expenses that occur in the normal course of a business, such as salaries, rent for buildings, research and development costs and advertising.

operating margin

Calculated by dividing a company's operating profit by net sales.

operating system

A program that allows software to run on a computer or another consumer electronics item such as a mobile phone or GPS device. Unix and Microsoft Windows are examples.

Technology

Operation Twist

A **Federal Open Market Committee** action that attempts to reduce long-term borrowing costs by buying and selling bonds. In September 2011, the Fed announced a plan to sell shorter-term bonds and buy longer-term issues. The name comes from the attempt to twist the shape of the yield curve. **($$)**

ophthalmologist, optometrist

An ophthalmologist is a medical doctor who specializes in treating eye-related illnesses and diseases as well as prescribing glasses and contact lenses. In contrast, an optometrist can diagnose and treat eye illnesses and prescribe glasses and contact lenses, but does not operate on eyes. The two are sometimes confused and incorrectly used interchangeably, and ophthalmologist is often misspelled.

Health care

option

A contract between a buyer and a seller that gives the buyer the right to purchase a security at a certain date at a predetermined price. In return, the seller receives a payment. This is called a call option, in contrast to a put option. Stock options are also commonly used as part of an executive's compensation package. **($$$$)**

Wall Street

Oracle Corp.

The computer technology company is based in Redwood Shores, Calif.

Company Name, Technology

order

An instruction by a customer to a broker to buy or sell a security, often at a specific price.

Wall Street

order backlog

An economic indicator that measures orders for goods and services that have not been filled. An increase in order backlogs can mean that the economy is growing, while a decrease could signal that the economy is slowing down or contracting.

Economy

Oreo

A trademarked product. The generic term is sandwich cookie.

Trademark

Organization of Petroleum Exporting Countries

An intergovernmental organization of 12 oil-producing countries founded in 1960. Its goal is to coordinate the pricing and supply of oil and maximize revenue for OPEC countries during the long-term. *OPEC* and cartel are acceptable on second reference.

Energy

organized labor
Another term for workers who belong to a union. Bloomberg News tells its journalists to refer to a specific union.

origination fee
A payment made to a financial services firm when applying for a loan. It can also be called an activation fee.

Finance, Real estate

orthopedist
Also known as an orthopedic surgeon, this type of doctor who treats injuries or illnesses related to the skeleton, tendons and ligaments. An orthopedist treats bone fractures while a podiatrist primarily treats ankle and foot disorders. Avoid calling the doctors orthopods, regarded as a slang term, and avoid the "ae" spelling (orthopaedist) unless your publication uses diphthongs.

Health care

Oshkosh Corp.
The truck manufacturer is based in Oskosh, Wis.

Company Name, Manufacturing, Transportation

osteopath
A physician who holds a doctor of osteopathy degree rather than an M.D. Typically osteopaths are primary care doctors.

Health care

otolaryngologist
A physician who specializes in the treatment and diagnosis of illnesses of the head and neck, particularly related to the ears, the nose and the throat. They are sometimes called otorhinolaryngologists. Because of the length of both names, these doctors are often called ear, nose and throat specialists. We agree. (**$$$$**)

Health care

Ouija
A trademarked product. The generic term is fortunetelling board game.

Trademark

outpatient care
Health care, including surgery, provided to a patient that does not require an overnight stay.

Health care

outperform
A rating given a stock by a sell-side analyst. An "outperform" rating is considered the second-highest rating for many brokerage firms, right behind a "strong buy" rating. It's equivalent to a **buy** rating in most cases.

Wall Street

outside director
A member of the board of directors who is not a current or former employee of the company and derives no significant income from

it. Regulators have been pushing companies to add more outside directors.

outsourced, outsourcing

When a company contracts with an outside business to have a job function previously performed by its employees. When jobs are outsourced to a location outside the company's country, it's called offshoring.

Economy, Manufacturing

over

Do not use when describing a company's financial results or stock market performance, such as revenue increasing by over 18 percent. Use more than instead.

over-the-counter

The market where stocks or debt instruments trade via a dealer network and not an exchange. *OTC* is acceptable on second reference. **($$)**

Wall Street

overbought

A situation in which demand to purchase an asset increases its prices to levels beyond what should be supported by its fundamentals. The opposite is **oversold**. **($$$)**

overcollateralization

A form of **credit enhancement**. It simply means that the face value of the loan portfolio is higher than the security it backs. **($$$$)**

Finance, Wall Street

oversold

A situation in which the price of an asset has fallen sharply to levels below its true value. The opposite is **overbought**. **($$$)**

oversubscribed

A situation in which the orders for shares of an offering exceed the number of shares available to be sold. Provide the specific amount in a story. **($$)**

Wall Street

overvalued

A stock price that is not justified by its current **price-to-earnings ratio**, asset value or its earnings projections. The opposite is **undervalued**. **($$$)**

Wall Street

overweight

A rating given a stock by a sell-side analyst. An "overweight" rating is considered the equivalent of an **outperform** or a **buy** . It also refers to when a portfolio has a higher percentage of a stock or group of stocks than an index it's tracking, such as the S&P 500.

Wall Street

Owens & Minor Inc.

The Mechanicsville, Va.-based company distributes medical and surgical supplies. Do not shorten to Owens to avoid confusion with **Owens Corning** and **Owens-Illinois Inc.**

Company Name, Health care

Owens Corning

The manufacturer of fiberglass and insulation is based in Toledo, Ohio. There is no hyphen in its name. Do not shorten to Owens to avoid confusion with **Owens & Minor Inc.** and **Owens-Illinois Inc.**

Company Name, Manufacturing

Owens-Illinois Inc.

The packaging company is not based in Illinois, but Perrysburg, Ohio. Use the hyphen in all references. Do not shorten to Owens to avoid confusion with **Owens & Minor Inc.** and **Owens Corning**.

Company Name, Manufacturing

O'Reilly Automotive Inc.

The auto parts retailer is based in Springfield, Mo. It has more than 3,500 stores, which are called O'Reilly Auto Parts.

Company Name, Retail

p&l

A shortened form of profit and loss. Acceptable on second reference.

P/E ratio

See **price-to-earnings ratio**. P/E ratio is acceptable on second reference.
Wall Street

Pablum

A trademarked product. The generic term is baby food. Tasteless, simplistic writing is pablum.
Trademark

Paccar Inc.

Capitalize only the first letter in the first name of the Bellevue, Wash.-based manufacturer of Kenworth, Peterbilt and DAF trucks.
Company Name, Manufacturing

Pacific Investment Management Co.

One of the largest money managers in the United States. PIMCO is acceptable on second reference.
Company Name, Wall Street

Pacific Life Insurance Co.

The Newport Beach, Calif.-based life insurance company can be referred to as Pacific Life. Avoid PacLife in all references.
Company Name, Insurance

page views

The number of downloads for a website, even if it is from the same user. One person who visits the same website 500 times in one day, or who visits 500 different pages within one domain, will register as 500 page views but only one unique visitor for that day.
Technology

panic

Wide-scale selling of an investment without regard for the price, and a disregard for the investment's fundamentals. **($$)**
Wall Street

Pantry Inc.

The convenience store operator is based on Cary, N.C. Its main locations are called Kangaroo Express.
Company Name, Retail

par

The face value of a bond, such as $1,000 or $10,000. For common stocks, the par value has no relationship to the market price.

parent company

A parent company controls a subsidiary through stock ownership, but has operations of its own. **Walt Disney Co.** is the parent company of ESPN. Compare with **holding company**.

parentheses

They are used in Securities and Exchange Commission filings to indicate a negative number. However, when writing a business news story, exclude the parentheses and write that the number was negative or a loss. For example, a company may record that it had net income of ($12.5 million) in the third quarter in its filing, but write it as a net loss of $12.5 million.

Parker Hannifin Corp.

The manufacturer of motion and control technologies is based in Mayfield Heights, Ohio. Parker is acceptable on second reference.

Company Name, Manufacturing

partnership

An unincorporated business in which two or more people manage and operate the business. All of the owners are liable for the debts of the business.

passthrough

A mortgage-backed security where the owner receives the principal and interest payments on the home mortgages. (**$$$$**)

Finance, Real estate

patent

A government designation that gives the holder the sole right to use the process, design or invention for a specified time period. In the United States, most patents last for 20 years.

Patient Protection and Affordable Care Act

The law passed in 2010 designed to expand Americans' access to health care. It's allowable to let others call it Obamacare, but avoid the term in neutral reportage. On the other hand, avoid calling it health care reform. Also avoid PPACA. Call it the health care act, or the act, instead.

Health care

payday lender

A finance company that provides small, short-term loans to borrowers to cover expenses until their next paycheck, often at high interest rates. Payday lenders typically require a recent paycheck stub. (**$**)

PayPal Inc.

The eBay subsidiary spells its name as one word.

Company Name

payrolls

The common term used for nonfarm payroll employment, which is the number of all goods-producing, construction and manufacturing employees in the economy. The number is released every month along with the unemployment data by the Department of Labor. If the payrolls number is increasing, then it can be considered a sign that the economy is expanding. (**$$$**)

Economy

PCI compliance standards

Mandatory standards to protect personal information and ensure security when transactions are processed using a payment card. These standards are regulated by the industry, not a government agency. Explain somewhere in your story that PCI stands for payment card industry. **($$$$)**

Finance, Retail

PDF

Stands for Portable Document Format. Created by Adobe Systems, it allows computer users to view documents through its universal format.

Technology

Peabody Energy Corp.

The coal mining company is based in St. Louis.

Company Name, Energy

pediatrician

A doctor who specializes in children, from birth to the age of 21.

Health care

penny stock

A stock that trades at a very low price or has a very small market capitalization. Penny stocks may trade for more than $1 a share, but they are considered highly speculative and generally trade in the **over-the-counter** market. **($$$$$)**

Wall Street

Pension Benefit Guaranty Corp.

A part of the **Department of Labor** that guarantees the payment of certain pension benefits. A list of the largest pension plans it insures can be found online.

pension plan

A retirement plan where the employer sets aside money for the benefit of its workers and promises them a benefit based on salary and years of service. Also known as a defined contribution plan.

Penske Automotive Group Inc.

The operator of automobile dealerships is based in Bloomfield Hills, Mich. Avoid the PAG abbreviation in all references.

Pep Boys - Manny, Moe & Jack

Use the full name of the Philadelphia-based auto parts retailer only on first reference. Pep Boys is acceptable on second reference.

Company Name, Retail

Pepco Holdings Inc.

An electric utility based in Washington, D.C.

Company Name, Energy

PepsiCo Inc.

The food and beverage company based in Purchase, N.Y. The C is capitalized in its name.

Company Name

per share earnings

A company's net income, less preferred stock dividends, divided by the total number of outstanding shares. It's also called **earnings per share**, which is more common on first reference.

percent

Always spell out. Do not use the %
sign, except in headlines and in **The
Wall Street Journal** and **Fortune** magazine or when your publication's style
requires it. Numerals are also always
used with percents.

percentage point

The difference between two percents.
A change in consumer confidence to
80 percent from 70 percent is a change
of 10 percentage points. (The term is
not interchangeable with percent. A
change in consumer confidence to 80
percent from 70 percent is a change
of 14.3 percent.)

perform, performance

Avoid using these terms when referring to an investment. A performance
implies some sort of act or presentation. The terms results or returns are
preferable.

Wall Street

peripheral

A piece of computer hardware added
to a computer to expand its capabili-
ties, such as a scanner or a printer.

Technology

personal finance

Advice to readers and viewers on
matters related to investing, retirement, savings, and other money-re-
lated issues. Some publications, such
as **Money** and **Worth**, focus exclusively
on personal finance coverage.

Petco Animal Supplies Inc.

Capitalize only the first letter in the
first name of the San Diego-based
pet supply retailer, which is privately
held.

Company Name, Retail

PetSmart Inc.

The Phoenix-based animal products
retailer spells its name as one word
with a capital S.

Company Name, Retail

Pfizer Inc.

The New York-based pharmaceutical
company has its research operations
in Groton, Conn.

PG&E Corp.

A San Francisco-based energy
company. Its main subsidiary is
Pacific Gas and Electric Co. Use
the PG&E abbreviation only when
referring to the parent company.

Company Name, Energy

Philip Morris International Inc.

The New York-based tobacco company spells Philip with only one L.

Company Name

Photoshop

A trademarked name from Adobe
Systems. The generic term is photo
manipulation.

Trademark

physician

Any doctor other than a surgeon,
who holds an M.D. or a D.O. degree
and treats patients.

Health care

Pier 1 Imports Inc.
Always use the numeral when writing the name of the Fort Worth, Texas-based retailer.
Company Name, Retail

Pilgrim's Corp.
The chicken producer is based in Greeley, Colo. It formerly was known was Pilgrim's Pride.
Company Name

Ping-Pong
A trademarked product. Note the hyphen. The name of the game is table tennis.
Trademark

Pink Sheets
A daily publication from the National Quotation Board that lists the prices of **over-the-counter** stocks and their **market maker.**
Wall Street

pink slip
A term that refers to being fired or laid off from a job. It comes from the former practice, now nearly extinct, of human resources departments putting pink pieces of paper in people's pay envelopes when they were terminated.
Economy

pit
A designed place on the market floor for the trading of a **futures** or **options** contract.
Wall Street

Pitney Bowes Inc.
The business services company is based in Stamford, Conn.
Company Name

pixel
One dot on a computer screen or one dot in an image from a digital camera. Short for PICture ELement. The resolution of a photograph or computer is stated in pixels per inch, or PPI. The size of an image is stated in megapixels, or 1 million pixels. It is determined by multiplying the width of an image in pixels times its depth in pixels. A camera with a 14-megapixel sensor can produce a larger-size sharp photographic print than can an 8-megapixel camera. In printing, pixels per inch roughly translate into dots per inch. **($$$)**
Technology

Pizza Hut Inc.
The company operates nearly 10,000 Pizza Hut restaurants in more than 90 countries. Pizza Hut Inc. is a subsidiary of **Yum Brands Inc.**
Company Name, Restaurant, Retail

plain vanilla
The basic version of a financial investment, such as an option or a bond. The opposite is an **exotic instrument.**
Finance, Wall Street

Plains All American Pipeline LP
A limited partnership based in Houston that operates oil pipelines. Note there is no hyphen in the name.
Company Name, Energy

planned community

1. A development in which homeowners are obligated to pay the upkeep of common property such as a clubhouse, swimming pool, playground and special lighting and street signs. The board of the homeowners association manages the common property once the property is fully developed.
2. A town or city that has been carefully planned and developed from its beginning, typically on a barren piece of land. Celebration, Fla., is an example.

Real estate

plasma

A type of flat-panel display commonly used with large televisions. Plasma displays are not to be confused with LCDs.

Technology

PLC

An abbreviation for a public limited company based in the United Kingdom. Acceptable on all references. The German equivalent is AG, while the French and Spanish equivalent is SA. The Italian equivalent is S.p.A.

PLU code

The numbers on a sticker placed on fruits and vegetables to identify them for purchase and for inventory control. PLU code stands for price look-up code. Can also be called *produce codes*.

Restaurant, Retail

PNC Financial Services Group Inc.

The Pittsburgh-based financial services company should be referred to as PNC Financial Services on second reference. Its bank is known as PNC Bank.

Company Name, Finance

podiatrist

A doctor who treats disorders of the ankle, foot and lower leg. A podiatrist is a doctor of podiatric medicine (DPM) and should not be called a physician. While an **orthopedist** typically treats bone fractures, a podiatrist treats ingrown toenails, calluses, fallen arches, heel spurs and foot or ankle injuries. (**$$**)

Health care

poison pill

A strategy by a corporation to discourage a hostile takeover. Sometimes, a poison pill will allow existing shareholders to purchase more shares of company stock at a discounted price if an offer is made for the company. (**$$$$$**)

Ponzi scheme

A fraudulent investment scam. It provides returns to the early investors by giving them the funds that later investors put into the scheme, but collapses when the scheme runs out of investors. The term originated with Boston-based Charles Ponzi and came back into popularity with the scam run by Bernard Madoff. It's slightly different from a **pyramid scheme**. (**$$$$$**)

pooling

A practice where health insurers underwrite a number of small groups as if they were one large group. **($$)**

Health care, Insurance

pooling of interests

An accounting method commonly used in the past during the combination of companies after mergers and acquisitions. It is not a valid accounting method anymore. **($$$$$)**

Popeyes Louisiana Kitchen

A subsidiary of Atlanta-based AFC Enterprises. There is no apostrophe in the name. It formerly was Popeyes Chicken & Biscuits.

Company Name, Restaurant

Popsicle

A trademarked product. The generic term is flavored ice on a stick.

Trademark

portable mortgage

A mortgage that the borrower can transfer from one house to another.

Real estate

portfolio

A term used to describe a group of financial assets, such as stocks, bonds and commodities, managed by an investor, fund manager or a financial planner. Describe the investments instead of using the word portfolio.

Finance, Wall Street

portfolio manager

A person who invests a mutual fund's assets.

Finance

POS

An acronym commonly used in retailing that stands for point of sale. It refers to where the transaction occurs, and can also be used as an adjective for in-store advertising. POS is acceptable on second reference.

POS (point-of-sale) advertising

Posters, electronic signs and other advertising devices positioned in the sight of customers when they place an order.

Restaurant, Retail

POS (point-of-sale) systems

The suggested first reference for computerized "point-of-sale" stations where counter personnel enter orders, take payments and print out receipts. Increasingly, customers use POS terminals to place their orders. Use POS as an adjective on second reference.

Restaurant, Retail

Post-It

A trademarked product. The generic term is self-stick note.

Trademark

poverty rate

The rate at which a person or family lacks the income and material possessions taken for granted by a society. The poverty threshold is set by the Census Bureau. For a single adult, the threshold in 2010 was $11,344 in pretax income. For a family of four, it's $22,133.

Economy

power of attorney

A document that allows one person to act on behalf of another. The person does not have to be an attorney.

PowerBar

A trademarked product. Note that it is one word. The generic term is energy snack. (**$$$**)

Trademark

PPG Industries Inc.

The Pittsburgh-based company manufacturers paint, glass and chemicals. PPG is acceptable on second reference.

Company Name, Manufacturing

PPL Corp.

An energy company based in Allentown, Pa. Its name comes from Pennsylvania Power & Light, the former name of its main subsidiary, which is known now as PPL Electric Utilities.

Company Name, Energy

Praxair Inc.

The chemicals company is based in Danbury, Conn.

Company Name, Manufacturing

pre-existing condition

A medical condition where the patient received coverage in the three months before the effective date of a health insurance policy. In some cases, pre-existing conditions are excluded from coverage.

Health care

pre-existing condition insurance plan

A federal-state program that makes health insurance available to people who can't get other health insurance because of a pre-existing condition.

Health care, Insurance

pre-market trading

Trading that occurs before the exchanges open.

Wall Street

Precision Castparts Corp.

The cast-metal parts manufacturer is based in Portland, Ore. Avoid using the PCC abbreviation in all references.

Company Name, Manufacturing

predatory lending

Providing loans to individuals who can't afford the monthly payments or understand the terms of the loan, which may have high interest rates or high fees. A company making such loans is called a predatory lender. The term comes from creatures that prey on other creatures. (**$$$**)

Real estate, Wall Street

preferred provider organization

A managed-care plan similar to a **health maintenance organization** in which the patient can pick the physician and health care provider he or she wants as long as the provider is in the health insurance company's "preferred provider" network. The PPO enrollee will pay higher rates to receive health care from providers

outside the network. *PPO* is acceptable on second reference. **($)**
Health care, Insurance

preferred stock
Shares issued in a company where the owner has more rights than the owners of regular, common stock. The preferred stock may require that it be paid a dividend before the common stock receives a dividend. However, preferred stock usually does not have voting rights. *Preferred shares* is also acceptable. **($$$$)**

premium
The difference between the actual cost for acquiring a target firm versus its value before the acquisition.

prepackaged bankruptcy
A situation where a company and its significant creditors agree to a reorganization plan before the company files for bankruptcy court protection. **($$$$$)**

prepayment
The early repayment of a loan by the borrower. Some loans may require the borrower to pay a penalty if the loan is paid off early. Sub-prime mortgages often carry prepayment penalties.
Real estate

president
The officer responsible for the day-to-day management of a company who usually reports to the **chief executive officer**. This person is often called the chief operating officer as well.

price point
The retail price set for an item. The price point may have to fit into a standard pricing scheme, such as a value menu. In most cases, use "price" and drop the "point."
Restaurant, Retail

price target
The price a **sell-side analyst** believes a stock will reach within the next 12 months. The price target is usually listed on the front page of a **research report**. **($$)**
Wall Street

price-to-book ratio
Used to compare a stock's market value with its book value, calculated by dividing the current closing price of the stock by the most recently available book value per share. P/B is acceptable on second reference. **($$$)**

price-to-earnings ratio
A stock analysis statistic in which the current price of a stock is divided by the company's earnings per share. P/E is acceptable on second reference. **($$$)**

Priceline.com Inc.
Capitalize the name of the Norwalk, Conn.-based online company. The company lowercases the P.
Company Name

PricewaterhouseCoopers LLP
The name of the London-based accounting firm is all one word. It uses

PwC as a brand name, but Pricewa-terhouseCoopers remains the full name for legal purposes, and it is the name used by the firm to sign company audits.

Company Name

primary care physician

A doctor who usually sees patients with undiagnosed illnesses, diseases or injuries. This is the type of physician who most people see on a regular basis. A primary care physician conducts annual physicals, for example. Though many primary care physicians specialize in family practice, many other specialists, including internists and gynecologists, may also offer primary care.

Health care

primary care provider

A physician who provides general medical care without requiring a reference from another physician.

Health care

prime rate

The interest rate that banks charge their most creditworthy customers, such as large corporations.

Finance

principal

This word has a number of different meanings when writing about business. It could mean: The amount owed on a loan, minus interest; The original amount invested; The face value of a bond; or An owner of a public or private company.

Finance, Real estate, Wall Street

Principal Financial Group Inc.

The insurance and financial services company is based in Des Moines, Iowa.

Company Name, Finance, Insurance

principals only

A property sale involving only the buyer and seller and not a real estate agent. May also mean that a seller doesn't want to be contacted by an agent. See also **FSBO**.

Real estate

private company

A business whose ownership is confined to a handful of people, or whose ownership cannot be traded on a stock exchange. It can also be referred to as privately held.

private equity fund

Typically a limited partnership that makes investments in companies, sometimes private, with the idea of selling the company in five to seven years for a higher price. Such funds are operated by private equity firms. A private equity fund is a Wall Street euphemism for "leveraged buyout fund." **($$$$)**

private placement

The process by which a company raises money by selling stock to a small number of investors, such as insurance companies, pension funds and large banks. The stock is not registered with the **Securities and Exchange Commission**. **($$$)**

privately held

A company whose shares are not traded on an exchange or through a dealer network. The company's shares may be held by one person, a group of shareholders, or employees.

pro forma

A Latin term used to describe financial results that would have occurred given a merger, acquisition or other change in a company. When an acquisition is announced, the companies will typically provide pro forma financial numbers to show the combined operation's revenue and net income. ($$$)

Procter & Gamble Co.

The consumer goods company based in Cincinnati is often misspelled as Proctor. P&G is acceptable on second reference. Proctor-Silex (note the "or") makes small kitchen appliances.

Company Name

producer price index

A measure of price change from the perspective of the seller, it measures selling prices for goods and services and is compiled by the **Bureau of Labor Statistics**. The data is released about two weeks after the end of the month, and the story focuses on the monthly percentage change. Use index on second reference. Do not use PPI on any reference. ($$$)

Economy

product

Avoid using this term for something being sold by a company that has not actually been produced, such as parking.

productivity

Output divided by input, with output being the goods and services produced and input being the number of worker hours. It's a measure of how the workforce is producing goods. The data is compiled by the **Bureau of Labor Statistics** and comes out about five weeks after the end of a quarter. The story focus is on the annualized quarterly percentage change in nonfarm business productivity, unit labor costs and compensation per hour.

profit

When revenue exceeds expenses and all other costs. **Income** is the preferred synonym.

profit margin

Earnings after taxes divided by revenues. This is a number that is usually displayed as a percentage. Also referred to as the *net profit margin*. ($$$)

profit-sharing plan

A plan where the employees of a company share in its profits. The business typically decides what profits will be shared. ($$)

profit-taking (n., adj.)

A Wall Street euphemism for selling to take advantage of a sharp rise in price.

program trading

Computerized trading that institutional investors use to execute large trades, typically when an index has reached a certain level. **($$)**

Wall Street

Progress Energy Inc.

A Raleigh, N.C.-based energy company currently in the process of being acquired by **Duke Energy Corp.**

Company Name, Energy

Progressive Corp.

The property and casualty insurance company is based in Mayfield Heights, Ohio. Its primary subsidiary is Progressive Casualty Insurance Co.

Insurance

promissory note

An agreement in which one party agrees to pay a sum of money to another party during a period of time, or on demand of the payee. It differs from an IOU because there is a promise to pay. **($$$)**

Real estate

property and casualty insurance

Insurance purchased by an individual or corporation that protects a business or property from loss. Auto and home insurance are examples. Do not use the ampersand when writing property and casualty. Avoid using P&C as well.

Insurance

property tax

A tax placed on the value of a piece of property. A property tax is written as a percentage, such as 2 percent. In the United States, property tax is usually levied by local governments to help pay for services such as schools, police and fire protection. A property tax is also called an ad valorem tax or a millage tax, though we prefer the property tax.

Economy, Real estate

prospectus

A document filed with the **Securities and Exchange Commission** when a company wants to sell stocks or bonds to investors. **($)**

proxy fight

When shareholders or would-be acquirers try to force a change in control at a company. A proxy fight could be on the election of directors, the sale of a company, or the ouster of a **CEO.** Proxy battle is also an acceptable term. **($$)**

proxy statement

A document sent to shareholders of public companies to invite owners of the company's stock to its annual meeting. The proxy statement will include information about proposals to be voted on at the annual meeting and executive salaries. It's formally known as a DEF 14A. Use the term proxy statement and not DEF 14A. **($$$)**

Prudential Financial Inc.

The Newark, N.J.-based company's main subsidiary is Prudential Insurance Co. of America. When referring to the parent company, write Prudential Financial.

Company Name, Finance, Insurance

public company

A business whose ownership interests, either shares or partnership units, are publicly traded.

Public Service Enterprise Group Inc.

The electric and gas utility company is based in Newark, N.J. The PSEG abbreviation is acceptable on second reference.

Company Name, Energy

public utilities commission

State agencies that regulate water, natural gas, electrical and telephone companies. In some states, the agency may be called the Public Service Commission.

Energy

Public-Private Investment Program

A plan by the U.S. Treasury Department, in conjunction with private financiers, to buy and sell **toxic assets** from troubled companies. Avoid using the PPIP abbreviation. On second reference, call it the program. **($$$$$)**

Economy, Finance

Publix Super Markets Inc.

The Lakeland, Fla.-based grocery store chain spells supermarket as two words in its name.

Company Name, Retail

pump and dump

An illegal strategy used by investors where false and misleading statements are made about a stock to increase its price. The investors then sell their stock before the information is proved false and the price decreases. The Securities and Exchange Commission reports that this strategy occurs often with companies with small market capitalizations. **($$$)**

Wall Street

purchasing managers index

An index compiled by the Institute of Supply Management and released on the first business day of the following month that measures new orders, inventory, supplier deliveries, production and employment at companies as a way to assess the health of the economy. The story focuses on the index and new orders. An index number above 50 means that the economy is expanding. Purchasing managers index is acceptable on first reference even though the Institute of Supply Management only uses PMI. *PMI* is acceptable on second reference.

Economy

pure play

A company that has only one line of business, as opposed to a company that has different business lines. Coca-Cola is considered a pure play because it produces only beverages, whereas PepsiCo Inc. also has food businesses. **($$$$)**

put option

A contract giving the holder the right, but not the obligation, to sell a security or property at a specific price within a certain time period. The buyer of a put is betting that the price of the equity will fall below the exercise price before the contract expires. **($$$$$)**

Wall Street

put-back

A mortgage sold back to the lender that originally made the loan because of problems with its documentation or because it has gone into default. **($$$)**

Real estate

pyramid scheme

An illegal investment scheme in which the initial members recruit new members, who must themselves recruit new members to receive a payment. The scheme collapses when not enough new members can be found. The difference between a pyramid scheme and a **Ponzi scheme** is that in a Ponzi scheme, the person running the scam does not ask the participants to find more members. **($$$$$)**

Q-Tips

A trademarked product. The generic term is cotton swabs.

Trademark

Qdoba Mexican Grill

A subsidary of **Jack in the Box Inc.**, the Wheat Ridge, Colo., company has more than 500 **fast-casual** restaurants in 43 states.

QR code

A square code box that can be scanned by a mobile phone equipped with a camera, allowing customers to quickly obtain more information about a business or a product. QR stands for "quick-response." **($)**

Restaurant, Retail

Quaalude

A trademarked drug. The generic term is methaqualone.

Health care, Trademark

quadruple witching

When contracts for stock index futures, stock index options, stock options and single stock futures all expire at the same time. The day occurs on the third Friday of March, June, September and December. **($$$$$)**

Wall Street

Qualcomm Inc.

Capitalize only the first letter in the first name of the San Diego-based cell phone manufacturer.

Company Name, Manufacturing

qualified opinion

Suggests that the information provided was limited in scope or the company being audited did not maintain GAAP accounting principles. Contrary to its connotation, a qualified opinion is not a good thing. Auditors that deem audits as qualified opinions are advising that the audit is not complete or that the accounting methods used by the company do not follow GAAP. **($$$$$)**

quality of earnings

A company with high quality of earnings typically has conservative accounting methods. Earnings quality is also a common term. The factors that can create low earnings quality include unusually low tax rates, a reversal of large reserves, a reduction in the allowance for doubtful accounts and share repurchases. **($$$$)**

quantitative easing

A government monetary policy designed to increase the amount of money in the economy by purchasing government securities or other securities in the market. Avoid using the term QE in all references. **($$$)**

Economy, Wall Street

quarter

A three-month time period that acts as the basis for a company reporting its financial results. Do not abbreviate as Q1, Q2, etc., or as in the first Q. Quarter should be spelled out in all references.

quarterly services survey

An **economic indicator** that the Census Bureau began collecting data for in 2003. It measures four services sectors: information; professional, scientific and technical services; administrative and support; and hospitals and nursing homes. Avoid QSS on all references. **($$$)**

Economy

Quest Diagnostics Inc.

A clinical laboratory company based in Madison, N.J.

Company Name, Health care

quick serve (n.), quick-serve or quick-service (adj.)

Any restaurant not offering table service but providing fast meals. **($$)**

Restaurant

quiet period

The period of time during which the issuer of an offering cannot publicly issue any promotional statements or documents. Also known as the waiting period. **($$$)**

quitclaim deed

A document in which one person disavows any interest in a piece of property and gives all rights to the property to another person. Such deeds are used in divorce cases, for example, where one person gives the sole rights to a home to the other. **($$$)**

Real estate

Quotron symbol

The stock ticker for a mutual fund or an index. The name comes from the company Quotron Systems Inc., which provided stock information.

Wall Street

R.R. Donnelley & Sons Co.

Use the periods in the name of the Chicago-based commercial printing company even though it sometimes does not use them. R.R. Donnelley is acceptable on second reference.

Company Name

radiologist

A physician who specializes in obtaining and interpreting medical images such as X-rays, sound waves or the body's magnetic properties. An example of a sound wave would be an ultrasound to determine the gender of an unborn fetus. A magnetic resonance imager, or MRI, can be used by a radiologist to examine internal injuries.

Health care

RadioShack Corp.

The Fort Worth, Texas-based retailer's name is one word.

Company Name, Retail

raider

An individual or company that tries to take over another company through a **hostile takeover**. Short for corporate raider.

rainmaker

An employee or executive who typically brings in a lot of business to the company. Avoid unless it can be quantified. **($$$$)**

raised

Do not use to describe an increase in a dividend payment or in prices. Instead, say that dividends or prices rose.

rally

A substantial increase in the value of stocks, bonds or equities, or an overall market, following a decline.

Wall Street

Ralph Lauren Corp.

The clothing company is based in New York no longer includes "Polo" in its name.

Company Name

ranges

Write $10 million to $15 million, not $10 to $15 million.

rate spread

The ratio of the highest and lowest rates that a health insurer charges small groups. The National Association of Insurance Commissioners limits the spread to 2 to 1.

Health care, Insurance

Raytheon Co.

The military contractor and industrial company is based in Waltham, Mass.

Company Name, Manufacturing

real dollars

The price of a good or service adjusted for inflation. **($$$)**

Economy

real estate investment trust

A company that invests in real estate, either through property or mortgages, and must pay out virtually all its profits. *REIT* is acceptable on second reference. **($)**

Finance, Real estate

realized gain/realized loss

The amount of money made, or lost, from selling an asset.

Realtor

A trademarked name. The generic term is real-estate agent.

Real estate

recapitalization

The restructuring of a company's debt and equity in an attempt to make its capital structure more stable. A company issuing shares of stock to pay off some of its debt would be an example of a recapitalization.

receiver

The person appointed by the bankruptcy court to run a company for a short period so that creditors will be repaid as much as possible.

receivership

A situation where the state insurance commissioner or bankruptcy court takes control of and administers a company.

Health care, Insurance

recession

A period of diminishing economic growth. Recessions are officially determined by the **National Bureau of Economic Research**'s business cycle dating committee. The actual recession would have likely begun three to six months before it is declared.

Economy

record high/record low

Terms used when a company's stock price, or the price of any equity, hits an all-time mark. Be careful to discern for readers the time element involved with the record. A stock that has hit a new high or low in the past 12 months is said to have reached a 52-week high or a 52-week low. The price of a barrel of oil hit an all-time high in 2008. Be careful, however, to figure in inflation when reporting commodity price records. Avoid using the terms high or low for equities if it's just within the past week.

Wall Street

recovery

The end of a **recession** or **depression,** marked by renewed economic growth.

Economy

red herring

A slang term used to describe when a company files a **prospectus** with the **Securities and Exchange Commission** because there is red lettering on the cover that states the company is not yet attempting to sell stock. **($$$)**

Redbox

The full name of the movie rental company is Redbox Automated Retail LLC, and it is a subsidiary of Coinstar Inc. Redbox is acceptable on first reference when referring to its locations. Use the full company name on first reference when referring to the business, but then Redbox is acceptable in all other references.

Retail

redemption

The return of an investor's principal on a bond or preferred stock. A redemption occurs when the fixed-income security is paid off by the issuer. **($$)**

Wall Street

redemption charge

A fee charged by a **mutual fund** when investors redeem their shares. The redemption charge may be reduced or waived if the investor has held the money in the mutual fund for a long time. **($$)**

Finance, Wall Street

redlining

The unethical practice by a financial institution of not doing business with customers who live in a low-income neighborhood. Redlining can involve mortgages or any other financial product, including auto and home insurance. In 1988, Atlanta Journal-Constitution business reporter Bill Dedman uncovered redlining in banks in the Atlanta area and won a Pulitzer Prize. **($$)**

Finance, Insurance, Real estate

refinance

A process whereby a borrower replaces an existing debt obligation with a new one, typically at a lower interest rate. The most common type of refinancing is with a home mortgage.

Finance, Real estate

Regions Financial Corp.

The bank holding company is based in Birmingham, Ala.

Company Name, Finance

Regulation Fair Disclosure

A rule passed by the **Securities and Exchange Commission** in 2000 in an effort to prevent selective disclosure by public companies to market professionals and certain shareholders. The rule has made conference calls and investor meetings held by companies open to business journalists. *Regulation FD* is acceptable on second reference. The rule can be read on the SEC's website. **($$$$)**

reinsurance

Insurance purchased by insurance companies to protect them from excessive losses on the policies they have written. **($$)**

Insurance

Reinsurance Group of America Inc.

The reinsurance company is based in St. Louis. Avoid the RGA abbreviation in all references.

Company Name, Insurance

reinsurer

An insurance company that provides insurance to other insurance companies. Munich Re and Swiss Re are two of the largest reinsurers in the world. **($$)**

Insurance

Reliance Steel & Aluminum Co.

The metals company is based in Los Angeles. Reliance Steel is acceptable on second reference.

Company Name, Manufacturing

Rent-A-Center Inc.

The Plano, Texas-based rental center operator hyphenates its name.

Company Name, Retail

reorganization

A process designed to revive a financially troubled or bankrupt firm. It typically involves the restatement of assets and liabilities in order to make arrangements for maintaining repayment. In some cases, the length of repayment terms is extended. Specify what the reorganization entails in a story. **($$)**

repetitive strain injury

An injury that occurs from a repeated process, typically in a work environment. Carrying heavy equipment or typing on a keyboard for long periods of time has been known to cause repetitive strain injuries. **Ergonomics** attempts to eliminate repetitive strain injuries.

Manufacturing, Technology

repo market

A place where securities are sold with the promise that the seller can repurchase them at a later date. There are three types of repo markets — overnight, term and open. The overnight repo market is a one-day market, while the term repo market is for a specific time period. The open repo market has no set time period. The difference between the price at which the securities are sold and then repurchased can be considered an interest rate, with the initial buyer being the lender. The term "repo" is short for "repurchase," but repo market is preferred. **($$$)**

Finance, Wall Street

Republic Services Inc.

The second-largest garbage collector, behind **Waste Management Inc.**, is based in Phoenix.

Company Name

repurchase agreement

A form of short-term borrowing where an investor sells a security to a lender and agrees to buy back the security at a later date for a predetermined price. Do not use "repo agreement," but the **repo market** is acceptable on second reference to repurchase. **($$$$$)**

Wall Street

request for proposal

An invitation from a company or government entity for bids on providing goods or services. The process theoretically puts all bidders on equal footing, and the request typically has guidelines that the bid must meet. *RFP* is acceptable on second reference.

Company Name

research and development

Activities undertaken by companies to discover new products or business lines. Companies in technology and pharmaceutical businesses typically spend a lot of money on research and development. R&D is acceptable on second reference.

Technology

research note, research report

Information compiled by a sell-side analyst and sent to the clients of the analyst's firm about a company's performance. A report is considered longer than a note. A research note or report will include the analyst's estimate of the company's future earnings, a recommendation on the stock and a 12-month target for the company's stock price, as well as a statement about whether the analyst holds the stock or the analyst's firm has done any investment banking for the company in question. The terms note and report are acceptable after first reference.

Wall Street

reserve

Money theoretically set aside by a company from earnings to pay for other expenses, such as a pending lawsuit or other contingencies. It most cases, it is really just an accounting entry, as cash is not actually set aside.

residential mortgage-backed securities

A type of bond that is backed by residential mortgages instead of commercial mortgages. Those who purchase such securities are paid interest and principal by the holders of the mortgages. Avoid using RMBS in all references. On second reference, use mortgage-backed securities. **($$$)**

Finance, Real estate, Wall Street

restaurateur

The owner or operator of a restaurant. There's no "n."

Restaurant

restricted stock

A restricted stock award is a grant of stock by an employer to an employee in which the employee's rights to the shares are limited until the shares "vest." Typically, the employee may not sell or transfer the shares of stock until they vest — frequently a defined period of time — and forfeits the stock if the employee's employment ends before the stock vests. **($$$$$)**

restructure

General term for major corporate changes aimed at greater efficiency and adaptation to changing markets. A restructuring can be a sign that a company is having problems, but that's not always the case. This can also be called a downsizing, a recapitalization and a major management realignment, but avoid these terms. Specify what the restructuring entails.

restructuring charge

A one-time expense that a company takes to reorganize its operations. A restructuring charge is typically related to the closing of plants or warehouses, or the writing down of the value of assets. **($$$$)**

results

The financial performance of a company. Be more specific and write about earnings or losses.

retail sales

The sale of retail goods, as compiled by the Census Bureau, on a monthly basis. The data is released two weeks after the end of the month, and it breaks down sales into various categories, including food and beverage and auto, the most volatile sales number.

Economy, Retail

retained earnings

The profits that a company retains after paying dividends. Retained earnings are listed on a company's balance sheet. **($$$$)**

return on assets

A measure of profitability for a company. It is calculated by dividing a company's net income by its assets. The number is a percentage, and the higher the percentage, the more profitable a company's operations are. *ROA* is acceptable on second reference. **($$$$$)**

return on equity

A measure of a company's profitability calculated as net income divided by shareholder's equity. *ROE* is acceptable on second reference. **($$$$$)**

return on investment

A performance measure for an investment. It is calculated by subtracting the cost of an investment from the gain of an investment, and dividing that sum by the cost of the investment. If an investor purchased a stock for $10, and it was now worth $15, the gain would be $5. The difference between the cost and the gain is also $5. Dividing that number by the original cost gives a return on investment of 50 percent. *ROI* is acceptable on second reference. **($$$$$)**

Reuters

A general news service that has a major business news component. It was founded in Europe in 1851 by Paul Julius Reuter. It is now a subsidiary of Thomson Reuters. When referring to the parent company, use Thomson Reuters as two words. When referring to the wire service, use Reuters.

Company Name

revenue

The amount of money that a company receives or will receive for the sale of its goods and services, by renting goods or property, and through investment. The term sales cannot be used as a synonym because not all revenue is sales.

revenue bond

A municipal bond that is payable only from the revenue of a project, such as a toll road or a stadium. (**$$$**)

Wall Street

revenue recognition

A determination when a company can record money it receives or will receive from the sale of a product or service as revenue. A company whose products experience a high return rate that cannot be estimated may have to wait a certain time period before it can recognize the sale as revenue. (**$$$$$**)

reverse stock split

A reduction in the number of outstanding shares of a company in an attempt to boost its stock price or its **earnings per share**. For example, a 1-for-2 reverse stock split means a shareholder owning two shares of a stock will now own only one. The stock price doubles, but the shareholder has half as many shares. A company will employ such a tactic sometimes when it is in danger of being de-listed by an exchange for having too low a stock price. (**$$$$**)

reverse takeover

A strategy used by a private company to become a public company without having to go through the **initial public offering** process. The private company buys enough shares of the public company to gain control, and then the shareholders of the private company exchange their shares for shares in the public company. Can also be called a reverse merger or reverse IPO. (**$$$$$**)

revolving credit

A line of credit where the customer pays a fee and then is allowed to use the money, up to a limit set by the bank, whenever it is needed. Can be referred to as a revolver on second reference. (**$$$**)

Finance

Reynolds American Inc.

The Winston-Salem, N.C.-based company is the parent of R.J. Reynolds Tobacco Co.

Company Name

rheumatologist

A doctor who specializes in nonsurgical treatment of rheumatic illnesses, particularly arthritis. (**$$$**)

Health care

rich text

Text that has been enhanced with formatting, such as boldface, or multimedia. E-mail messages with graphics are considered rich text.

Technology

right of way

A type of **easement** that gives over people the right to travel across another person's property.

Real estate

right-to-work state

States that prevent unions and companies from having an agreement that requires a worker to belong to the union to be employed. Right-to-work states are primarily in the South and Southwest. **($$)**

rights offering

When a company issues rights that give holders the ability to buy additional shares of stock, typically at a discounted price. **($$$$)**

risk

The concept that the return on an investment may not be the same as the investor's expectations. High-risk investments could cause investors to lose all their money, but they could also result in oversized returns.

risk capital

The money that an investor places in risky investments.

risk management

The identification and assessment of risk to determine ways in which a company can mitigate potential losses from the risk. The term can be used to describe how insurance companies attempt to limit their losses from policies to investors, and it can be used to describe financial firms assessing their investment portfolios to determine how much money they could lose on an investment.

Finance, Insurance, Wall Street

risk manager

A job title for someone whose job is to decrease the risk associated with a line of business. In insurance, a risk manager could determine whether the prices of policies should be raised or lowered to reflect changing risk. In investment, a risk manager's job is to determine whether the firm has taken on too much risk in its portfolio.

Finance, Insurance

Rite Aid Corp.

The drugstore chain is based in East Pennsboro Township, Penn. Its major competitors are **CVS** and **Walgreen's**.

Company Name, Health care, Retail

roadshow

When investment banks and executives of a company going public visit potential investors in an attempt to persuade them to purchase shares in the offering. The term **dog-and-pony show**, although a synonym, should be used sparingly. **($$$)**

Wall Street

robber barons

A term that became popular in the late 19th century to describe businessmen who used unethical business tactics to amass large fortunes. John D. Rockefeller and J.P. Morgan were examples of robber barons. Today, the term has only the rare usage.

RockTenn Co.

The paper and packaging company is based in Norcross, Ga., and acquired rival Smurfit-Stone Container Corp.

in 2011. Do not hyphenate and capitalize the T in all references.

Company Name, Manufacturing

Rockwell Automation Inc.

The industrial automation company is based in Milwaukee, Wis.

Company Name, Manufacturing

Rockwell Collins Inc.

The aerospace company is based in Cedar Rapids, Iowa.

Company Name

Rollerblade

A trademarked product. The generic term is in-line skates.

Company Name

Rolodex

A trademarked product. The generic term is address-card file.

Trademark

Ross Stores Inc.

The clothing store chain is based in Pleasonton, Calif. Its stores are called Ross Dress for Less.

Company Name, Retail

Roth 401(k)

An employee-sponsored savings account that is funded with after-tax money. A Roth 401(k) plan allows the individual to begin withdrawing the money tax-free at age 59 and a half.

Finance

RSS

Stands for Really Simple Syndication, which allows material from the Web to be published in a standardized format.

Technology

runoff

When an insurer stops selling a line of polices or an entire operation, usually because the business is losing money. During runoff, the insurer continues to pay claims until the policies expire. The industry organization for such insurers is the Association of Insurance & Reinsurance Run-Off Companies.

Insurance

runoff

The posting of the end-of-the-day stock prices for every stock on an exchange.

Russell 3000 Index

An index that measures the performance of the largest 3,000 U.S. companies, representing about 98 percent of the U.S. equity market.

Wall Street

Rust-Oleum

A trademarked product. Note the hyphenation and capitalization. The generic term is moisture-resistant paint.

Trademark

Ryder System Inc.

The trucking company is based in Miami.

Company Name, Transportation

S

S corporation

A company that has met the requirements under subchapter S of the Internal Revenue code, allowing the company to be taxed as if it were a partnership. These businesses must be domestic, have 100 or fewer shareholders, and only one class of stock.

S&P 500

The Standard & Poor's 500 Index is considered one of the best barometers of the overall U.S. stock market. It should be considered as the stock index that provides the most accurate gauge for readers. S&P 500 is acceptable on all references.

SA

See **PLC** entry.

SABEW

The Society of American Business Editors and Writers, located at Arizona State University. Acceptable to use SABEW on second reference.

Safeway Inc.

The grocery store chain is based in Pleasanton, Calif.

Retail

SAIC Inc.

The McLean, Va.-based company is a large defense contractor. Its name stands for Science Applications International Corporation, but use SAIC in all references.

Company Name, Manufacturing

salary

Payment given to employees at regular intervals in exchange for the work they have done. Traditionally, a salary is a form of remuneration given to professional employees on each month. When writing about executive compensation, salary is but one part. Focus on the total compensation package of an executive, not just the base salary.

sale

The disbursal of a good or service by a company in exchange for money. The term sales cannot be used as a synonym for **revenue**.

sales per square foot

A measure of a retailer's performance. It is calculated by dividing the retailer's total sales, or often revenue, by the total amount of square feet in its stores. Jewelry stores typically have the highest sales per square foot, while book and sporting goods retailers have the lowest. Compare a retailer's sales per square foot of the current quarter with the same quarter last year to determine whether the retailer has improved its performance. **($$)**

Retail

sales tax

A tax added to the purchase price of a good or service when the product is obtained. A sales tax can vary depending on the product.

Economy

Sallie Mae

Acceptable on all references for SLM Corp., the student loan company based in Newark, Del.

Company Name, Finance

same-store sales

A measurement of the strength of a retailer's locations. Same-store sales compares the sales of stores open at least a year. A retailer can increase its overall sales by opening new locations, but if the same-store sales are declining, that means that its locations open more than a year aren't selling as much merchandise as they did during the first year of operation. Same-store sales are written about as a percent: Same-store sales for Target rose 3 percent during the third quarter.

Retail

Samurai bonds

A debt issue sold in Japan by a non-Japanese company or government.

Finance, Wall Street

Sam's Club

Capitalize only the first letter in the first name of the warehouse division of **Wal-Mart Stores Inc.**

Company Name, Retail

Sandler O'Neill & Partners LP

Use an ampersand, not a plus sign, in the name of this New York-based boutique investment bank.

Company Name, Finance, Wall Street

Sanmina-SCI Corp.

The electronics services company is based in San Jose, Calif. Use the hyphen in all references.

Company Name

Sanyo Electric Co.

Capitalize only the first letter in the first name of the Japan-based electronics manufacturer.

Company Name, Manufacturing

Sara Lee Corp.

The consumer products company is based in Downers Grove, Ill. It is in the process of spinning off its international coffee and tea operation.

Company Name

Sarbanes-Oxley Act

A set of regulations passed by Congress in 2002 in an attempt to protect investors from fraudulent companies. The act requires company executives to sign off on their financial statements and calls for stricter disclosures and harsh enforcement action. Do not refer to it as SOX on any reference.

Save-A-Lot

A grocery store chain based in St. Louis that is a subsidiary of Super-Valu Inc. Capitalize the A between

Save and Lot even though the logo uses a lowercase letter.

Company Name, Retail

savings and loan

A financial institution that focuses on deposits and originating home mortgages with access to low-cost funding from the Federal Home Loan Bank system. Savings and loans, also known as thrift banks, have a community focus. S&L is acceptable on second reference.

Finance

SCANA Corp.

The electric and natural gas utility is based in Cayce, S.C. Use all capital letters in all references.

Company Name, Energy

Schedule 13D

A form filed by any party acquiring an ownership of 5 percent or more of any equity registered with the SEC. The form must also be filed with the exchange on which the stock is traded. A Schedule 13D filing may indicate an investor who wants to make a change at the company — with its management, its board or its overall strategy — but most investors who file the document are simply taking a big stake in the company.

Schedule 13G

A form filed by any party acquiring a beneficial ownership of 5 percent of more of any equity registered with the SEC. The difference between it and a **Schedule 13D** is that the filer of a Schedule 13G is considered a passive investor, like a mutual fund, that does not seek to exert control on the company.

Scotch tape

A trademarked product. The generic term is cellophane tape.

Trademark

Sealed Air Corp.

The packaging company is based in Elmwood Park, N.J. It is best known as the manufacturer of **Bubble Wrap**, a trademarked brand.

Company Name, Manufacturing

Sears Holdings Corp.

The retailer based in Hoffman Estates, Ill., has two major retail subsidiaries — Sears and Kmart. It also operates Lands' End stores.

Company Name, Retail

seasonal adjustment

A change in an economic indicator to reflect the rises and falls due to seasonal factors. The adjustments are made by deducting an average of the change in a set number of previous years from the latest change, showing whether a rise or fall is unusual or purely seasonal.

Economy

seat

A term used to indicate membership in the New York Stock Exchange.

Wall Street

second mortgage

A subordinated mortgage made on property while the original mortgage is still in effect. The original mortgage has first claim on the property. A second mortgage typically has a higher interest rate. **($$)**

Finance, Real estate

secondary offering

When stock is sold by existing shareholders. An additional stock offering by a company is a follow-on offering.

Secretary of State's Office

A state agency that registers a variety of business organizations, including corporations, assumed business names, banks, insurance companies, limited liability companies, limited liability partnerships and limited partnerships. Other business-related filings include trade and service marks, auctioneer's licenses and legal newspaper registrations, among others.

sector

An area within the economy where the companies all sell the same product or service.

Economy

sector fund

A mutual fund that invests primarily in companies that are in the same industry. **($$$)**

Wall Street

secured creditor

People or companies owed debt that is backed by collateral, such as a car loan or a home mortgage. **($$$)**

Finance

secured lending

The process by which a lender such as a bank gives a consumer money but the loan is secured by collateral or some sort of asset.

Finance

Securities and Exchange Commission

The regulatory agency that oversees all publicly traded companies and investing. The SEC requires all public and some private companies to file documents regularly so investors can gauge the performance of the business. In addition, the SEC protects investors from manipulation and fraud by requiring the registration of securities sold by wire or on the Internet. It also maintains an online database of filings from companies. *SEC* is acceptable on second reference. The SEC has a handbook on clearer writing in its filings.

securitization

The process where an issuer packages a group of assets and markets the package to investors. Mortgage-backed securities sold to investors are an example of an asset that has gone through the securitization process. **($$$$)**

Finance

security

Any type of financial instrument that has value, such as bonds, stocks, futures, derivatives and options.

Finance, Wall Street

Seeing Eye dog

A trademarked product. There is no hyphen. The generic term is guide dog.

Trademark

self-insurance plan

An insurance strategy used by some companies where they set aside money to pay future claims, using actuarial tables, instead of buying a policy from an insurance company. The intent is to lower the company's insurance costs.

Health care, Insurance

sell

A rating given a stock by a sell-side analyst. A "sell" rating is the lowest rating an analyst can give. There are generally far fewer "sell" ratings than "buy" ratings.

Wall Street

sell-off (n.), sell off (v.)

The fast selling of a stock, bond or commodity, which causes the price of the equity to decline.

Wall Street

sell-side analyst

Used to describe the retail brokers and research departments that sell securities and make recommendations for the brokerage firm's customers. Do not use interchangeably with **buy-side analyst**.

Wall Street

seller's agent

An agent who represents the seller in a real estate transaction.

Real estate

seller's market

A situation in which the demand for real estate outstrips the supply, allowing sellers to raise the asking price for a piece of property.

Real estate

selling, general and administrative expense

An expense incurred by a company to operate. Such expenses include marketing and advertising costs, salaries, telephone bills, electricity and heating, and rent. The term is a line on a company's income statement. *SG&A* is acceptable on second reference.

Sempra Energy

The San Diego-based utility has no Inc., Co. or Corp. after its name on first reference.

Company Name, Energy

senior debt

A bond or other form of debt that has precedence over other debt issued by the same issuer. If the entity files for bankruptcy protection, the senior debt is repaid first. It can also be called a senior security. (**$$$$**)

Wall Street

settlement date

The date at which payment is made to settle a trade. For stocks, the settlement date is three days after the trade. For mutual funds, the settlement date is the day after the trade.

Wall Street

settlement statement

A document at the closing of a real estate transaction that discloses all of the fees and charges paid for by the buyer and the seller. It's also known as the HUD-1, but avoid this term. (**$**)

Real estate

7-Eleven

The operator of convenience stores is based in Dallas. Its parent company is Japanese.

Retail

share repurchase plan

A company's plan to buy back its own shares, reducing the number of outstanding shares. Also referred to as a buyback plan. (**$$**)

shareholder

An investor who owns at least one share of a company. Can also be called a *stockholder*. Shareholders are some of the most important sources when following a company. Go to annual meetings and hand your business card to them, and call them regularly to ask them about events going on at the company.

shareholder activist

An investor who uses his or her position as a shareholder in a company to attempt to force a change at the business. Shareholder activists will submit proposals to be included in the company's proxy statement and to be voted on at the annual meeting. They are often about issues such as the company's business in developing countries and how workers in those areas are treated. A shareholder activist, often a euphemism for corporate **raider**, is not the same as a **gadfly**. Do not use the terms interchangeably.

shareholder equity

A firm's total assets minus total liabilities. Also known as capital or net worth. (**$$**)

shareholder rights plan

A written document that outlines the rights of shareholders in a corporation. In most cases, the plan includes provisions that allow a company's board of directors to act on behalf of the shareholders to prevent a **hostile takeover**. A **poison pill** is a type of shareholder rights plan. (**$$$$$**)

shareholder value

The value that shareholders of a company receive by management's ability to increase earnings, the stock price and dividends. "Increasing shareholder value" is often a euphemism for "getting the stock price up." Simply write that the company wants to increase its stock price.

Sharpie

A trademarked product. The generic term is permanent marker.

Trademark

Shaw Group Inc.

The energy and construction company is based in Baton Rouge, La.

Company Name, Energy

Sheetrock

A trademarked product. The generic term is gypsum wallboard.

Real estate, Trademark

shelf registration

A **Securities and Exchange Commission** regulation that allows a company to file documents to sell shares but wait up to three years before actually executing its stock offering, i.e. keeping it "on the shelf." The regulation allows companies to avoid bad market conditions and take advantage of favorable investment trends. The documents can be referred to as a shelf filing. **($$$$)**

Sherwin-Williams Co.

The Cleveland-based paint company's name is hyphenated.

Company Name, Manufacturing

short interest

The percentage of shares in a company that are held by investors shorting the stock divided by the number of outstanding shares. A company with a large short interest may indicate negative investor sentiment about the company. **($$$$$)**

Wall Street

short selling

The selling of a security that the seller does not own but has borrowed, or any sale that is completed by the delivery of a security borrowed by the seller. Short selling is a legitimate trading strategy. Short sellers bet that they will be able to buy the stock at a lower price than the price at which they sold short. Short sellers generally employ this strategy if they believe there is a disconnect between the share price and the underlying fundamentals. However, it is also part of various hedging strategies and stock arbitrage. Can also be referred to as *shorting a stock*. The percentage of stock in a company that has been borrowed by short sellers is called the short interest. See **naked shorting. ($$$$$)**

Wall Street

short squeeze

A situation in which a lack of supply and an increase in demand force a stock price to rise. A short squeeze can be a strategy encouraged by a company, or forced by long investors, to reduce a short position in a stock. It hurts investors who are **shorting the stock**, forcing them to cover their short positions at substantial losses. See also bear trap. **($$$$$)**

Wall Street

short term

Bonds that mature in less than one year, or liabilities that are due in less than one year. Specify the time period in a story.

shortfall

Amount by which a financial objective has not been met.

sick building syndrome

When a building's ventilation or air-conditioning systems are flawed, causing workers to become ill with a number of maladies.

skin in the game

A term used to describe when executives use their own money to purchase stock in the company they're operating, or a fund manager puts his or her own money into the fund, or a company that owns stakes in assets it has securitized. **($$$)**

skirt length theory

The humorous idea that skirt lengths are an indicator of the stock market's direction. If skirts are becoming shorter, then the market is supposed to rise, and vice versa. **($$$$)**

Wall Street

sloppy payer

A consumer who pays only some bills on time. Delinquent payer is also an acceptable term.

Economy

small business

A business that is typically privately owned and has a few employees. The legal definition is a business with fewer than 100 employees in the United States and fewer than 50 employees in the European Union. A small business needs to have at least 10 employees for the term to be used. Otherwise, it's a **microbusiness**.

Small Business Administration

A federal government agency that provides support to small businesses in the form of loans or loan guarantees. *SBA* is acceptable on second reference.

small business investment company

A private company that is licensed by the **Small Business Administration** and makes investments in small businesses, generally at more favorable terms than **venture capital** funds.

small cap

A stock with a market capitalization between $300 million and $2 billion.

small groups

Health care plans that typically have fewer than 100 members.

Health care, Insurance

SmartMoney

A monthly personal finance magazine started in 1992 as a joint venture between **Dow Jones & Co.** and Hearst Corp. The magazine is now wholly owned by Dow Jones.The M is capitalized in the name although it's spelled as one word.

Company Name

smartphone

A hand-held computer device that has many of the same functions as a PC but also operates as a telephone.

Technology

Smithfield Foods Inc.

The world's largest pork producer is based in Smithfield, Va. It operates the world's largest meat processing plant in Tar Heel, N.C.

Company Name

Social Security Administration

A federal government agency designed to provide disability, retirement and survivor benefits. It was founded in 1935 and has been funded by taxes taken out of employee paychecks and from employers. The administration is located in Woodland, Md., not in Washington, D.C. Avoid SSA on all references.

soft goods

Goods that may only be used once or have a lifespan of less than three years. Examples are cosmetics, fuel, food and clothing. Also called nondurable goods. **($$$)**

Economy

soft money

Funding from a government or a corporation on a one-time-only basis for a project or a special purpose. It's also sometimes used to refer to paper money. Either usage is acceptable.

Economy, Finance

sole proprietorship

An unincorporated business that is owned by one person who pays personal income taxes on any profit the business makes.

solvent

A situation in which a company's assets exceed its liabilities. The antonym is **insolvent**.

Sonic Automotive Inc.

The owner and operator of automobile dealerships is based in Charlotte, N.C.

Company Name, Retail

Sonic Inc.

The drive-in hamburger chain features carhops. Sonic has more than 3,500 outlets coast to coast and is based in Oklahoma City.

source code

The underlying code that makes up a software program.

Technology

sourcing

A hot issue in business journalism. In some ways, sourcing of information when writing about business is easier than in other fields because there are plenty of government documents, such as **Securities and Exchange Commission** filings. But in other ways, sourcing for stories can be extremely complicated, particularly when using sources such as company employees whose jobs could be lost if their superiors knew they were talking to a journalist. In addition, sources in the business world always have an agenda — whether it's to make their company look better or worse in the public eye, or to make money in the markets.

Here are some general rules that should be applied when sourcing business news stories:

1. Limit off-the-record sourcing as much as possible. If a source tells you something off the record, verify the information from another source or two before feeling comfortable using it.

2. Use caution with sources who don't want information attributed

to themselves. Such sources would like a journalist to publicize the information, but don't want their names attached to it. Ask yourself why that's the case.

3. Back up what people say as much as possible with information contained in documents.

4. Avoid using company spokesmen and spokeswomen whenever possible. A manager or executive of the company should be the ones speaking for the company, particularly when the questions involve its day-to-day operations.

5. That said, realize that PR people within companies can be valuable sources of information and willing to provide excellent fact nuggets if you gain their trust as a responsible business journalist.

6. Feel free to use internal company documents as sources of information. Cultivate sources willing to provide such information.

7. Disclose potential conflicts for on-the-record sources in your stories during the first attribution. Explain that the hedge fund manager quoted about a company's poor management is shorting the stock, or that the sell-side analyst works for a firm that performs investment banking for the company.

8. Avoid using the same sources over and over again about the same topic or when writing about the same company. Find new sources to use. Long-time readers will recognize that you're going back to the same quote hounds and get turned off.

9. Realize that virtually everyone you encounter while reporting a story has a potential conflict. Independent industry consultants may want to curry favor with a company. Business school professors may want a spot on the company's board.

10. Always verify the source of information, particularly information from the Internet. Bloomberg News has a policy of attributing breaking news to the company's press release and how the release was distributed, such as via PR Newswire or Business Wire, if it is unable to verify the release with the company before publishing the first story. This policy is based on a hoax where a story was written based on a fake release.

Southern Co.

The Atlanta-based utility company is the parent of Georgia Power and Alabama Power.

Company Name, Energy

Southwest Airlines Co.

The airline is based in Dallas.

Company Name, Transportation

sovereign fund

A fund that is owned by a country's government. These funds typically invest in multiple types of financial instruments and in multiple countries.

Economy, Finance, Wall Street

Spam

A trademarked product. The generic term is luncheon meat. Lowercase, spam is acceptable for unsolicited e-mail.

Trademark

special purpose acquisition company

A publicly traded company that raises money to pursue the acquisition of another company. These companies raise money from the public for an unspecified deal, but may say they're targeting a specific industry. Avoid using the acronym SPAC in all references. On second reference, refer to is as the company. (**$$$$**)

Wall Street

specialist

A health care provider whose practice is limited to a certain branch of medicine, such as a specific disease (an oncologist treats cancer) or specific age categories (a pediatrician treats children). An exchange member who buys and sells a particular stock, holding inventory to trade with investors. There is at least one specialist in every major stock traded.

Health care, Wall Street

Spectra Energy Corp.

The natural gas company is based in Houston.

Company Name, Energy

Spectrum Group International Inc.

The Irvine, Calif.-based company trades precious metals and is an auctioneer of stamps, coins and other collectibles.

Company Name

speculator

An investor who takes large risks, hoping for a return that vastly exceeds the norms of a market. Speculators often invest in sophisticated equities such as futures and options or in shorting stock.

Wall Street

spinoff (n.)

A subsidiary or a division of one company that becomes its own separate company. Spinoff companies are intended to be worth more separately than they were as a subsidiary of a larger company. The verb is spin off.

split-adjusted price

A stock price that reflects historical stock splits. For example, a stock that was worth $10 in 2000 has since undergone two 2-for-1 stock splits, and the stock price is currently trading at $15. While the price may have appeared to have gone up 50 percent, it's actually risen more than that. The 2000 stock price, on a split-adjusted basis, is actually $2.50. (**$$$$$**)

Wall Street

spokesman, spokeswoman

Acceptable terms when referring to company public relations personnel. *Representative* is an acceptable gender-neutral substitute. The term also can be applied to a celebrity who appears in advertising to endorse a product.

spot market

The commodities market in which goods are sold for cash and delivered immediately. It's also called the cash market. **($$$)**

Wall Street

spread

The difference between the **bid** and **ask** prices of a security.

Sprint Nextel Corp.

The Overland Park, Kan.-based telecommunications company does not capitalize the letters in Nextel after the N. Sprint is its main wireless brand.

Company Name

SPX Corp.

The industrial conglomerate is based in Charlotte, N.C.

squawk box

An intercom speaker on the desks of brokers that allows them to hear sell-side analysts at the firm's research department discuss stocks. When used as the name of the **CNBC** show, it should be capitalized and placed in quotation marks. **($$$)**

Finance

squeeze

Used to describe a time period when lending is difficult, or when higher costs cannot be passed on to customers. During such a time,

profits are said to be squeezed. **($$)**

St. Jude Medical Inc.

The medical device company is based in Little Canada, Minn.

Company Name, Health care

stagflation

An economic period of high inflation and high unemployment but low economic growth. **($$)**

Economy

stake

A term used to describe how much an investor owns in a company.

stand-alone (adj.)

A restaurant or other business operating in its own freestanding building rather than being in a mall or in a storefront. **($$)**

Restaurant, Retail

Standard & Poor's Corp.

A New York-based company that rates stocks and bonds. Its parent is McGraw-Hill Cos.

Company Name, Finance

standard of care

A diagnostic process used by a health care provider for a certain type of illness or care.

Health care

standard of living

A level of wealth, ownership of material goods and income required to obtain a specific socioeconomic standing in a community. The standard of living fluctuates depending on a community. A high standard of living in Atlanta is less expensive than an equivalent high standard of living in New York.

Economy

standstill agreement

Can refer to a contract that stops a **hostile takeover,** or to when a lender stops demanding the payment of a loan from a borrower and new loan terms are then negotiated. **($$$$$)**

Stanley Black & Decker Inc.

The manufacturer of tools and hardware is based in New Britain, Conn.

Company Name, Manufacturing

Staples Inc.

The Framingham, Mass.-based company is the largest office supply retailer in the country.

Company Name, Retail

Starbucks Corp.

The coffee maker and retailer is based in Seattle.

Company Name

startup

A new company, sometimes one without any revenue. Start up is the verb.

Starwood Hotels and Resorts Worldwide Inc.

The hotel company is based in White Plains, N.Y. Starwood is acceptable on second reference.

Company Name

State Children's Health Insurance Program

A health insurance plan administered by the U.S.Department of Health and Human Services designed to provide health insurance to uninsured, low-income children. Some insurance companies specialize in selling such coverage. *SCHIP* is acceptable on second reference. **($$$)**

Health care, Insurance

State Farm Insurance Cos.

A group of insurance and financial services companies based in Bloomington, Ill. The main company is State Farm Mutual Automobile Insurance Co.

Finance, Insurance

State Street Corp.

The financial services company is based in Boston.

Company Name, Finance

Steak 'n Shake Co.

The Indianapolis-based restaurant chain usesonly one apostrophe in its name.

Company Name, Restaurant

stock

Ownership in a company that is represented by shares. A holder of stock (a shareholder) has a claim on a part of its assets and earnings. Also known as an **equity.**

stock index

A method of measuring the performance of the stock market. Indexes will also measure the performance of stocks in certain industries or countries. Do not call the **Dow Jones Industrial Average** a stock index. It is an average. Indexes are price-weighted.

Wall Street

stock market stories

Too often reporters overplay or underplay a daily change in the stock market by how it is described. The following guidelines should be applied when using verbs to describe how a broad market index has fluctuated:

1 percent drop or less: Use "fell" or "dropped," as well as "declined." And we're even OK with "moved downward."

2 to 4 percent decline: Any of the above, as well as "dipped" and "slumped," which are slightly more serious grades of a fall.

5 to 10 percent decline: "sell-off" is appropriate here, as is "retreated." On Wednesday, Oct. 15, 2008, the market "retreated" by 7.87 percent.

Drop of 10 percent or more: The term "rout" is correct. The stock market fell by 12.8 percent on Oct. 28, 1929, the first day of the decline that preceded the Great Depression. "Rout" needs to convey the suddenness of the move. On Oct. 19, 1987, the market was "routed" when the Dow Jones Industrial Average fell 22.6 percent that day.

Multi-day drops that total more than 10 percent would also equal a "rout" as long as it's clear that the term refers to more than one day. Do not use "correction" in any instance.

It is a euphemism.

Here are the verbs recommended when writing about increases:

Rise of up to 1 percent: Again, "gained," "increased" or "advanced" is fine here, as are "rose" and "grew."

2 to 4 percent increase: Again, "gained," "increased" or "advanced" is fine here, as are "rose" and "grew."

5 to 10 percent increase: "Jumped" and "soared" are appropriate here.

10 percent or more: "Surged" is the best antonym for "was routed." When the Dow rose by 936 points on Oct. 13, 2008, it surged by 11 percent, the fifth-largest one-day percentage gain in the market's history. The market has only had six one-day surges in its history.

Wall Street

stock options

The opportunity, given by your employer, to purchase a certain number of shares of your company's common stock at a pre-established price, known as the exercise price, during a specific period of time. The options mature during various periods, known as *vesting periods*. **($$$)**

stock split

Increase in a corporation's number of outstanding shares of stock without any change in the shareholders' equity or the aggregate market value at the time of the split. In a split, the share price declines. In a reverse split, the stock price rises. Begin with the number of shares an investor will have after the split. (**$$**)

stock symbol

A series of letters that an exchange assigns to represent the stock of a specific company. For example, Coca-Cola Co.'s stock symbol is KO. No two stock symbols are alike. Also called a *stock ticker* or a *ticker symbol*. Avoid using a stock symbol in a story to refer to a company.

Wall Street

stockbroker

A person who executes buy and sell orders on securities in return for a fee or a commission. Not to be confused with a **financial planner** or **financial adviser.**

Wall Street

stockholder

A person who owns at least one share of stock in a company. Also called a shareholder.

Wall Street

stop order

An order to buy or sell a stock when the price passes a particular point. It allows investors to lock in profits or limit their losses. Also called a stop-loss order. (**$$$**)

Wall Street

straddle

An options strategy in which the investor holds a call and a put option for the same security. It's an investment strategy that some investors use when they believe the price of a stock will move, but are unsure which way. (**$$$$$**)

Wall Street

strategic alternatives

A term used by a company when it announces a review of its operations, which may include a sale of some or all of its operations. It's often a euphemism for a company putting itself up for sale. Specify what the company is exploring instead of using the term strategic alternatives.

strategic defaulter

A consumer who walked away from a home when its value dropped below what was owed on the **mortgage.** Such consumers may still be considered prudent risks by lenders. (**$$$**)

Economy, Real estate

streaming

The transmission of digital audio or video on a website.

Technology

street account

The brokerage account where an investor's securities are held in the name of the brokerage firm. Street accounts make it easier for the brokerage to sell the securities when the investor wants. (**$**)

Wall Street

street name

When securities are held in the name of the broker instead of the specific investor. Such a move makes it easier

to transfer the stock to another investor if it is sold.
Wall Street

TheStreet.com
A Wall Street-focused financial news site co-founded in 1996 by Jim Cramer. When writing the name, capitalize the S and use the .com.
Company Name

strike price
The price at which a derivatives contract, such as a call option, can be exercised. Also known as the exercise price. **($$$)**
Wall Street

structured finance
Highly complex financial transactions such as a **collateralized debt obligation** or a **collateralized mortgage obligation**.
Finance

structured investment vehicle
A pool of investments created by a finance company that attempts to take advantage of the difference in value between short-term debt and long-term financial products such as mortgage-backed securities. They were popular until the decline in home values that began in 2008, which caused the value held by the vehicles to decline. *SIV* is acceptable on second reference. **($$$)**
Finance, Real estate, Wall Street

Stryker Corp.
The medical device manufacturer is based in Kalamazoo, Mich.
Company Name, Health care

style creep
An unflattering term applied to mutual funds that wander outside their advertised area of investment expertise. **($$)**
Wall Street

Styrofoam
A trademarked product used mainly for insulation. The generic term is foam plastic. There is no such thing as a Styrofoam cup.
Trademark

sub-prime mortgage
A loan with a higher-than-average interest rate offered to a consumer who presumably cannot qualify for a loan at the normal rate because of credit ratings or other problems. **($$)**
Finance, Real estate

subordinated debt
A bond or other debenture that ranks behind **senior debt** in terms of being repaid. Also called subordinated security. **($$$)**

subsidiary
A company where more than 50 percent of the voting stock is controlled by another company.

SunGard Data Systems Inc.
The information technology company based in Wayne, Pa., spells SunGard as one word with a capital G.
Company Name, Technology

Sunoco Inc.

The Philadelphia-based petroleum company has used the acronym of Sun Oil Co. Inc. since 1998.

Company Name, Energy

SunTrust Banks Inc.

There is no space between Sun and Trust in the name of the Atlanta-based bank holding company.

Company Name, Finance

Super Bowl indicator

An indicator based on the belief that when a team from the old National Football League wins the Super Bowl, the stock market will rise in the coming year; conversely, when a team from the old American Football League wins the Super Bowl, the stock market will fall in the coming year. It is not meant to be taken seriously. **($$$$$)**

Economy, Wall Street

Superfund

The federal government's program to clean physical sites such as closed manufacturing plants contaminated with hazardous materials. The name comes from the Comprehensive Environmental Response, Compensation, and Liability Act of 1980, which required the federal government to determine who should clean such sites. The Environmental Protection Agency's Superfund keeps an online database of such sites.

Company Name

SuperValu Inc.

Spell the name of the Eden Prairie, Minn.-based grocery retailer as one word, with only the S and the V capitalized. The company spells its name with all capital letters.

Retail

supply side economics

An economic theory that argues that economic growth can be created by decreasing barriers such as taxes and regulation. The theory believes that consumers will benefit from more goods and services available and lower prices. **($)**

Economy

surety bond

A type of insurance that protects against a default. For example, a surety bond protects a construction project's owner against a **contractor** failing to perform the work. The insurance company determines for the project's owner that the contractor has the financial wherewithal to complete the work. **($$)**

Insurance, Real estate

surplus

A situation in which exports exceed imports or assets exceed liabilities.

suspended trading

The stoppage of trading in a security, primarily due to a lack of material important information. A stock can be suspended because a company has failed to file recent financial information with the **Securities and Exchange Commission.** **($$$)**

Wall Street

swap

The exchange of one security for another. A swap can also occur with currencies and with interest rates. Explain what is being swapped in the story.

Wall Street

swap execution facility

A **derivative** trading venue mandated by the Dodd-Frank Wall Street Reform and Consumer Protection Act of 2010. A swap execution facility, such as an exchange, must monitor derivative swaps to make sure the market is not being manipulated. **($$$$$)**

Finance, Wall Street

sweetheart deal

An offer or agreement that is so advantageous to one party that it is difficult to turn down. It can be an acquisition offer, a compensation package or any other type of business deal.

Symantec Corp.

The manufacturer of security software is based in Mountain View, Calif.

Company Name, Technology

syndicate

A group that works together on a large project, such as a corporate loan. **($$$)**

synergy

Used mostly in the context of mergers and acquisitions, synergy is the idea — often erroneous — that the value and performance of two companies combined will be greater than the sum of the separate parts.

Synnex Corp.

Capitalize only the first letter in the first name of the Fremont, Calif.-based supply chain services company.

Company Name

Synovus Financial Corp.

The Columbus, Ga.-based financial services company can be referred to as Synovus after first reference.

Company Name, Finance

synthetic

A financial instrument that simulates another. For example, a synthetic stock can be created by purchasing a **call option** and selling a **put option** on the stock.

Finance, Wall Street

Sysco Corp.

Lowercase all but the first letter of the Houston-based food supplier's name.

Company Name

Tabasco

A trademarked product. The generic term is hot-pepper sauce.

Trademark

Taco Bell Corp.

Based in Irvine, Calif., the Mexican-style fast food chain has about 5,600 restaurants in the United States. It is owned by Louisville, Ky.-based **Yum Brands**

Company Name, Restaurant, Retail

takeover

Change in controlling interest of a corporation. A takeover may be a friendly acquisition or an unfriendly bid that the target company may fight. If the company is publicly traded, then the acquiring company will make an offer for the outstanding shares. Take over is the verb.

takeover artist

An investor who tries to find companies that are attractive to purchase and that can be turned around and sold for a profit. Carl Icahn is an example of a takeover artist.

tangible net worth

A measure of the worth of the physical assets of a company, excluding intangible assets such as **goodwill**, patents and brand names. **($$$)**

Target Corp.

The Minneapolis-based retailer has sold off its other locations and now just operates stores with the Target, Target Greatland and SuperTarget names.

Retail

target date fund

A mutual fund where the investment portfolio becomes more conservative as the fund gets closer to its target date. The fund is commonly used by people who are investing for retirement.

Finance, Wall Street

TARP

The Troubled Asset Relief Program originally created by the federal government in 2008 to purchase troubled assets from financial companies to improve their finances, but later used to provide capital to banks and to companies such as **General Motors Co.** and **American International Group Inc. ($$$$)**

Finance

Taser

A trademarked product. The generic term is stun gun.

Trademark

tax-free bond

A bond issued by a municipal, county or state government where the interest payments are not taxable by the federal government. Also called tax-exempt bonds. **($$)**

Wall Street

taxable income

The amount of income by an individual or a company that's taxable by the federal, state or local government.

TD Ameritrade Holding Corp.

Capitalize only the first letter in Ameritrade, in contrast to the all capitalization used by the Omaha, Neb.-based broker. Use TD Ameritrade on second reference.

Company, Finance, Wall Street

Tech Data Corp.

The Clearwater, Fla.-based company is a distributor of information technology.

Company Name, Technology

technical analysis

A method of evaluating an equity by looking at data such as historical prices and volume traded. **($$$)**

technology terms

The growing use of technology in all forms of business, and the increasing importance of the technology industry itself, has resulted in many technology-related words, phrases, acronyms and abbreviations entering the language. Still, many people are unfamiliar with much of this terminology. When writing about technology or mentioning technology, we recommend explaining as much as possible. If you think a word or term might be unfamiliar to any of your readers or viewers, then explain or define it.

Technology

Telephone and Data Systems Inc.

The telecommunications company is based in Chicago. Do not use an ampersand in the name.

Company Name

Temporary Liquidity Guarantee Program

A plan adopted by the **Federal Deposit Insurance Corp.** in 2008 to guarantee the debt of banks. The plan was designed to encourage bank lending to consumers and businesses. Avoid using the TLGP abbreviation. On second reference, call it the program. **($$$$)**

Finance

tender

As a verb, to make or accept a formal offer, such as a takeover. It can also be a noun meaning a bid to purchase **Treasury securities**.

tender offer

An offer to shareholders to purchase some or all or their shares. The price offered is usually at a premium to the market price. Tender offers may be friendly or unfriendly. **($$$)**

Wall Street

Tenet Healthcare Corp.

The Dallas-based health care company spells health care as one word.

Company Name, Health care

Tenneco Inc.

The auto parts manufacturer is based in Lake Forest, Ill.

Company Name, Manufacturing

Terex Corp.

The heavy equipment manufacturer is based in Westport, Conn.

Company Name, Manufacturing

term life insurance

A policy with a specific duration, such as 10 years. When the policy term ends, the policyholder must decide whether to renew for another term, often at a higher premium. Term insurance carries no cash value.

Insurance

term to maturity

The remaining time of a bond's life. **($)**

Wall Street

Tesoro Corp.

The San Antonio, Texas-based company operates refineries and gasoline stations.

Company Name

Texas Instruments Inc.

The Dallas-based manufacturer of semiconductors and electronics. Avoid calling it TI on second reference.

Company Name, Technology

Texas ratio

A term used to describe the credit problems of a bank. The ratio takes the amount of a bank's nonperforming assets and loans, as well as loans delinquent for more than 90 days, and divides this number by the firm's tangible capital equity plus its loan loss reserve. A ratio of more than 100 is considered problematic. **($$$$)**

Company Name, Finance

Textron Inc.

The conglomerate is based in Providence, R.I. Among its businesses is Cessna Aircraft Corp.

Company Name, Manufacturing

Thermo Fisher Scientific Inc.

The life sciences company is based in Waltham, Mass.

Company Name

thinly traded

When a few shares of a security are traded on a daily basis. A stock that is thinly traded may see more dramatic changes in its price than a stock that is widely traded.

Wall Street

third-party administrator

A company that provides administrative services for a health insurer or managed care plan but does not assume any financial responsibility for paying benefits.

Health care, Insurance

3M Co.

The St. Paul, Minn.-based company uses the numeral 3 and the capital M in all references to its name.

Company Name, Manufacturing

thrift

A financial institution that focuses on taking deposits and making mortgage loans in the local community. It can also be called a **savings and loan**

or a savings bank.
Finance

Thrivent Financial for Lutherans
The financial services company has headquarters in Minneapolis, Minn., and Appleton, Wis.
Company Name, Finance

TIAA-CREF
Stands for Teachers Insurance and Annuity Association — College Retirement Equities Fund. It's a nonprofit organization that manages retirement funds for employees in the education, medicine and research fields. TIAA-CREF is acceptable on all references.
Finance

ticker symbol
Do not use the stock ticker symbol of a company as a shortened version of its name in any reference except in charts.

ticker tape
A computerized device that delivers market information — the ticker symbol, amount of shares traded and latest price of a stock — to investors around the world. The term "ticker" comes from a telegraph machine invented in 1867 to distribute stock prices that was later updated by Thomas Edison, who fixed the Gold Indicator Co.'s telegraph that relayed gold prices to customers. (**$**)
Finance, Wall Street

Time Warner Cable Inc.
The New York cable television operator was spun off from **Time Warner Inc.** in 2009 and is now a separate company. Use cable when referring to the company in all references to distinguish between the two companies.
Company Name

Time Warner Inc.
The New York media company is the parent of **Fortune** and **Money** magazines. It is also the parent of HBO and TBS. It spun off its cable operations in 2009.
Company Name

title
A document that serves as evidence of ownership of a piece of property.
Real estate

title insurance
A policy purchased by home buyers that protects the lender from pre-existing liens against the property. (**$**)
Insurance, Real estate

titles
Capitalize all business titles when used before a person's name. **CEO** is acceptable on first reference. Other title abbreviations, such as **CFO**, COO and **CIO**, are acceptable on second reference. Lower case and spell out titles when they stand alone or after a person's name. Occupational titles should be lower case in all references. Although a company may capitalize a title, follow these rules.

TiVo

A trademarked product. The generic term is digital TV recorder.

Trademark

TJX Cos.

The Framingham, Mass.-based company is the parent of the T.J. Maxx and Marshalls retail chain.

Company Name, Retail

tombstone

An advertisement by an investment banker of the offering of a security that gives details such as how many shares were sold and who other underwriters are. A tombstone can also be run by an investment banker that provides services for a merger or acquisition. **($$$)**

too big to fail

A concept in current U.S. economic policy that the largest companies are so interconnected that the government cannot allow them to go under because the financial system and the economy would go into a downward spiral. An example of a company deemed "too big to fail" is the insurer **American International Group Inc.**

top line

The line on a financial statement that shows how much revenue or sales is being produced. It's typically the first line in a financial statement, hence the name. **Revenue** is the preferred term, although top line can be used in casual references. It's also used as an adjective to describe inves-tors, such as a mutual fund manager seeking to invest in companies with strong top line growth.

total return

The **dividend** plus any gains or losses in a stock investment. A stock with a return of 30 percent on the year has a higher return if it also pays a dividend.

toxic assets

Financial assets whose values have dropped dramatically and no longer attract much interest from investors. A slang term, it's generally used to refer to **collateralized debt obligations** and **credit default swaps. ($$$$)**

Finance

Toys R Us Inc.

There is no need for the apostrophes around the R in the Wayne, N.J.-based retailer's name.

Company Name, Retail

tracking stock

Stock issued by a parent company that rises or falls based on the performance of a specific division, not the entire company.

Retail

trade

The buying or selling of a security, such as a stock or bond. Also, the buying and selling of goods and services between economies. Trade statistics are measures taken by the Census Bureau and released six weeks after the end of a month. The story focuses on the change in the overall balance of trade as well as total imports and total exports. The latest trade data can be found on the Census Bureau website.

Wall Street

trade deficit

When the buying and selling of goods and services result in a country importing goods worth more than what it exports.

Economy

trade surplus

When exports exceed imports. The United States has not had a trade surplus for an entire year since 1975.

Economy

trademark names

Use the generic equivalent unless the trademark name is essential to the story. Never use a trademark as a thing; for example, it's Scotch-brand adhesive tape, not Scotch Tape.

trading floor

Where equities are traded. Trading can occur at an exchange or at a brokerage house or investment bank. The area is also called the pit.

Wall Street

tranche

A piece or portion of a structured finance investment such as a **collateralized debt obligation** or a mortgage-backed security. It's the French word for slice or portion. Tranches can have different risks or different maturity dates. Mortgage-backed securities can have tranches that include **sub-prime mortgages** and tranches that include AAA-quality mortgages. **($$)**

Finance, Real estate, Wall Street

transfer agent

A financial institution that keeps a record of all investors and their account balances in a company. Some companies will act as their own transfer agent. **($$$$)**

transumer

It has at least two meanings: A consumer who tends to rent, rather than buy, consumer goods. Transumers may rent cars from Zipcar and even rent such items as high-fashion handbags.A consumer who tends to shop heavily in transit, for example, while waiting for a plane connection. **($$$)**

Retail

TravelCenters of America LLC

The truck stop operator is based in Westlake, Ohio. TravelCenters is one word with a capital C.

Company Name

Travelers Cos.

The **property and casualty** insurer has two headquarters — St. Paul, Minn., and Hartford, Conn. Delete "the" before its name in all references.

Company Name, Insurance

Treasury bill

Short-term debt issued by the federal government that has a maturity of less than one year. Bills are sold in $1,000 denominations. The term T-bill is also acceptable.

Wall Street

Treasury bond

Debt issued by the federal government that has a maturity of more than 10 years. It can also be referred to as a T-bond on second reference.

Wall Street

Treasury Department

The federal government agency responsible for the issuing of Treasury bonds, notes and bills. The U.S. Mint, however, prints money.

Treasury Inflation-Protected Securities

A special type of Treasury note or bond that offers protection against inflation. TIPS pay interest on a principal amount that rises or falls based on the consumer price index. *TIPS* is acceptable on second reference. (**$$$$$**)

Wall Street

Treasury note

Debt issued by the federal government that has a maturity between one year and 10 years. It can be referred to as a T-note on second reference.

Wall Street

Treasury securities

The term covers Treasury bills, bonds and notes and Treasury Inflation-Protected Securities. Together, they may be referred to as Treasurys.

Wall Street

trend analysis

A segment of technical analysis that attempts to predict the future price of a stock based on past data. (**$$$**)

Wall Street

triple net lease

A lease agreement in which the tenant is responsible for costs associated with the building, such as property taxes, insurance and the cost of repairs and maintenance. The rent payment is generally lower for such leases. (**$$$$$**)

Real estate

triple witching

The date when contracts expire for stock index futures, stock index options and stock options. It occurs four times a year, on the third Friday of March, June, September and December. It can be referred to as freaky Friday after it's been explained. (**$$$$$**)

Wall Street

trustee

A court-appointed representative who administers a business or estate. Can be assigned if creditors or others argue that the company is unfit to manage its operations. (**$**)

Truth in Lending Act

A federal law that requires lenders to disclose specific information to consumers borrowing money, such as the **annual percentage rate** of the loan.

Finance, Real estate

TRW Automotive Holdings Corp.

The Livonia, Mich.-based company makes parts for automobiles. Its former parent company was TRW Inc., but that was sold to **Northrop Grumman Corp.** in 2002. The automotive parts business was then sold.

Company Name, Manufacturing

tuck-in acquisition

A deal made by a company where the acquired business is folded into an existing division, often to expand its product line or geographic territory. It can also be called a bolt-on acquisition. **($$)**

turnaround

A situation where a company that has struggled in the past has turned around and improved its operations dramatically. Explain how the turnaround has occurred in a story.

turnover

The number of times an asset is replaced during a financial period. A retailer wants a high turnover number because it means that its inventory is not sitting on shelves. It can also be called the turn. **($$)**

Retail

Tutor Perini Corp.

The general contractor is based in Sylmar, Calif.

two-step mortgage

A mortgage that offers a fixed rate for a specific period of time, such as five or seven years, and then an ad-justable rate for the remaining years of the **mortgage. ($$)**

Finance, Real estate

Tyson Foods Inc.

The food processing company is based in Springdale, Ark.

Company Name

U.S. Bancorp

When writing about the Minneapolis-based parent company, write U.S. Bancorp. When writing about its commercial banking operation, use U.S. Bank.

Company Name, Finance

U.S. Green Building Council

The nonprofit trade organization behind LEED certification. Try to avoid USGBC, referring instead to the organization. It is based in Washington, D.C. **($$$$)**

U.S. Tax Court

A special federal court that decides issues of taxation, such as litigation involving federal income taxes not paid. A company charged with failing to pay enough taxes to the government could go to U.S. Tax Court to resolve the dispute. Tax court is acceptable on second reference. The tax court maintains an online database of cases that can be searched by name.

UGI Corp.

The energy company sells propane, butane, natural gas and electricity. It is based in King of Prussia, Pa.

Company Name, Energy

under water

When a lender owes more money on the loan than the value of what was purchased. It's commonly used to describe a home loan where the consumer owes more on the home than the home's value.

Finance, Real estate

undercapitalized

A description for a company that does not have enough money to support an expansion. **($)**

underperform

A rating given a stock by a sell-side analyst. An "underperform" rating is slightly better than a "sell" rating, but not as good as a "neutral" rating.

Wall Street

undersubscribed

When demand for a new stock offering is less than the number of shares available to be purchased.

Wall Street

undervalued

A stock that is trading below its perceived value. The opposite is **overvalued. ($$)**

Wall Street

underwater options

Stock options where the exercise price is higher than the current price on the market. **($$$)**

Wall Street

underwriter

The Wall Street firm that works with a company to sell its shares to the investment world. The underwriter helps determine a price for the stock, then acquires the stock and sells it to investors, who are often its clients. An underwriter receives a fee from the company selling the stock for its services and also receives commissions when selling the stock. **($)**

Finance, Wall Street

underwriter discount

The difference between the price the lead underwriter pays for the initial public offering shares and the price it resells those shares to other members of the syndicate. **($$$$)**

Wall Street

underwriting

A process used by an insurance company to determine what it will charge for coverage. It's also a term used to describe when investment banks raise cash for companies or governments by selling securities.

Health care, Insurance

underwriting income

The difference between the premiums charged by an insurance company to its customers and the cost to settle claims. An insurance company that reports an underwriting income is considered a solid underwriter.

Insurance

unemployment rate

A measure of how many people are out of the labor force but are looking for work. Measured by the Bureau of Labor Statistics, the monthly data comes out the first Friday of the following month. When writing about unemployment, reporters can write about the unemployment rate, which is the total number of people out of work but looking for work divided by the total workforce. They may also write about the change in the total number of people working, which in some cases might be the more relevant number. For example, the unemployment rate can decline in a month where the total number of people working also declines if the number of discouraged workers — those who have stopped looking for work — increases. Local unemployment data can be found on the Bureau of Labor Statistics website. **($$)**

Economy

Uniform Commercial Code

A set of laws regulating commercial transactions, especially those involving the sale of goods where money is borrowed. A UCC filing is a document submitted to the state Secretary of State's Office indicating that the filer has a claim against an asset. *UCC* is acceptable on second reference to the code.

Uniform Franchise Offering Circular

Predecessor to the **Franchise Disclosure Document**. Avoid UFOC.

Restaurant, Retail

union

An organization of workers who have joined together to benefit the entire group.

Union Pacific Corp.

There is no hyphen in the name of the Omaha, Neb.-based railroad operator.

Company Name, Transportation

union shop

An employer that requires new workers to join the union within a certain time period.

Unisys Corp.

The information technology company is based in Blue Bell, Pa.

Company Name, Technology

United Continental Holdings Inc.

The parent company of United Air Lines and Continental Airlines, based in Chicago. UAL is no longer an acceptable abbreviation for this company.

Company Name, Transportation

United States Steel Corp.

The Pittsburgh-based steel manufacturer can be called U.S. Steel in all references.

Company Name, Manufacturing

United Stationers Inc.

The business products company is based in Deerfield, Ill. Avoid the USI abbreviation in all references.

Company Name

United Technologies Corp.

The Hartford-based conglomerate has a number of businesses, but is best known for Carrier air conditioners, Otis elevators and Sikorsky helicopters.

Company Name, Manufacturing

UnitedHealth Group Inc.

The Minnetonka, Minn.-based health care company spells the first word in its name as one word. Capitalize the H in all references.

Company Name, Health care

Universal American Corp.

The health care benefits company is based in Rye Brook, N.Y.

Company Name, Health care

Universal Health Services Inc.

The King of Prussia, Pa.-based company manages hospitals. Avoid the UHS abbreviation in all references.

universal life

A **whole life insurance** policy where the insurance portion pays a competitive interest rate.

Insurance

unlisted stock

A stock that trades via a dealer network instead of through an exchange. It's also called an **over-the-counter** stock. These stocks don't trade on exchanges because they're often too small to meet the exchange requirements. In addition, such stocks often are considered volatile. (**$$$**)

Wall Street

unrealized gain/loss
A potential profit or loss from holding an asset. The opposite is **realized gain/loss**.

unsecured creditors
People or companies owed debt that is not backed by collateral. **($$$)**

Unum Group
The Chattanooga, Tenn.-based company sells **disability insurance**.
Company Name, Insurance

up zoning
Avoid this term because it can have opposite meanings. For example, the rezoning of a residential piece of property to a commercial usage can be considered an up zoning because it provides for wider using or a down zoning because the new usage is less restrictive. **($$$)**
Real estate

UPC code
The series of vertical lines on a product label used to identify and track items for sale in stores. UPC stands for universal product code. **($)**
Manufacturing, Restaurant, Retail

upgrade
The act of a sell-side analyst raising his or her rating on a stock. An upgrade could be from a "neutral" rating to an "outperform" rating, for example.
Wall Street

UPS
Acceptable in all references for Atlanta-based United Parcel Service of America Inc.
Company Name

upsell (n.,v.)
To encourage a customer to buy an add-on product to go along with a purchased item, often with a higher profit margin. Upsells range from the sale of a drink with a food item to a service contract to go along with an appliance. **($$$$)**
Restaurant, Retail

upside-down mortgage
A mortgage where the amount owed on the mortgage is more than the value of the home. This occurs in slumping real estate markets. **($$$)**
Real estate

uptick
An investment transaction occurring above the previous price. When a stock is purchased for $15 a share in one transaction and then $15.10 in the next transaction, this is considered an uptick. **($$)**
Wall Street

URL
Stands for Uniform Resource Locator. It's the address of a site on the Internet.
Technology

urologist
A physician who specializes in treating illnesses related to the urinary tract

and the male reproductive organs.
Health care

URS Corp.

An engineering company based in
San Francisco.
Company Name

US Airways Group Inc.

No periods are used in the name of
the parent company of US Airways.
Company Name

USAA

The San Antonio, Texas-based insurer
and banking company that does
business only with military members
and their families. Use all caps.
Company Name, Insurance

USB

Stands for Universal Serial Bus. It is
the most common type of connector
that allows consumers to download
photos, documents and other files
onto a computer.
Technology

Valero Energy Corp.

The San Antonio, Texas-based company operates gas stations using the Valero, Diamond Shamrock and Shamrock brands.

Company Name, Energy

value fund

A mutual fund that invests in stocks that are considered to be undervalued in price and often pay dividends. **($$$)**

Wall Street

value, worth

Although often used interchangeably, these words have different meanings. The worth of something is its relative merit or importance to an individual or organization. The value of something is how much it can be exchanged for in currency. A share of Coca-Cola stock can be valued at $45 a share but its worth to an investor could be more than the value because the investor is a descendant of the family that founded the company.

value-added tax

A tax that is added to a product or material based on the value of the finished good. The tax is added at each level of manufacture. A value-added tax is common in the **European Union**, but it is not used in the United States. *VAT* is acceptable on second reference, but do not use "tax" after the acronym. **($$)**

Economy, Manufacturing

vampire squid

A term first used by Rolling Stone writer Matt Taibbi to describe a Wall Street firm that uses its businesses to obtain as much money from every customer possible. It is a pejorative and should be used sparingly. **($$$$$)**

Finance, Wall Street

variable annuity

An insurance contract in which the insurance company guarantees a minimum payment, but actual payments depend on returns of the assets in which the premiums are invested. Variable annuities were popular purchases in the 1990s when the stock market rose, but have since fallen out of favor. **($$)**

Finance, Insurance

variable rate

An interest rate that is periodically adjusted.

Finance

Vaseline

A trademarked product. The generic term is petroleum jelly.

Trademark

Velcro

A trademarked product. The generic term is fabric fastener.

Trademark

venture capital

Funds made available to start-up companies and small businesses, typically in return for an ownership stake and a say in how the operation is managed. A venture capital firm invests money in such companies, expecting that the company receiving the funds will grow and become successful. **($)**

Verizon Communications Inc.

The New York-based company has a subsidiary named Verizon Wireless. Distinguish between the two parent company and the subsidiary.

versus

Abbreviate as v. when writing about lawsuits.

vest

To convey to a person a legal authority or possession. When **restricted stock** vests, it becomes the property of the employee. **($$)**

vested interest

A financial or personal stake in an operation. An investor in a company may take over as chief executive officer in an attempt to improve its operations because he or she has a vested interest in improving its performance.

VF Corp.

The Greensboro, N.C.-based company is the world's largest maker of blue jeans, including the Lee, Wrangler and Rustler brands. It uses no periods in its name.

Company Name, Manufacturing

Viacom Inc.

A media company based in New York. Its name is the shortened version of Video and Audio Communications. Use Viacom in all instances.

Company Name

vice chairman

A title given to a member of the board of directors who is second in command to the chairman. In reality, the vice chairman title is often given to executives who have lost out in a bid to become the chief executive officer of a company.

vice president

A title of a company executive. Capitalize when used before the name. Do not use VP.

Virgin Media Inc.

The telecommunications and media company is based in New York.

Company Name

Visa Inc.

Lowercase all but the first letter in the name of the credit card company, based in San Francisco.

Company Name, Finance

visibility

A term used when gauging a company's future performance. A company with low visibility means that analysts are having a hard term accurately predicting its earnings and revenue.

Finance, Wall Street

Visteon Corp.

The automotive parts manufacturer is based in Van Buren Township, Mich.

Company Name, Manufacturing, Transportation

VOIP

Stands for Voice Over Internet Protocol. It allows people to transmit their voices and talk to each other using the Internet with services such as Skype.

Technology

volatility

The measure of risk in an investment. The higher the volatility, the riskier the investment. One measure of volatility of a stock is its **beta**. **($$)**

Wall Street

volume

The number of units traded in a market or exchange during a certain point of time, such as a day or a week. An increase or decrease in volume may indicate investor sentiment has changed.

Wall Street

vulture fund

A fund that buys distressed securities, such as the bonds of companies that have filed for bankruptcy court protection or junk bonds of companies that are likely to default on its interest payments. **($$$$)**

W.R. Berkley Corp.

The **property and casualty** insurer is based in Greenwich, Conn. Berkley is acceptable on second reference.

Company Name, Insurance

W.W. Grainger Inc.

The industrial supply company is based in Lake Forest, Ill. It can be referred to as Grainger on second reference.

Company Name

Wal-Mart Stores Inc.

Wal-Mart is acceptable on second reference for the world's largest retailer, with headquarters in Bentonville, Ark. Though the company logo no longer contains a hyphen, the official company name does. Refer, however, to the stores as Walmart stores.

Company Name, Retail

Walgreen Co.

The name of the drugstores operated by the Deerfield, Ill.-based company is Walgreens, but the parent company name has no S. There is no apostrophe in the store name.

Retail

Wall Street

A term used to describe the financial and investment community in the United States. It comes from the original location of the New York Stock Exchange in lower Manhattan.

The term can also be used in writing to refer to the overall stock market, as in Wall Street fell Monday in heavy trading amid concerns about inflation and a drop in consumer spending. In such cases, the Street is acceptable. A variant meaning is a large financial institution.

Wall Street

The Wall Street Journal

A daily U.S. business newspaper founded in 1889, The Wall Street Journal is considered the leading source of business news in the United States. In 2007, its parent company, Dow Jones & Co., was sold to News Corp., leading some to question whether the paper's coverage would remain independent under Rupert Murdoch's ownership. The is always capitalized when used as part of the paper's name. The abbreviation WSJ is acceptable in headlines only. On second reference, use The Journal.

Company Name

Walt Disney Co.

The Burbank, Calif.-based company is commonly referred to as Disney on second reference.

Company Name

warehouse lender

A short-term lender for mortgage banks. (**$$$$**)

Finance

WARN Act

The Worker Adjustment and Retraining Notification Act. It was enacted in August 1988 and became effective February 1989. This law requires companies with 100 or more workers to give a state labor department or similar agency 60 days' notice when laying off employees. A WARN Act notice is a public record. WARN Act is acceptable in all references.

warrant

A derivative security that gives the holder the right to purchase securities from the issuer at a certain price and a certain time. The difference between a warrant and a **call option** is that a warrant is issued by the company. **($$$$$)**

Wall Street

Washington Mutual Inc.

WaMu is acceptable on second reference to the Seattle-based bank, closed by regulators in 2008, now part of JP-Morgan Chase.

Company Name, Finance

Washington Post Co.

The education and media company is based in Washington, D.C. Distinguish between the company and the newspaper when writing about both in the same story.

Company Name

Waste Management Inc.

A Houston-based garbage collector and recycling plant operator is the largest waste management company in the United States.

Company Name

weather derivative

A financial instrument used by a company to hedge against the possibility of weather-related losses, such as attendance at an outdoor concert being reduced by rain. If the losses do not occur, then the investor who purchases the instrument makes a profit. If the losses do occur, then the company receives payment from the investor. **($$$$$)**

Finance

Web 2.0

Used to describe a new generation on the Internet where pages are no longer static and content can be entered or manipulated on sites.

WebMD Health Corp.

Capitalize the MD when referring to the New York-based online medical information provider.

Company Name, Health care, Technology

WellCare Health Plans Inc.

The managed care provider is based in Tampa. The C is capitalized in all references.

Company Name, Health care

wellness program

A preventive care program designed to decrease the usage of health care by promoting healthy lifestyle choices. Also known as a health promotion program.

Health care

WellPoint Inc.

The Indianapolis-based health insurance company spells its name as one word and with a capital P.
Health care, Insurance

Wells Fargo & Co.

The San Francisco-based financial services company operates Wells Fargo Bank. It switched the name of all Wachovia Corp. branches it acquired to the Wells Fargo name in 2011 and 2012, so be careful when using Wachovia in reference to a branch.
Company Name, Finance

Wells notice

A notification sent to a company from the Securities and Exchange Commission that indicates that SEC investigators are recommending a lawsuit alleging a violation of federal securities laws. **($$)**
Company Name, Wall Street

Wendy's Co.

The company and its franchisees operate more than 6,500 restaurants Wendy's restaurants worldwide and is based in Dublin, Ohio.
Company Name, Restaurant, Retail

Wesco International Inc.

Lowercase the name of the maintenance, repair and service company based in Pittsburgh after the W. The company uses all capital letters.
Company Name

Western & Southern Financial Group

The Cincinnati-based company uses an ampersand in all references.
Company Name, Finance

Western Digital Corp.

The manufacturer of computer disk drives is based in Irvine, Calif. Avoid the WD and WDC abbreviations.
Company Name, Manufacturing, Technology

Western Refining Inc.

The oil refiner and marketer is based in El Paso, Texas.
Company Name, Energy

Western Union Co.

The financial services and communications company is based in Englewood, Colo. Do not use the before its name.
Company Name, Finance

Weyerhaeuser Co.

Note the spelling of the name of the paper and pulp company located in Federal Way, Wash.
Company Name

WH Smith PLC

The name of the British-based bookstore chain uses no periods.
Company Name, Retail

when-issued (adj.), when issued (v.)

A transaction that is agreed upon before a stock actually begins trading. Stock splits and new issues are traded on a when-issued basis.
Wall Street

Whirlpool Corp.

The household appliance manufacturer is based in Benton Charter Township, Mich. Its brands include Maytag and KitchenAid.

Company Name, Manufacturing

whisper number

An unofficial earnings-per-share estimate for a company that circulates on Wall Street before a company actually releases its earnings. The whisper number may be very different from the published earnings-per-share estimate from sell-side analysts, and it's sometimes given to favored investors. **($$$)**

Wall Street

whistle-blower

An employee who thinks he or she has knowledge of illegal activity within a company and "blows the whistle" by providing that information to a regulatory agency or media outlet.

white collar

A description of an employee who does no manual labor. Many Wall Street workers are white-collar employees.

white goods

A term for heavy consumer products such as air conditioners and refrigerators. Avoid using the term white goods.

Manufacturing

white knight

A company that makes a **friendly take-over** offer to another company that is the subject of a **hostile takeover.**

white-shoe firm

A slang term for an old-line, broker-dealer organization or law firm. The term should be explained in almost all references. **($$$$$)**

Finance

Whole Foods Market Inc.

The Austin, Texas, company is a grocery store chain. Whole Foods is acceptable on second reference.

Company Name, Retail

whole life insurance

A policy with both insurance and investment parts that pays a guaranteed amount upon the death of the policyholder and has a cash value.

Finance, Insurance

Wi-Fi

A trademark of the Wi-Fi Alliance, so it is always capitalized. The term is used to describe gadgets that can access wireless local area networks.

Technology

widow-and-orphan stock

A low-risk stock that pays dividends, such as utilities stocks. They are considered some of the safest stocks in the market, although they are not without risk. **General Motors Corp.** was once considered a widow-and-orphan stock, as were bank stocks. **($$$)**

Wall Street

Wieden & Kennedy

Use an ampersand, not a plus sign, in the name of the Portland, Ore.-based advertising agency.

Company Name

Williams Cos.

The energy company is based in Tulsa, Okla.

Company Name, Energy

wind down

A term used to describe a business that is shutting its doors. Chris Wienandt, the business copy chief of the Dallas Morning News, hates the term, and we agree. Use close or shut instead.

Windbreaker

A trademarked product. The generic term is lightweight jacket.

Trademark

Windex

A trademarked product. The generic term is glass cleaner.

Trademark

Winn-Dixie Stores Inc.

The grocery store chain is based in Jacksonville, Fla. Always use the hyphen, although the company's logo has a check mark instead of the hyphen.

Company Name, Retail

Winnebago

A trademarked vehicle name. The general term is recreational vehicle or motorhome.

Trademark, Transportation

wire house

A company whose offices are connected by communications systems that allow any piece of financial information or prices for financial products to be transmitted back and forth. A bank is considered a wire house, though the term bank is preferred. **($$$)**

Finance, Wall Street

Wired

A technology-oriented business magazine acquired by Conde Nast Publications in 1998 and founded in 1993.

Company Name, Technology

Wisconsin Energy Corp.

The utility is based in Milwaukee, Wis.

Company Name, Energy

Wite-Out

A trademarked product. Note the hyphen and capital O. The generic term is correction fluid.

Trademark

workers' compensation

Insurance purchased by companies that pays benefits to workers when they are injured on the job. This type of insurance is required by state regulators. Note that the apostrophe comes after the s. **($$)**

Insurance

working capital

Current assets minus current liabilities. Working capital is considered a measure of a company's financial health. Positive working capital means a company is able to pay off its short-term debt. **($$)**

World Fuel Services Corp.
The Miami-based company sells fuel to commercial airlines and shipping companies.

Company Name, Energy

World Trade Organization
The international body that governs rules of trade between countries. Its goal is to ensure that trade flows freely. The organization compiles international trade data.

Economy

WorldCom
The company that produced the largest bankruptcy court filing ever when the filing was made in July 2002, primarily due to accounting scandals. (That record has been surpassed by the Lehman Brothers filing in September 2008 as the largest bankruptcy filing in history.) The company emerged from bankruptcy court protection in 2004 as MCI Inc., which disappeared when it was acquired by Verizon in 2006. Use WorldCom only when referring to the pre-bankruptcy company.

Company Name

Worth
A personal finance magazine launched in 1992 by Fidelity Investments. It was purchased by Sandow Media in 2008 and relaunched in June 2009 aimed at individuals with a net worth of more than $2 million.

Company Name

WR Hambrecht & Co.
Use an ampersand instead of the plus sign, and no periods, in the name of the San Francisco-based investment bank.

Company Name, Finance

wrap
An account in which a broker manages an investor's money for a flat quarterly or annual fee. It avoids **churning**, the practice of a broker trading in an investment account to generate commissions. **($$$$$)**

Finance, Wall Street

wrap-up insurance
A policy that covers all liability for a number of businesses working together on a project. The coverage, however, applies only to losses for that project.

Insurance

write-down (n., adj.), write down (v.)
Reducing the book value of an asset because it is overvalued compared with market values. Also called a **write-off**.

write-off (n., adj.), write off (v.)
A reduction in the value of an asset to its actual worth. Write-offs can decrease earnings for a company. For example, if a company acquired some machinery in the purchase of another company but then discovered that the machines were outdated and couldn't be used to manufacture its products, it would write off, or lower, the value of those assets on its books.

Xcel Energy Inc.

The utility is based in Minneapolis.

Company Name, Energy

Xerox

A trademarked product. The generic term is photocopy. The name of the Rochester, N.Y.-based company is Xerox Corp. on first reference.

Company Name, Trademark

XTO Energy Inc.

The Fort Worth, Texas-based company produces oil and gas. It is now a subsidiary of **Exxon Mobil Corp**.

Company Name, Energy

Yahoo Inc.

Do not use the exclamation point in the name of the company.

Company Name, Technology

Yankee bonds

Debt sold in the United States by foreign governments and companies.

Finance, Wall Street

year to date

The period beginning Jan. 1 up until the current day. Do not use YTD on any reference.

year-over-year

A comparison that measures the financial performance during the same time period. A company may state that its first-quarter earnings have risen on a year-over-year basis for the past five years. That means that its earnings for the first three months of 2009 have been higher than the earnings for the first three months of 2008, which reported earnings slightly higher than the first quarter of 2007, when first-quarter earnings were higher than 2006's first-quarter earnings, which were higher than first-quarter earnings in 2005.

yield

The income return on an investment, divided by its market price. This word can be used to refer to both stocks and bonds.

yield curve

A line that plots the interest yields, on a set day, of debt obligations with the same credit rating but different maturity dates. The yield curve is used as a benchmark for other debt. **($$$$)**

yield to maturity

The rate of return for a bond if it is held until its maturity date. It can also be referred to simply as the yield. Avoid the abbreviation YTM. **($$$)**

YouTube LLC

The name of the San Bruno, Calif., company and its website is one word. It became a division of **Google Inc.** in 2006.

Company Name, Technology

YRC Worldwide Inc.

The transportation company is based in Overland Park, Kans. YRC stands for Yellow Roadway Corp., its previous name.

Company Name, Transportation

Yum Brands Inc.

Do not use the exclamation point after Yum for the restaurant company based in Louisville, Ky.

Company Name, Restaurant

Z

zero-coupon bond

A bond that doesn't pay any periodic cash interest but is sold for less than its face value and is redeemed at maturity for face value. (**$$$$$**)

Wall Street

Ziploc

A trademarked product. The generic term is zippered plastic bag.

Trademark

zoning

Government laws that regulate the use of land in an area. In most cases, a company must obtain zoning approval before building.

Real estate

II. Business News Legal Issues

I t's not enough for business journalists to know the ins and outs of corporate America and how it works. They also need to know a fair amount of how laws and regulations affect their ability to obtain and use information about companies and individuals in stories.

We cover some of the bigger legal issues involving business journalism in this section. It is by no means complete, but we do believe that it gives a business reporter an overview of what he or she needs to know when confronted with a legal issue.

Annual meetings

In May 2009, the St. Petersburg Times retail reporter was denied access to the annual meeting of the Home Shopping Network. That's not the first time a business journalist has been denied entry into a meeting being held by a company for its shareholders.

In 2006, retailer Target Corp. closed its annual meeting to reporters. In December 2005, New Jersey-based IDT Communications barred a New York Times reporter from attending its annual meeting. In 2001, Yahoo wouldn't allow reporters into its annual meeting, and in 1999, Exxon Mobil wouldn't allow reporters from gay publications into its meeting. In 2001, Pacific Gas & Electric Corp. would not let a reporter from the San Francisco Bay Guardian attend its annual meeting.

No part of federal laws governing publicly traded companies stipulates that the annual shareholders meeting should be open to the public. Shareholders are allowed to attend, but a company can prevent the media from attending.

Many companies, of course, do allow business journalists to attend their annual meetings. Some even provide access to their executives before or after the meeting. But there is no legal provision that states they must do so.

A number of business media outlets have taken the following step to avoid missing out on potential news at an annual meeting — they have bought a share of stock for each company they are interested in covering. With that one share, they can send a reporter to attend the meeting as their representative.

At the 2007 annual meeting of the Society of American Business Editors and Writers, 57 percent of the business journalists in attendance said the practice of a media outlet or a reporter owning shares to attend an annual meeting was acceptable. Another 15 percent said it was acceptable to obtain a proxy statement from a shareholder and use that document to attend the meeting.

Also note that a company holding an annual meeting can make stipulations on journalists attending the meeting. In February 2009, Apple prevented reporters from entering its annual meeting with cellular phones, laptop computers and other communication devices that would have allowed them to blog or report on the meeting as it was happening.

Defamation/privacy

Although defamation and privacy cases often concern themselves with individuals outside the business world, they can also be brought by a company or the executive of a company.

In 2006, real estate developer Donald Trump sued New York Times business journalist Timothy O'Brien, who had written a book about Trump. In his lawsuit, Trump alleged that O'Brien defamed him by stating in the book that his net worth was in the hundreds of millions of dollars, not in the billions of dollars that Trump asserts. A judge ruled in favor of O'Brien and his publisher in 2009 and dismissed the case, stating Trump had not been a victim of actual malice, although Trump vowed to appeal the ruling.

In addition, a number of states have product disparagement or trade libel statutes and also recognize such claims at common law that allow a company to sue business journalists when they have written stories about companies and their products.

Although not a business journalist, talk show host Oprah Winfrey was sued by cattle ranchers in Texas after airing a show in 1996 that called into question what cattle were being fed. The ranchers claimed the show caused a drop in the price of their cattle. A jury ruled in favor of Winfrey.

In the Jan. 13, 1997, edition of Forbes, writer Caroline Waxler wrote in the "Streetwalker" column that shares of Biospherics Inc. were overvalued. The company filed a defamation lawsuit six months later, claiming that its "reputation and business" had been injured. The court denied the company's claims, stating that the column was protected as a statement of opinion. An appeals court affirmed the court's ruling. See the appeal court ruling at: http://lw.bna.com/lw/19980825/981118.htm.

It's important for business journalists to realize that while opinion can be a defense in a defamation action, it does not enjoy blanket protection. Certain elements must be met first, such as disclosing the facts you're basing your opinion on, and not suggesting to your reader that you know other facts you aren't sharing.

HIPAA

Stands for the Health Insurance Portability and Accountability Act, which was enacted in 1996. In 2002, a privacy provision was added that governs the release of health status and coverage information related to individuals.

Essentially, the HIPAA privacy provision prevents the release of medical and health information about individuals to journalists, unless the person signs a waiver of HIPAA. Then, the information can be released to anyone noted in the authorization.

This provision has broad ramifications for business journalists, particularly those who report about the health care or pharmaceutical industries. Often, these reporters seek examples of consumers who suffer from certain illnesses or who are taking specific medications. The reporter cannot obtain information about the consumer's health status from anyone but the patient.

The privacy provision has yet to be tested in terms of other areas, such as what would happen if the health status of the CEO of a company became public interest. For example, in the past few years, the health of Apple CEO Steve Jobs has been a topic of stories for those covering the company. In January 2009, the company released information about Jobs' health when it stated that he would take a leave of absence from his leadership role.

An unanswered question regarding the HIPAA privacy provision remains: What would happen if a business journalist received from an anonymous source the medical records of a company CEO whose health was of great interest to shareholders and wrote an article based on those records? It could be argued that those medical records would be exempt from the privacy provision because of public interest — if the CEO was deathly ill, such news could cause the stock price to drop dramatically. In June 2009, The Wall Street Journal broke the story that Jobs had received a liver transplant at a Tennessee hospital. The story did not attribute the information, but was later confirmed by the hospital.

Insider trading

The connection between illegal insider trading and business journalism has unfortunately been in existence for more than 100 years.

"If a railroad baron wished to manipulate his company stock in the 19th century, he leaked a story to a news agency where it would be circulated at once and trading in the stock affected within an hour or so, bullish or bearish," according to an early history of Dow Jones and The Wall Street Journal. "The baron would pocket the profit, losers be damned."

At The Journal, reporters overseeing the "Broad Street Gossip" and "Abreast of the Market" columns wrote positive stories about specific companies and the stocks in return for money from investors in the 1920s. The revelations about the Journal reporters came out during hearings by the Senate Banking and Currency Committee in 1932, when Congressman Fiorello LaGuardia produced canceled checks written to the Journal reporters. The stories based on the bribes had gone as far back as 1923.

In June 1969, financial columnist Alex Campbell published an item in the Los Angeles Herald Examiner about Amer Systems Inc. Unbeknown to readers, Campbell had purchased 5,000 shares of the company shortly before the article ran. The article, which praised the company, caused the stock to rise. Campbell then sold his stock at a profit. Campbell was charged. A judge who ruled in Campbell's case called his actions "reprehensible." (Campbell and the paper were also sued by two people who sold their company to Amer Systems Inc., arguing that he should have stated his interest in the stock. Read the appeals court ruling in that case at: http://bulk.resource.org/courts.gov/c/F2/594/594. F2d.1261.76-1647.html)

The most famous illegal act involving using the media to profit financially occurred at The Wall Street Journal. In the 1980s, Journal reporter R. Foster Winans was writing the "Heard on the Street" column. He met some stockbrokers and agreed to provide them information about what was going to appear in the column before it was published. The brokers then used that information and made nearly $700,000. They also paid Winans some of their profits.

Winans and the two brokers were convicted of mail and wire fraud charges and for violating securities laws by using confidential information for personal use. A court ruling related to the Winans case, *Carpenter v. United States*, can be found at: http://caselaw.lp.findlaw.com/cgi-bin/getcase. pl$court=US&vol=484&invol=19.

In 1989, Seymour Ruderman, an editor at BusinessWeek, was sentenced to six months in prison for trading on information in the magazine before it was published. He had earned $39,000 in profits with the information. The SEC also brought charges against the editor. The information came from the "Inside Wall Street" column written by Gene Marcial. Ruderman pleaded guilty to two counts of mail fraud. His case can be found at: http://www.sec.gov/news/digest/1989/dig052689.pdf

And in early 2004, CBS Marketwatch.com commentator Thom Calandra resigned from the online financial journalism site after it was disclosed that the SEC was investigating his trading. The SEC accused him of "scalping," or selling stocks shortly after his positive recommendations about the stocks caused their prices to rise, without disclosing the sales.

Calandra allegedly made more than $400,000 through buying shares of 23 small-cap stocks while writing favorable profiles recommending the stocks, and then selling his shares when the stocks rose after his columns were published. The SEC also accused Calandra of failing to disclose that he was compensated from a stock promoter affiliated with two companies that he profiled.

In 2005, Calandra settled the charges, without admitting or denying the allegations, by paying more than $540,000 in penalties. The complaint against Calandra can be read at: http://www.sec.gov/litigation/complaints/comp19028.pdf

It should be apparent that although the majority of coverage about illegal insider trading in the business media has been about corporate executives, board members and others connected to a company, business journalists are also subject to the insider trading laws. A business journalist cannot use information that he or she gathers in the course of reporting a story to make investments before the story is published and the information is provided to readers or viewers.

Public records

Many federal and state government documents filed by public and private companies are public record by law and can — and should — be used by business journalists in the course of reporting stories.

The most important of these include:

1. Securities and Exchange Commission filings by public and private companies.

2. Documents filed by companies with many federal regulatory authorities, such as the Federal Trade Commission, the Federal Communications Commission, the Consumer Product Safety Commission and the Environmental Protection Agency. In addition, these regulatory agencies produce documents that are almost always public record, and they often have complaints filed by consumers and businesses against companies they regulate.

    Please note that there are at least two documents with federal government agencies that a journalist might want that are **NOT** public record and not available to business reporters. These are initial complaints of harassment or discrimination filed with the Equal Employment Opportunity Commission and information that a pharmaceutical company supplies to the Food and Drug Administration when asking the FDA for approval to sell a drug to consumers.

    Also, proprietary information or trade secrets filed by companies with federal agencies could be exempt from being produced by the agency pursuant to a Freedom of Information Act request under Exemption 4, which protects confidential business information. For instance, there may be trade secret information in a patent application filed with the U.S. Patent and Trademark Office.

3. State documents, such as information about a company filed with the Secretary of State's Office and information with state regulatory agencies, such as the insurance department.

4. Lawsuits filed in both state and federal courts. These documents include initial complaints, affidavits, exhibits and depositions. Sometimes, lawsuits are sealed by companies that want to keep certain disclosures from the public, such as trade secrets. When a lawsuit is settled out of court, a confidential settlement is not a public record. The court record will simply indicate a dismissal. In addition, the parties to the litigation might sign an agreement of confidentiality that prohibits each side from making the

terms of the settlement public — that happens all the time.

5. Form 990 filings by nonprofit organizations and foundations with the Internal Revenue Service.

6. State and federal government contracts with public and private companies.

7. Bankruptcy court filings for both individuals and businesses. These include lists of creditors, which often include their mailing address and phone numbers.

8. Real estate records such as the buying and selling of property and the rezoning of property for new uses. These records are kept at the municipal and county level.

Media organizations such as The New York Times, Bloomberg News and Fox Business Network filed lawsuits in 2008 and 2009 against the federal government, seeking access to records for the government's Troubled Asset Relief Program, or TARP, to gain access to details of financial bailout. While some of these lawsuits have been successful, the federal government resisted releasing much of this information.

Regulation Fair Disclosure

On Aug. 15, 2000, the Securities and Exchange Commission adopted Regulation Fair Disclosure to outlaw the selective disclosure of information by publicly traded companies and other issuers. Regulation FD provides that when an issuer discloses material nonpublic information to certain individuals or entities — generally, securities market professionals such as stock analysts or holders of the issuer's securities who may well trade on the basis of the information — the issuer must make public disclosure of that information. In this way, the new rule aims to promote the full and fair disclosure.

The full regulation can be read at: http://www.sec.gov/rules/final/33-7881. htm

In addition to helping investors, Regulation FD has been a boon to business journalism because it requires companies to provide access to its earnings conference calls and video conferences of investor presentations, among other events, to everyone, including reporters and editors who previously were not allowed to hear these calls. In fact, many business journalists argued in favor of Regulation FD before it became a rule for this and other reasons.

Companies typically provide the access by releasing information about a conference call at the end of a news release, or by posting the information on its website. In many cases, a company will post a link to a video conference on its site as well.

The Securities and Exchange Commission staff has also recently decided that disseminating information on company websites is also considered a way to comply with Regulation FD. This includes blogging by chief executive officers and other executives. See further details here: http://www.sec.gov/news/speech/2008/spch073008km.htm

What all of this means is that a business journalist should be aware of Regulation Fair Disclosure and how it now requires companies to provide information.

In addition, Regulation FD has been interpreted as not preventing journalists from obtaining scoops and exclusives from companies.

Sourcing

Increasingly, business journalists are under threat to divulge their sources for stories as companies want to know where information was obtained.

Journalists are also potentially liable if they divulge where they obtained information if the informant had a binding oral contract with the reporter not to have his or her identity disclosed.

In the case of *Cohen v. Cowles Media,* a campaign adviser who acted as a source for a story about a politician running for governor had his name used in a Minneapolis Star Tribune story even though the reporter had promised not to identify the source. The editor included the information against the reporter's wishes, and the source lost his job. The source sued the newspaper for breaching the reporter's promise and won a substantial jury verdict in 1988 that ultimately was upheld by the U.S. Supreme Court in 1991.

A business journalist, as well as a confidential source, needs to understand precisely what deal is being cut. In most cases, the deal needs to be defined as narrowly as possible. Many journalists tell a source, "I will keep your name out of the paper." Reporters should also refrain from — or be very cautious about — promising a source that "no one will be able to identify you," as that usually cannot be guaranteed. Instead, the reporter and source might agree that the source will identified as, say, a "high-ranking corporate official."

Business journalists and their sources should also be comfortable with the terms "off the record" and "on background." They should reach an agreement as to whether that means the information can be used in a story without being attributed to the source.

In addition, business journalists could be subpoenaed by readers or investors to force disclosure of their sources. A growing controversy in business journalism centers on the use of hedge fund managers as sources and the relationship between business journalists and short sellers, but this issue has been ongoing for more than three decades.

In 1977, a class-action lawsuit was brought against Barron's columnist Alan Abelson, his editor and parent company Dow Jones & Co. The lawsuit, which was later dismissed, questioned whether Abelson was using short sellers as sources for his stories, with the short sellers knowing that Abelson would write a negative article about the stock mentioned by the investors.

The charges were never proved. In fact, Abelson had sued BusinessWeek magazine in 1975 after it published an article alleging that the Barron's writer leaked information to investors about his column. BusinessWeek subsequently disclaimed the story and admitted that it had "no evidence that advance information on the contents of Barron's was intentionally leaked to investors by Abelson, Barron's, or Dow Jones."

Although it is a broader issue, reporters subpoenaed in state proceedings to reveal a source (i.e., subpoenaed to testify in a criminal or civil case) might or might not have statutory protection. That would depend on whether the state in which the proceedings are pending has a shield statute and, if it does, what the terms of the statute are.

If the reporter is subpoenaed in a federal proceeding in which state law is not being applied, then the reporter will not have statutory protection because there is no federal shield law — although the reporter might have some degree of First Amendment protection depending on the circumstances and facts and on the U.S. Circuit in which the proceedings are pending. The U.S. Supreme Court has never implicitly recognized a First Amendment right of reporters to refuse to testify when subpoenaed in a lawfully convened civil or criminal proceeding.

International law

Finally, any business journalist should be aware that international law is different when it comes to the media and their reporting about companies. In addition, although a company or a CEO of a company is based in the United States, a company could file a claim in another country claiming the foreign courts have jurisdiction over the matter because the company has a reputation in that country and transacts business in that country, where the laws are less friendly to media organizations.

The Wall Street Journal has, for example, been a defendant in the Singapore judicial system in recent years. In March 2009, the paper was ruled in contempt and fined a small amount for two editorials and a letter to the editor it published about the country's judiciary system. In November 2008, Singapore's high court found an editor of The Journal in contempt of court and issued a fine for damaging the reputation of its judiciary relating to the same items.

There's also increasing pressure by some countries in the Middle East and Asia to prevent publishing information by business media outlets that might negatively affect the economy.

III. Business Journalism Guidelines and Ethics

Not all aspects of business journalism are as cut and dried as the laws and rules that determine the release of information. That's why we're including this section on business journalism ethics.

There are no set guidelines in business journalism. Although many business journalists agree on certain issues, such as that trading in stocks of companies they report about is unethical, there are just as many other issues on which there is disagreement.

We're providing two sets of guidelines and ethical statements from two business media outlets — American City Business Journals and Bloomberg Businessweek — as recommended reading for any business journalist faced with an ethical issue.

Others can be found here:

1. Dow Jones Code of Ethics: http://www.dj.com/TheCompany/CodeConduct.htm

2. Thomson Reuters Code of Ethics: http://www.thomsonreuters.com/content/PDF/corporate/corp_govern/TR_COBC_English_20081028.pdf

3. American Business Media Code of Ethics: http://www.americanbusinessmedia.com/images/abm/pdfs/committees/EdEthics.pdf

4. American Society of Business Publication Editors Guide to Preferred Editorial Practices: http://www.asbpe.org/about/code.htm

5. Associated Press Statement of News Values and Principles: http://www.ap.org/newsvalues/index.html

6. Society of American Business Editors and Writers Code of Ethics: http://www.sabew.org/ethics/RevisedCodeofEthics.htm

When in doubt, however, let us emphasize that the best policy is to discuss the matter with your superior, or the editor-in-chief, before taking any action. An after-the-fact discussion won't undo any harm that might arise from your actions.

a. American City Business Journals Conflict of Interest Policy

This policy statement is designed to provide all employees with guidelines which will enable them to avoid conflicts of interest that might be construed to be detrimental to the best interests of ACBJ. It is important for all employees to keep in mind the tremendous embarrassment and damage to the Company's reputation and that of fellow employees that could come about through a lapse in judgment by one person, or someone closely associated with that person, no matter how well-intended that person may be. Because we think it is essential that every employee be above suspicion, we consider any slip in judgment in the areas covered in this policy statement to be serious enough to warrant dismissal.

Confidential Information

Employees should not use, directly or indirectly, for their own or any other person's financial gain, any information about ACBJ which the employee obtained in connection with ACBJ employment. Further, employees should not disclose to anyone confidential information obtained in connection with ACBJ.

Gifts, Purchases of Goods or Political Contributions

Employees should not requisition, order, approve or otherwise participate in the purchase of goods or services on behalf of ACBJ from any company in which the employee or a family member has any financial interest, whether stock ownership or loans or otherwise.

Employees should not accept, directly or indirectly, any gift, entertainment or reimbursement of expenses of more than twenty dollars or that exceeds customary courtesies, nor should they accept, directly or indirectly, payment, loan, services, employment or any other benefit from any company or individual that furnishes or seeks to furnish news, material, equipment, supplies or services to ACBJ.

Employees are not permitted to accept free transportation or lodging ("so-called junkets") offered by companies, individuals or governmental agencies.

Employees should not offer to provide, directly or indirectly, any gift, entertainment or reimbursement of expenses for more than nominal value or that exceeds customary courtesies, nor should they offer, directly or indirectly, any material, equipment or services to any company or person in position to make or influence any business or governmental decision affecting ACBJ.

ACBJ does not contribute directly or indirectly to political campaigns or to political parties or groups seeking to raise money for political parties or political campaigns, and ACBJ does not and will not reimburse any employee for any political contribution made by an employee.

Security Transactions

ACBJ has a strict policy on security transactions by employees who have access to inside information regarding unpublished stories or advertising schedules. It also has a strict related policy on the conduct of news and advertising staff members dealing with corporations we cover or whose advertising we carry. Each employee is expected to bend over backwards to avoid any action, no matter how well-intentioned, that could provide grounds even for suspicion:

(i) that an employee, his family or others close to the employee made financial gains by acting on the basis of "inside" information obtained through a position on our staff, before it was available to the general public. Such information includes hold-for-release material, our plans for running stories, items that may affect price movements, or projected advertising campaigns;

(ii) that an employee is financially committed in the market so deeply or in such other ways as to create a temptation to biased writing or scheduling of advertising;

(iii) that an employee is beholden to brokers or any other group we cover or advertisers. Such indebtedness could arise through acceptance of favors, gifts or payments for performing writing assignments or other services for them.

We do not want to penalize our staff members by suggesting that they not buy stocks or make other investments. We do, however, want employees to avoid speculation or the appearance of speculation. We reiterate that it is not enough to be incorruptible and act with honest motives. It is equally important to use good judgment and conduct one's outside activities so that no one — management, our editors, an SEC investigator, or a political critic of the Company — has any grounds for even raising the suspicion that an employee misused a position with the Company.

With these general propositions in mind, here are some further specific guidelines:

(i) First and foremost, all material gleaned by you in the course of your work for ACBJ is deemed to be strictly the Company's property. This includes not only the fruits of your own and your colleagues' work, but also information on plans for running items and articles on particular companies and industries and advertising schedules in future issues. Such material must never be disclosed to anyone outside of the Company, including friends and relatives. Viewing information as the Company's property should avoid a great many of the obvious pitfalls.

(ii) No employee regularly assigned to a specific industry should invest, nor should his family, in any company engaged in whole or significant part in that industry.

Serving on the Board of Directors of Other Companies

ACBJ employees are prohibited except with written approval of the chief executive officer from serving as directors or officers of any other company devoted to profit-making. Employees may not receive payment for serving on a board which is not devoted to making a profit. If an employee is involved in a family-owned profit-making business, clearance should be obtained in advance from the chief executive officer. If an employee's participation on a board of directors, of either a profit-making or nonprofit organization, creates the appearance of a potential conflict of interest with the company or a conflict of the editorial integrity of the newspaper, that person may be required by the chief executive officer to resign from that board of directors.

Accounting Procedures

No ACBJ fund, asset or liability which is not fully and properly recorded on the books and records shall be created or permitted to exist.

All employees will comply with ACBJ's accounting principles, procedures and controls and no false, artificial or misleading entries in our books and records shall be made for any reason whatsoever.

No ACBJ employee will:

(a) issue or authorize any official company document that is false or misleading;

(b) knowingly accept and treat as accurate a false or misleading document prepared by a person outside ACBJ; and

(c) knowingly make false or misleading statements to our external, internal or other auditors.

Only those corporate managers authorized to do so may release information regarding ACBJ. Management of individual papers may release information pertaining solely to their own market as outlined in the Company's policy manual.

We believe these guidelines should be easily understood. They aren't intended to deter any employee from participating actively in civic or charitable organization, provided they have no impact on or connection with ACBJ. The same applies to political organization or government advisory boards for the average employee — but editorial employees and company executives would be expected to refrain if there were a connection with issues covered by his or her publication or if his or her superior didn't provide prior clearance.

We would like to emphasize that we have complete confidence in all of our employees. It is essential, however, that all of us maintain the highest standards of ethics in the conduct of ACBJ business in actuality and also in appearances by acting within the framework of these guidelines. Please retain this policy statement in your files.

Every ACBJ employee will be given a copy of this Conflict of Interest policy annually and acknowledge by signature that they understand and abide by it. All new employees will receive the policy at the time of hiring and acknowledge same.

Your cooperation is greatly appreciated.

b. The BusinessWeek Code of Journalistic Ethics

The code was last updated online on December 2, 2009. It is an abridged version of the document BusinessWeek journalists are required to sign annually.

What We Stand For

In our society, the press enjoys a remarkable degree of freedom. With that freedom comes the responsibility to practice our craft in accordance with the highest standards, to be accountable for what we publish, and to avoid conflicts of interest.

Ever since BusinessWeek was established in September, 1929, we have striven to fulfill these responsibilities. And with good reason. Otherwise, we could lose our most important asset: the trust of our readers, online visitors, viewers, and listeners in the credibility of the information and insights we provide.

We believe that our future depends upon preserving and enhancing this trust. Therefore, we must ensure that:

1. The integrity of our journalists is of the highest caliber.
2. We base our unique brand of journalism on accurate information, gathered honestly and presented fairly.
3. Our journalists' professional conduct is unassailable.
4. Our journalists' personal conduct, as it reflects on BusinessWeek, is beyond reproach.

All members of the BusinessWeek editorial staffs must uphold these principles. This means everyone who works on the magazine, the Web site, or in our multimedia operations (including members of the art, production, and systems departments, all Web developers and programmers, and all assistants and clerical workers), be they full-time, part-time, interns, or freelancers.

Here are the rules by which they must live:

INTEGRITY

1. "Church and State."

Unquestionable integrity is at the heart of BusinessWeek's effort to serve our audiences with the best business journalism in the world. One way we achieve this is to strictly observe an invisible wall that separates our editorial operations from our advertising and other business departments, so as to avoid any chance that one will inappropriately influence the other.

In every medium, our reporters, editors, and producers prepare and place stories, graphics, and interactive features based solely on their editorial merits. Thus, we treat companies that advertise with us exactly the same as those that don't. We don't favor any company or subject of a story, or discriminate against any — for any reason.

Moreover, editors and editorial imperatives dictate the design of our products. Obviously, we make allowance for the presentation of revenue-generating elements. However, the design must always make clear the distinction between editorial and commercial material. In the spirit of that rule, for example, we do not link, for any reason other than editorial purposes, from within the text of electronic versions of our stories to an advertiser's Web site.

2. ASME guidelines.

The American Society of Magazine Editors has created guidelines for both print and digital media that establish a minimum standard of behavior for reputable magazines and Web sites. BusinessWeek and its employees, both editorial and business, must honor the ASME guidelines. (Editorial Guidelines: http://www.magazine.org/Editorial/Guidelines/. Best Practices for Digital Media: http://www.magazine.org/Editorial/Guidelines/Best_Practices_for_Digital_Media/). We will treat violations of them as violations of our journalistic ethics.

OUR JOURNALISTIC STANDARDS

BusinessWeek specializes in valued-added, interpretive journalism. This gives us license to go beyond a traditional, just-the-facts approach. At the same time, it puts an extra onus on us in the following areas:

1. **Accuracy.**

   For the reader to believe our interpretations, we must start with accurate information, honestly and professionally gathered. Moreover, our interpretation must flow from the facts and be reasonable.

   Inaccurate or sloppy reporting of material that appears anywhere under the BusinessWeek name violates the spirit of this Code. The responsibility for accuracy lies with everyone who touches the editorial product.

2. **Honesty.**

   All of our journalists' dealings with sources — and with other editorial staff — must be truthful.

   As an institution, moreover, BusinessWeek will always be an independent voice, with no ax to grind. We do not support political candidates or political parties. We are not Keynesians, monetarists, or supply-siders. On all matters of politics, economics, and social policy, we try to bring our own judgment to bear, based on thorough reporting and reasonable analysis. We do not do stories that are designed to hew to any ideological agenda.

3. **Fairness.**

    We give the subjects of a story — people, companies, and institutions — an opportunity to have their views presented. We include relevant portions of those views — or report that the subject declines to comment. We also present differing or dissenting opinions, though they may be subordinate to the main thrust of the story.

    If someone complains about a story, we will investigate promptly and even-handedly. If we are right, we will stand by the story regardless of who is complaining. If we are wrong, we will say so forthrightly and make whatever amends seem appropriate.

    Because we do analytic journalism and commentaries, we do not strive for perfect objectivity. But we must always strive to be fair.

4. **Attribution.**

    We use the following ground rules when seeking information from sources:

    On the record:

    Journalists are free to use all material from the interview, including information and quotations, and to identify the source. We prefer this approach.

    Not for attribution:

    Journalists are free to use information and quotations, but they agree not to identify the source. "Not for attribution" is an acceptable method of gathering information, though not the one we prefer.

    Journalists generally should have more than one source for information that you can't attribute, both to double-check its veracity and to guard against being used or misled by a single source.

    Off the record:

    Journalist agrees not to use information from the source. Or journalist may agree not to use the information unless he/she checks with the source before publication. We ask our journalists to avoid this method unless it's the only way to interview a one-of-a-kind source.

    Routine attribution:

    "He said" means the journalist got the quote from the source — in person, at a press conference, or on the phone. "He said in a statement" or "in a report" means the quote came from a written statement or press release, or from a document such as an analyst's report. "He said in an e-mail interview" means exactly that. If the quote comes from another news outlet, the journalist must credit it: "President Smith told the Associated Press."

How to Join SABEW

When you join the Society of American Business Editors and Writers (SABEW), you are among the largest organization of business news people in the world, more than 3,400 members in the United States and Canada. Those eligible for membership are persons for whom **a significant part of their occupation involves writing, reporting, editing or overseeing business, financial or economic news** for newspapers, magazines, newsletters, journals, books, press or syndicated services, radio or television, online publications, or other media approved by the SABEW Board of Governors and to teachers and students of business journalism or business media subjects at recognized colleges or universities or other organizations approved by the Society's board.

If your request for membership is denied, you will receive a refund of your membership dues. A member may **retain full membership status** after being assigned to another news position at news organizations, even if the new position is not directly involved in business news, or if he or she leaves journalism entirely, **so long as his or her dues remain current.** Questions about new memberships or renewals may be directed at Mark Scarp, membership coordinator, at 602-496-5183, or scarp@sabew.org.

Individuals

Those seeking first-time **individual regular membership** should please fill out the Online Individual Membership Registration Form at https://membership.sabew.org/join/individual-application

Application processing could take up to 5 business days after SABEW receives your application. **Individual membership is $55 per year. Students pay $10 per year. Associate members pay $75 per year (see next paragraph).**

Associates

Application for first-time associate membership is open to those who do not meet requirements for regular membership but who demonstrate a desire to support the mission and goals of SABEW.

Those seeking **associate membership** should please fill out the Online Individual Membership Registration Form at https://membership.sabew.org/join/individual-application

Application processing could take up to 5 business days after SABEW receives your application. **Associate membership** is $75 per year.

Institutions

SABEW's Institutional Membership program allows business desks or business publications, broadcasts and websites, and university journalism schools, to provide membership benefits to business staffers and students and is an economical way to stay connected to the industry. Full access to the SABEW website, including the searchable database, is available to all individuals who are included by the institution as members. Membership rates for institutions vary depending on the size of the membership list:

Those seeking first-time **institutional membership** should please use our Online Institutional Membership Registration Form at https://membership.sa-bew.org/join/institutional-application

Institutional membership rates as of Jan. 1, 2011

1-5 members	$105.00
6-10 members	$165.00
11-15 members	$225.00
16-20 members	$285.00
21-25 members	$345
26+	$345 plus $13.50/person after first 25